EISENHOWER PUBLIC LIBRARY
3 1134 00300 9040
P9-CAJ-381

THE TURKEY

A list of books in the series appears at the back of this book.

The Turkey

An American Story

ANDREW F. SMITH

UNIVERSITY OF ILLINOIS PRESS
CHICAGO AND URBANA

Manufactured in the United States of America
c 5 4 3 2 1
∞ This book is printed on acid-free paper.

Library of Congress Cataloging-in-Publication Data
Smith, Andrew F.
The turkey : an American story.
p. cm. — (The food series)
Includes bibliographical references and index.
ISBN-13: 978-0-252-03163-2 (cloth : alk. paper)
ISBN-10: 0-252-03163-6 (cloth : alk. paper)
1. Turkeys—United States—History. 2. Cookery (Turkey)
I. University of Illinois (Urbana-Champaign campus). Press.
SF507.T84 2006
641.3'65920973—dc22 2006022790

This book is dedicated to the old turkeys I've known—Frank Dantona, Fred Czarra, Midge Longley, Tom Collins, Larry Condon, Bruce Kraig, Joe Carlin, David Finn, and Alan Boorstein—and to the young chicks I look forward to knowing better—Meghanne, Reilly, Ethan, and Owen.

Contents

Historical Recipes

Preface

My fondest childhood food memories relate to the traditional Thanksgiving feast and its centerpiece, the turkey. In southern California in the 1950s the celebration started at school with Thanksgiving-related arts and crafts such as tracing our hands on construction paper and then coloring in the gobbler's features and tail feathers. Frequently, there were dramatic reenactments of the "First Thanksgiving," with students playing Pilgrims and their gracious friends the American Indians, who kindly supplied much of the food. At lunch, the school cafeteria dished up tasteless turkey, nondescript gravy, overcooked vegetables, and pastel mashed potatoes produced from powder, but we knew it was just a feeble foretaste of what was to come on our family tables on Thanksgiving Day.

Thanksgiving was the one holiday when the extended family—grandparents, aunts, uncles, cousins, and friends—came together. The Thanksgiving meal, served in the dining room or if more space were needed in a rearranged living room, was shared late in the afternoon. Everyone brought something: potato salad, wine, baked beans, cranberry sauce, and apple, mincemeat, or pumpkin pie. The hosts (my parents alternated with grandparents and aunts) provided the turkey, gravy, candied sweet potatoes (called yams in our family), stuffing (usually called dressing), and anything that had to be served hot. The turkey was always stuffed, and gravy was made from the drippings.

Hours before dinnertime, savory aromas emanated from the kitchen, where the women scurried about, an innate sense of choreography keeping them out of each other's way as they sliced, chopped, grated, sautéed, strained, boiled, mashed, and baked their ways through a mountain of groceries. The men chatted in the living room or sat outside in the patio, weather permitting, and occasionally asked if they could do anything to help. Unless something needed to be acquired from the market the answer was usually no until time to carve the bird. Carving was the prerogative of the senior male in the host family (grandfather, father, or uncle), who could, of course, assign the task to someone else. But first the turkey was placed on tantalizing display in the kitchen for at least half an hour, "resting" to cool and be easier to carve and letting the juices redistribute themselves, ensuring more succulent white meat. Nobody could resist at least one glance into the kitchen to admire the fragrant, crisp-skinned holiday symbol soon to be gobbled up.

Children were seated at a separate table from the adults, far enough away to form our own conversational group but near enough so they could chasten us when our table manners, eating habits, language, or other unpleasantries made it necessary. When we sat down, side dishes and condiments were already on the table, and everyone gazed in awe as the enormous platter was reverently brought forth from the kitchen, bearing steaming slices of light and dark meat flanked by the wings and two giant drumsticks. This platter was strategically placed in the middle of the adults' table, but turkey was liberally dished out to children.

Once the turkey arrived the meal began with grace—usually a nondenominational prayer—usually led by the youngest child. Even though Thanksgiving was not a religious day, occasionally grace took the form of a litany of the things for which we should be thankful. The final item on the list was the bountiful meal set before us. With grace over, the food was passed around or served more formally by one or two of the women. I always ended up with a drumstick after most of the meat had been removed. It sounds somewhat pathetic, but I was happy to pick up and gnaw what to me was a gargantuan bone; I also enjoyed violating the usual taboo against eating with my hands. Of course, everyone over-ate. It was an obligation to demonstrate how much you liked each dish. The person who prepared each delicacy might be offended if it wasn't enthusiastically received.

After the slowest eater had finished and the table was cleared, everyone looked for some comfortable place to sit or, if possible, lie down. After a "decent interval," dessert—usually apple pie with vanilla ice cream or pumpkin pie with real whipped cream piled high—was served. No matter how much they had already eaten, everyone always found room for at least one slice of pie. Of course, Thanksgiving didn't end with dessert: leftovers were packed up and distributed among the families. For days afterward turkey turned up in casseroles, sandwiches, salads, soups, and stews made from the scraps, bones, and carcass.

These memories were surely the beginning of my lifelong fascination with the turkey, a fascination that persists decades after these extended family Thanksgiving celebrations receded into memory. Although my interest in turkey initially sprang from childhood memories, now, as a food historian, I am concerned with what the turkey tells us about larger social, historical, cultural, and culinary issues and also what it reveals about what it means to be an American.

To explore these broader issues I have divided this book into two parts. The first is a history of the turkey, which has played an important role in North America for thousands of years. The second offers a tantalizing selection of more than a hundred historical recipes that feature turkey. The bibliography provides a listing of selected books, agricultural bulletins, commercial booklets, and cookbooks as well as organizations or programs that specialize in turkeys or issues related to turkeys.

From a culinary standpoint, the common turkey (*Meleagris gallopavo*) was the only important domesticated animal in the Americas in pre-Columbian times. Wild turkeys ranged from Mexico to the east and west coasts of North America. There are many unknowns about its early history. It isn't known, for instance, where the turkey originated, where or how it was domesticated or why many species disappeared. Although wild turkeys were easy to capture, various American Indian groups were widely divergent in their esteem for the bird. Some ate turkey with great gusto, whereas others wouldn't eat the birds even when faced with starvation. The wild turkey was likely first domesticated in the highlands of central Mexico and in the American Southwest, although much about the domestication process is shrouded in mystery. The first chapter relates how and why pre-Columbian groups responded so differently to the turkey and discusses the wild turkey's domestication.

Common wisdom has it that hundreds of years passed before New World foods were integrated into European diets. This is not true of the turkey. The Spanish encountered domesticated turkeys in Mexico by 1518, and within a few years they had been introduced into the West Indies and Spain. Shortly thereafter, turkeys were widely disseminated throughout Western Europe, the Mediterranean, and Asia. The second chapter tells how and why the North American turkey so quickly conquered the Old World.

Before 1541 the turkey arrived in England, where it was immediately adopted by the upper classes. Domesticated birds were easy to raise, and turkey farms proliferated throughout England. By 1577 English growers raised vast flocks of turkeys, which were driven like cattle hundreds of miles to market. As turkeys became plentiful they became affordable to the middle class and soon were the least expensive bird on the English market. British cookbooks from the sixteenth century onward featured recipes for preparing turkeys for the table. The third chapter describes how the turkey conquered England and became the basis for the traditional English Christmas dinner.

European settlers and travelers were fascinated by the wild turkey, which was larger than its domesticated counterpart. Plentiful along North America's East Coast and in the South, the river valleys of the Midwest, and the Southwest, wild turkeys were an extremely important food source for early European colonists. Aggressive hunting and the destruction of its habitat, however, brought the wild turkey near extinction. By the 1930s they vanished completely from twenty of thirty-nine states of their original range and were fast disappearing elsewhere (chapter 4).

Before English settlers arrived in North America, turkey recipes appeared in British cookbooks. With the demise of the wild turkey, domesticated fowl—imported from Europe—came to the culinary forefront in Colonial America. As the birds became more abundant in America, colonists perfected the art of turkey cookery. The many recipes that appear in early American manuscripts and cookbooks advise how to roast, boil, fry, and steam turkeys; how to bake turkey pies; how to select, prepare, and stuff turkeys in dozens of ways; and what to do with leftovers. Chapter 5 describes how the turkey has fared on the American menu.

The single most important role of the turkey in American life is as the centerpiece of Thanksgiving dinner. How the turkey achieved and has maintained this position is the focus of chapter 6, which reveals how Sarah Josepha Hale invented Thanksgiving, how the holiday was "hijacked" by long-dead Pilgrims, and how Turkey Day was widely celebrated.

Shortly after British colonies were established in North America, domesticated turkeys were imported from Europe. By accident, these birds bred with wild turkeys, and new turkey varieties emerged. During the nineteenth century, poulterers deliberately bred turkeys to produce specific traits. Several varieties were elevated to "breed" status: Bronze, Narragansett, White Holland, and many more. Then Jesse Throssel, an English poultry raiser who immigrated to Canada, created what became the Broad-breasted Bronze. The American turkey has never been the same. Chapter 7 tells of the rise and fall of traditional turkey breeds and how Broad-breasted white turkeys conquered America.

Until the early twentieth century turkeys were raised on family farms and marketed locally. After World War II, growers began to expand their operations. One way of lowering costs and increasing efficiency was through vertical integration—combining all aspects of turkey farming and processing into one operation and thus eliminating middlemen. That tended to concentrate the industry in fewer hands, and most small farmers dropped out of the turkey business. Commercial turkey production became a highly centralized national industry (chapter 8).

In addition to its role as a culinary centerpiece, the turkey has been viewed as an American icon and was interwoven into the American social fabric. When Americans want to have a serious discussion they talk turkey. When Americans fiddled or danced, it might be to the popular tune "Turkey in the Straw." Later, the turkey's comically awkward strut provided the inspiration for a dance called the turkey trot. A failed Broadway show is called a turkey, but when luck is needed, a fortunate break of the turkey's wishbone is necessary. Chapter 9 tells the action-packed tale of how the turkey became a significant symbol in the nation's gastronomical, historical, social, economic, and cultural stew.

The final chapter looks at the turkey in America today. Wild turkey has been saved from oblivion, and heritage turkeys may survive as well. Some growers have begun raising free-range and organic turkeys, and others focus on preserving traditional breeds. The turkey remains a powerful American symbol and culinary treat.

The historical turkey recipes in the second section of this book date from the sixteenth to the twentieth centuries and are intended to reflect the diverse ways in which wild and domesticated birds have been prepared for the table. Also in this section are safety procedures related to turkey preparation and handling. The selected bibliography and list of resources is a guide to books, agricultural reports, and commercial booklets as well as turkey-related organizations.

During the course of my research, culinary "fakelore" emerged. The Aztecs, for example, did not domesticate the turkey. Despite repeated stories to the contrary, the frequently cited "First Thanksgiving" dinner never happened—at least not the way it has been described in textbooks and popular magazines. Benjamin Franklin did not propose that the turkey be America's national emblem. Free-range and organic turkeys may or may not be more flavorful than frozen turkeys purchased in supermarkets. Yet another myth deals with the belief that drowsiness after eating turkey is caused by tryptophans, amino acids known to cause an overload of serotonin in the brain, thus inducing sleep. But a person would be physically incapable of eating the amount of turkey required to induce such a state. Sleepiness that comes after consuming a big turkey dinner is more likely caused by the stress of the day and a heavy work load as well as by the large quantities of carbohydrates consumed.

Due to the frequently regurgitated culinary fakelore, I have extensively documented this work. It is likely that future researchers will uncover additional information that may lead in new directions—or contradict conclusions I have presented here. Future culinary historians and writers will make better judgments if they can easily check the sources upon which I have relied. I hope this book encourages others to revise, challenge, and improve the turkey's story and the social and cultural history in which it is embedded.

Acknowledgments

Many problems confront anyone writing about the history of the turkey. Among the mass of information available are tens of thousands of references, descriptions, and depictions in American and European literature, newspapers, diaries, letters, legal documents, paintings, engravings, poems, zoological works, and cookbooks. It is impossible for any one individual to examine each of these. Another problem is that Arlie William Schorger, a professor at the University of Wisconsin, Madison, collected 2,600 historical citations and published them in his monumental *The Wild Turkey: Its History and Domestication* (1966). Anyone attempting to write about turkey history needs to avoid being a footnote to that masterful work.

I am indebted to others who have explored the history of the turkey: Albert Hazen Wright, whose four-part series "Early Records of the Wild Turkey" appeared in *Auk;* Karen Davis, author of *More Than a Meal: The Turkey in History, Myth, Ritual and Reality* (2001); and Sabine Eiche, who wrote *Presenting the Turkey: The Fabulous Story of a Flamboyant and Flavourful Bird* (2004), a beautiful book filled with spectacular illustrations and extensive sources and insights into turkey history. As with Schorger's work, I have borrowed sources liberally from these as well.

This story could not have been told without the assistance of many others who have passed on information about turkeys: James Baker, former vice president and chief historian, Plimoth Plantation, Plymouth, Massachusetts; Karen Goldstein, also at Plimoth Plantation; Peggy M. Baker, director and librarian, Pilgrim Hall Museum, Plymouth, Massachusetts; Sandra Oliver, editor, *Food History News,* Isleboro, Maine; Kathleen Curtin, food historian, Plimoth Plantation; Barry Popik, independent researcher, New York City; Janet Clark, culinary historian, Brisbane, Australia; Cathy Kaufman, culinary historian, New York City; Barbara Kuck, then at Culinary Archives and Museum, Johnson and Wales University, Providence, Rhode Island; Karen Hess, New York, New York; and Joseph Carlin, Food Heritage Press, Ipswich, Massachusetts. Ken Albala, professor of history, University of Pacific, Stockton, California, helped with translations and location of Renaissance turkey recipes, specifically those of Bartolomeo Scappi's *Opera Dell'Arte del*

Cucinare; Nanna Rögnvaldardóttir forwarded turkey recipes from Iceland; Carolin Young assisted with the translation of sixteenth-century French sources; Cara De Silva, New York, New York, supported of this project and helped with Italian turkey connections; Mario Zannoni, Parma, Italy, assisted in researching turkey linguistics in Italy; Susan Rossi-Wilcox, Cambridge, Massachusetts, helped with Charles Dickens and the turkey; and Richard Wright, Balmain, Australia, provided information about turkey recipes in British cookbooks. I also thank James G. Dickson, editor of the *Proceedings of the Seventh National Wild Turkey Symposium* and Merritt Professor of Forestry at Louisiana Tech University, Ruston, Louisiana; Karen Davis, author of *More Than a Meal: The Turkey in History, Myth, Ritual and Reality* and president of United Poultry Concerns, Machipongo, Virginia; Mark Zanger, culinary historian, Boston; Fritz Blanc, chef and culinary historian, Philadelphia; Nick Aretakis, William Reese Company, New Haven; James Earl Kennamer, senior vice president for Conservation Programs, National Wild Turkey Federation, Edgefield, South Carolina; Tom Hughs, biologist, National Wild Turkey Federation, Edgefield, South Carolina; Marjorie Bender, research and technical program manager, American Livestock Breeds Conservancy, Pittsboro, North Carolina; Paula Lambert, Society for the Preservation of Poultry Antiquities, Las Cruces, New Mexico; Christy Marr, National Turkey Federation, Washington, D.C.; Walter Levy, Accord, New York; Malcolm Thick, historian, United Kingdom; and Bonnie Slotnick, who patiently commented upon each chapter with intelligence and constructive criticism. All comments and responses have been appreciated, but not all have been accepted or incorporated; I accept all responsibility for errors that may appear in this work.

I'd also like to thank Bill Regier, director and editor-in-chief of the University of Illinois Press, for his constant encouragement and right-on-target advice; Mary Giles for her excellent and prompt editing of the book's manuscript; and all the staff at the Press for their behind-the-scenes work.

PART 1
The History of the Turkey

1

THE PREHISTORIC TURKEY; OR, HOW THE TURKEY CONQUERED NORTH AMERICA

More than twelve thousand species of birds are dispersed throughout the world, and virtually all of them are edible. Fowl were an important part of early human diets. Their eggs were easily gathered, but the fowl themselves were more difficult to procure. Because it is not easy to hit birds on the wing, hunters devised methods of capturing them with traps, nets, and snares. Land or gallinaceous birds—heavy-bodied fowl that roost and largely feed on the ground—were easier to catch, especially when humans joined in group efforts. Some flushed birds from thickets while others clubbed, hit, or netted them. Once acquired, the flesh was prepared in many ways—from raw and roasted to boiled, baked, fried, and braised when these cooking techniques developed.

In addition to eating their flesh and eggs, humankind has used birds in many practical, artistic, social, and symbolic ways. Chickens, doves, ducks, geese, and storks, for instance, have all borne religious symbolism. Chicken entrails have been used for divination and magic. Many cultures and religious groups have imbued eggs with special significance, such as fertility, and some vestiges of these ancient traditions have survived in modern Easter and Passover celebrations. Roosters or cocks have been set against one another in cockfights, providing an opportunity for gambling and a source of entertainment for millennia. Cockscombs have been used for medical purposes, and feathers have been fitted on arrows, sewn into blankets, and woven into clothing, while birds' bones have been fashioned into tools, buttons, and ornaments. In all, humankind has greatly benefitted from birds.

The Americas

The Americas were particularly well endowed with edible wildfowl. At the top of the list were migratory ducks, geese, partridges, pheasants, and carrier pigeons, which were numberless according to many early European observers. Nonmigrating land birds such as ruffed grouse and turkeys were also plentiful in parts of North America and especially important from a culinary standpoint after migratory birds departed during the winter and other game and edible plants were scarce.

Only two fowl were domesticated in the New World in pre-Columbian times. One was the Muscovy duck (*Cairina moschata*), which originated in tropical South America. Precisely when, where, and how it was domesticated is unknown. By the time Europeans arrived it was an important part of the diets of people inhabiting the tropical regions of Central and South America. During the sixteenth century Europeans widely disseminated the Muscovy duck, but it never became an important food source anywhere. Today, its culinary contribution is insignificant except to subsistence farmers in tropical areas of the world.[1]

The other fowl domesticated in the Americas was the turkey—a large, nonmigratory land bird. Turkeylike birds have inhabited North America for several million years, but the earliest archaeological evidence for the modern turkey dates back only about fifty thousand years. The turkey's closest living relatives are the Asian pheasant and the African guinea fowl. The American turkey and the Asian pheasant are close enough genetically so that they can be mated through artificial insemination and produce offspring. Researchers have proposed that these two species evolved from a common ancestor, but if so, no intermediate fossils have been found in Asia or North America.

Fossils of various turkey species have been unearthed, but only two survived into historical times. The ocellated turkey (*Meleagris ocellata,* formerly *Agriocharis ocellata*) and the common turkey (*Meleagris gallopavo*).[2] The ocellated turkey is found today in Mexico's Yucatán Peninsula, Belize, and Guatemala. It is slightly smaller and has shorter legs than the common turkey. The male ocellated turkey has no beard—coarse, long, black hairs that protrude from the upper part of the breast—but it does have large spurs—strong, sharp, and pointed appendages that protrude from the back of legs. Its head feathers are blue or white, and it has wattles, the pouchlike appendages that descend from the neck. Its body plumage is copper or bronze-green, and its tail feathers have a purple cast with blue-green eyespots. Its snood—the floppy growth on the front of the head that flops over the beak—has a roundish protuberance tipped with yellow.[3]

Stylized figures of ocellated turkeys have been found in Mayan manuscripts and codices, which suggests that ocellated turkeys were consumed by Mayan priests and aristocracy.[4] Although easily tamed, the ocellated turkey does not reproduce in captivity. Today, they are frequently found around rural homesteads and tourist areas.

The Wild Turkey

Historically, the ocellated turkey was not found in areas inhabited by the wild turkey, which ranged throughout much of North America from the Canadian province of Ontario to the area around Veracruz, Mexico, and extended from the Atlantic coast to the American Southwest.[5] By the time Europeans arrived in what is today the United States, wild turkeys inhabited the territories of thirty-nine states.[6] A closely related species, the *Meleagris californica,* survived on the West Coast until about ten thousand years ago, when it disappeared from the fossil record. Its extinction was perhaps the result of early hunters, diseases, or climatic changes at the end of the last ice age.

Wild turkeys are natural foragers and eat almost anything, but they prefer mast (acorns, chestnuts, nuts, and seeds), plant tops, grapes, rose haws, and berries. As they are omnivores, they also eat spiders, tadpoles, snails, slugs, worms, grasshoppers, crickets, beetles, caterpillars, and ants as well as small snakes and lizards. When food is scarce during winter, wild turkeys eat wild rye, Kentucky bluegrass, and almost anything else they can find.[7]

By any standard a wild turkey is an impressive bird of unusual appearance. The adult ranges in size from ten to almost forty pounds and stands three to four feet tall; its wingspan can reach almost six feet. Their wings may seem long, but they are comparatively short for the bird's weight. Wild turkeys can fly but are neither aerodynamic nor graceful when they do. The shape of their wings and their powerful wing muscles permit rapid acceleration, and they have been clocked at speeds of fifty-five miles per hour. They can fly distances of up to a mile, but they mainly use flight to escape predators. Wild turkeys also use their wings to leap into trees, where they prefer to roost at night. For normal locomotion, they prefer to use their powerful legs. With a long, straddling gait, they can trot at twelve miles per hour; when frightened, they can accelerate to twenty-five miles per hour. Wild turkeys can also float on water and swim, which makes it possible for them to traverse wide rivers and large bodies of water.

Wild turkeys have excellent hearing and eyesight. Without moving their heads, they can see 320 degrees.[8] They make many sounds and have a relatively complex set of speech patterns, the word for one of which, "gobble," has entered the English language. According to the *Oxford English Dictionary,* the word has been used since 1680 to describe the sound male turkeys make during mating season. Male turkeys are called gobblers as well as cocks or toms, whereas females are usually called hens.[9]

Wild turkeys have distinctive physical features. Their wrinkled heads and necks are without feathers. They have caruncles—a reddish, pliable growth on the head and upper neck, snoods—which are more pronounced in the males, and wattles, which are attached below the beak and down the throat. Male turkeys (and some hens) have a beard—a long, hairlike appendage hanging from their chests. In addition to its unusual appearance, a wild turkey's habits and behavior are also remarkable, particularly during the mating season in March and April when cocks strut about, call to hens, and display their tail feathers. During this time a male's head, neck, snood, and wattle turn bright red. When a hen signals readiness by separating herself from other hens, she may engage in a dance of her own before she invites the cock to mount her from behind.

Along with some lizards, snakes, and a few other animals, the turkey's most unusual aspect is that the hen has the ability to reproduce by parthenogenesis. Without having mated, hens can produce fertilized eggs under certain conditions. All chicks produced from these eggs are male, and about 20 percent of them will be able to reproduce as adults. Although parthenogenesis has only been documented in domesticated turkeys, it is thought that wild turkeys have this ability as well.[10]

Wild turkey hens lay between eight and twenty eggs, colored white to a cream with brown speckles, in a single clutch. The hen carefully conceals them on the ground. Should something happen to the eggs, hens can lay an additional clutch or two. The hen incubates and turns the eggs for twenty-eight days. Hatching takes place over a twenty-four-hour period, and the hen remains in the nest during that time. For the first four or five weeks, chicks roost on the ground, protected by the mother's wings. Poults learn to leap into low-hanging tree branches, again spending the night under their mother's wings in the tree. Poults stay with their mothers until they are about nine months old, when they are considered adults. They are highly adaptable, preferring thick woods, brushland, and swampy lowlands, but have difficulty with deep snow. Their natural life span is from ten to fifteen years.

Geographic isolation has fostered six major subspecies of wild turkeys, which differ as to plumage coloration and range: the Mexican turkey (*M. g. gallopavo*) is found mainly in southern Mexico from Puerta Villarta and Acapulco on the Pacific Coast to Veracruz and Tuxpan on the Gulf of Mexico, and is quite rare; the eastern wild turkey (*M. g. silvestris*), the most numerous subspecies, ranges widely from the eastern coast of North America to the Mississippi River; the Florida turkey (*M. g. osceola*) is found in the southern half of Florida; Merriam's turkey (*M. g. merriami*) is native to the mountain regions of the west from Colorado to Mexico; the Rio Grande turkey (*M. g. intermedia*) inhabits the south central Plains states from South Dakota to Texas and northeastern Mexico; and, finally, Gould's turkey (*M. g. mexicana,* which also now incorporates *M. g. onusta*) is found in northwestern Mexico and parts of Arizona and New Mexico.[11]

The Domesticated Turkey of Mexico

The concept of "domestication" of animals is subject to extensive academic debate. Some scholars define domestication as any change in animal behavior caused by human interaction. For others, domestication means the point at which animals discontinue behaviors that harm humans and begin to breed easily in captivity. New World–domesticated quadrupeds include the American dog, which may have accompanied early hunters from Asia and was occasionally consumed; the New World camelids—the alpaca and the llama—which were rarely eaten in pre-Columbian times; and the guinea pig, which was an important food animal in parts of South America. Of these, none made any significant global culinary contribution. The American dog was replaced by the Old World dog that arrived with Europeans. Camelids emerged from South America mainly as zoo or circus animals. The guinea pig serves mainly as a pet or subject in medical experiments and remains a food source only in limited areas of South America today.

The wild turkey is a very inquisitive animal and readily congregates with humans. As one observer has noted, it was "aggressively begging to be domesticated."[12] Relatively little is known about how or where the turkey was first domesticated. Part of the problem in determining its point of domestication is that wild turkey bones do not differ greatly from those of domesticated turkeys. Without corroborative evidence it is difficult to determine if turkey bones unearthed in archaeological sites are from domesticated or wild birds. There are plenty of signs of domestication, however, at sites of human habitation: the presence of turkey egg shells, which suggests that chicks were born in captivity; turkey pens, which suggests intentional caging; and the remains of turkeys of different ages, which suggests they were indeed being raised at that location. Feathers are also helpful indicators. White tips can result from a diet strong in corn, which lacks lysine. Because corn does not grow in the wild and can only be grown with human help, turkey feathers with white tips are another indicator of domestication.[13]

Richard MacNeish, a Canadian archaeologist who worked extensively in Mexico, is credited with finding the oldest evidence of the domesticated turkey at sites in the Tehuacán Valley. These remains date to 200 B.C.E.–700 C.E.[14] Domesticated turkey bones, dating to about 700 C.E., have also been unearthed at a Guatemalan archaeological site far beyond the pre-Columbian range of the wild turkey. That is not likely to have been the point of domestication, but it does point to early trade in domesticated turkeys in Central America.[15] Aldo Leopold, who studied wild turkeys in Mexico during the 1940s, speculated that domestication had occurred north of the Rio Blasas Valley, but that was based on reports of sightings of wild turkeys in the twentieth century and a few historical documents. Others have surmised that the turkey was domesticated in Michoacán, but no convincing evidence has been offered to support that (or any other) view.[16]

When the turkey was domesticated is also mysterious. Pre-Columbian domesticated turkeys were much smaller than wild turkeys, which suggests a relatively short period of domestication because size reduction is observed in many animals early in the process of domestication. Also, when Europeans arrived in the Americas, domesticated turkeys were found in a relatively small geographic area in Central America. Because other domesticated foods such as maize, beans, squash, chili peppers, peanuts, sweet potatoes, and Muscovy ducks were widely disseminated in pre-Columbian times, the turkey's limited range suggests that it had not been long domesticated before the arrival of Europeans.[17] The exact date of domestication in Mexico is unknown, but it likely occurred during the past 2,500 years.

What is clear is that the Aztecs did not domesticate the turkey, as many writers, incorrectly, have reported. The Aztecs are thought to have been closely related nomadic groups who lived in northern Mexico before migrating into the Valley of Mexico around 1200 C.E. The Aztecs arrived in Mexico's central valley well after others domesticated the turkey. Because the Aztecs were familiar with the wild turkeys that inhabited northern Mexico, they readily adopted domesticated turkeys when they settled down. When Europeans arrived in 1519, both domesticated and wild turkeys played an important role in the cuisine of indigenous people of Mexico. At that time, the Aztec empire was at its zenith, and Europeans naturally associated turkeys with Aztecs.

Eating Turkey in Pre-Columbian Mexico

Because the Aztecs did not develop a system of writing, all we know of the pre-Columbian turkey is what can be surmised from a limited number of archaeological artifacts and the reports that Europeans wrote after the Conquest in 1519. By all surviving accounts, turkeys were extensively raised in ancient Mexico. The Aztec word for a male turkey, *huexoloti,* survives in modern Mexico as *guajolote.* Much of what we know today about the Aztec consumption of turkeys comes from Bernardino de Sahagún, author of the *Historia General de las Cosas de la Nueva España* (General History of the Things of New Spain). Sahagún was a Franciscan priest who went to Mexico in 1529 and for the next forty-eight years recorded information on what Aztecs said about their pre-Columbian customs, politics, and daily life. He had much to say about the turkey, which "leads the meats; it is the master. It is tasty, fat, savory." Specifically, the hen "is tasty, healthful, fat, full of fat, fleshy, fleshy-breasted, heavy-fleshed."[18]

The Aztecs cooked turkey in many ways—roasting it over a fire as well and incorporating it into soups and stews. Sahagún describes one layered dish that merchants made and sold in markets. At the bottom was dog meat, followed by turkey meat covered by a sauce.[19] The Aztecs also made a turkey stew, *totolmolli,* that is similar to today's *mole de guajolote.*[20]

Turkeys did more than provide sustenance. Client cities gave large numbers of them as tribute to the Aztec emperor. His household consumed many, and it was reported that five hundred were fed daily to wild carnivores who resided in the emperor's menagerie.[21] Merchants gave turkey heads as religious offerings upon their safe return from travels.[22] The wattle was believed to cause impotence, says Sahagún, so it was ground, combined with chocolate, and given to enemies.[23] Finally, the Aztecs deified the turkey as Chalchiuhtotolin, the Jeweled Bird. A representation of that deity appears in the Codex Borbonicus, which was prepared shortly after the Spanish Conquest. According to Karl Young, who has spent years studying the codex, the deified turkey could cleanse humans of contamination and absolve guilt.[24]

It's also difficult to know the precise appearance of "original" domesticated Mexican turkeys from the stylized ways in which they have been depicted. Relatively few depictions have been found in pre-Columbian art although some have been located in codices.[25] Depictions also appear, although rarely, on pottery. A jar from Costa Rica, for instance, possesses a turkey-head handle, and a turkey-shaped clay whistle was unearthed in southern Veracruz.[26] Turkey representations also appear in jewelry. The Aztec emperor Montezuma, for instance, sent Hernán Cortés six turkeys made of gold.[27] The gift was intended to appease Cortés but only inflamed his desire to capture Mexico City and possess the wealth therein.

The surviving *criollo* (or *pavo creollo*) turkeys of Mexico today are thought to be the descendants of these original domesticated turkeys. They are about half the size of modern turkeys and have diverse color combinations of white, bronze, and black.[28] European-bred domestic turkeys were reintroduced into Mexico, however, and there has been extensive cross-breeding among them, wild turkeys, and criollo turkeys, making it difficult to extrapolate from modern-day criollo turkeys to early pre-Columbian ones.

Another source of evidence of the original turkey's appearance comes from early sixteenth-century European sources. Illustrations in Sahagún's manuscript show gray and white fowl.[29] The several color depictions that originated in Europe within a few decades of the turkey's arrival suggest that pre-Columbian domesticated birds were diverse in coloration. In many images the turkeys are slate or have black feathers tipped with white; in others they are white, brown, or buff.[30]

Domesticated Turkeys in the American Southwest

Turkeys have been associated with humans in North America for millennia. Remains have been found at human habitation sites dating back to 3700 B.C.E. In the Southwest, turkey bones first appeared in the Mogollon culture area of New Mexico about 300 B.C.E. and in the Anasazi culture area about 400 C.E. A number of indicators suggest that at least some turkeys were domesticated and not just tamed; the remains of more than three hundred young and old birds dating to 400–700 C.E. were uncovered at a single archaeological site in Arizona.[31] Depictions of turkeys are common at Hopi archaeological sites, and a mural on a cliff-dwelling wall in Arizona, dated 1100–1300 C.E., features three large turkeys. The site has been aptly named after the murals: the "House of Three Turkeys."[32] Pueblo and other Indians penned turkeys to prevent them from raiding their food supplies.[33] The shells of turkey eggs have been unearthed at archaeological sites, offering further evidence that Pueblo Indians bred the birds. In addition, turkey bones have been found at Arizona pueblo sites where wild turkeys were not known to thrive in prehistoric times, which suggests that turkeys were raised at that location.

Across the Mexican border at an archaeological site in Casas Grandes, evidence indicates that a large number of diverse birds were penned by about 1300 C.E. Some observers have concluded that these turkeys were acquired from different locations in the Southwest and that turkeys had been bred at the site. One reason for that viewpoint is the variation in feather coloration, which American Indian groups greatly appreciated.[34]

These observations have led many researchers to conclude that turkeys in the American Southwest were domesticated and most likely derived from Merriam's subspecies. These domesticated turkeys, however, were not hardy and died out by the mid-eighteenth century. Southwestern turkeys therefore did not contribute to the heritage of commercial turkeys raised in modern times.[35]

Diverse American Indian Approaches to Turkeys

When the Spanish explored vast sections of what is today the United States they found wild turkeys in great abundance. Francisco Vásquez de Coronado's 1540–42 expedition located turkeys in what is now Kansas, Oklahoma, Texas, and New Mexico. When Coronado arrived at pueblos in the American Southwest he found "large numbers" of turkeys, many of which provided meals for the men of his expedition. These turkeys were larger and tastier than those in Mexico reported the Spaniards, but the Pueblo people told them that the birds were kept for their feathers and not consumed. Coronado, who could not imagine that anyone would forgo turkey meat, concluded that the natives were lying to him.[36] In fact, the Pueblo and other American Indians used feathers extensively to make cloaks, blankets, headdresses, religious symbols, and many adornments. An adult bird has about 3,500 feathers, but the best were plucked from the wings and tails of live birds. Feathers grew back over time, only to be plucked again. At least one observer concluded that feathers may have been the reason why indigenous people in the Southwest domesticated turkeys.[37]

Many American Indian groups hunted and ate wild turkeys, but they did so in diverse ways. The Lipan Apaches, for instance, ate no other fowl but wild turkeys.[38] The Navajo only ate the birds roasted, believing that boiling destroyed their flavor.[39] Boiling was fine with other groups, but at least one refused to boil turkey in the same vessel with "land animals" for fear of offending "the Guardian of the Forest."[40]

Other Indian groups such as the Pima and Papago (now called the Tohono O'odham) refused to eat turkey flesh.[41] The Cheyenne eschewed the bird because they believed it to be cowardly, and "they claimed it would make cowards of them" if they ate it.[42] The Hopi did not eat turkey meat but were delighted, as were most other American Indians, with its eggs, which were considered a delicacy.[43] The Navajo, however, who ate turkey flesh, never ate turkey eggs.[44]

From New England to the American Southwest, turkey feathers were employed to make mantles, coats, and blankets. In prehistoric times such garments were considered important enough to be placed around the bodies of those interred in the nitre caves of Kentucky. European colonists were extremely impressed with the garments. One observer reported that turkey-feather fabrics felt like velvet. Another said they were "so prettily wrought and woven with threads, that nothing could be discerned but the feathers, which were exceeding warme and handsome." The feathers were secured with twine made from wild hemp or nettle. Double threads of hemp or coarse twine were used on the outside of blankets and turkey feathers on the inside. In some groups, women made turkey-feather coats; in others, old men were charged with constructing them. Despite their great beauty and utility, the making of turkey-feather mantles, blankets, and coats declined during the late eighteenth century, replaced by cotton and wool blankets and garments supplied by the Europeans.[45]

Many groups that did not eat turkey still valued parts of the bird for utilitarian and other purposes. Bones, for instance, were used for making tools.[46] In southern Arizona, the Papago constructed spoons, awls, beads, and other decorations from turkey bones.[47] Turkey feathers were employed to make fans and umbrellas. In Louisiana, then controlled by France, Native Americans made blankets by weaving turkey feathers. Then they would "fasten them to an old covering of bark, which they likewise line with them, so that it has down on both sides." They also made fans of turkey tails.[48] Many indigenous people used turkey feathers on their arrows and turkey spurs as arrowheads.[49] The Cheyenne, "the striped arrow people," specifically used barred wing feathers.[50] The Papago, however, refused to feather their arrows with them because they considered the turkey to be a cowardly bird and believed the arrows would be adversely affected. The Papago did use turkey feathers for particular ceremonial dances, however, and to make prayer sticks, as did the Hopi, Pima, Pueblo, and Navajo. Among many American Indian groups, headdresses were usually composed of eagle and hawk feathers, but the Navajo made them from turkey feathers.[51]

Wild turkeys were relatively easy to catch; some Native Americans used snares and pole traps to secure one bird at a time.[52] In areas of large numbers of wild turkeys, Native Americans and European colonists used funnel-entrance traps, open-front traps, and drop-net traps, but none of those methods captured a large number of birds at one time.[53]

American Indians and colonists lured wild turkeys into the open by using decoys and imitating appropriate turkey sounds. Decoys were constructed from turkey skins and feathers. During the mating season hunters would follow turkey trails until they discovered a flock and then place the decoy in the open and hide behind logs, imitating a hen in the hope of attracting a cock.[54] It was a necessary part of children's education to learn turkey calls, which were used to communicate among hunting parties and also set up ambushes in times of conflict.[55]

Turkeys were also relatively easy to hunt, particularly where they were plentiful. Some Chiricahua Apaches did not bother to hunt them but would shoot at those they happened upon; still other Chiricahua organized turkey hunts. Some Indians flushed turkeys, and others waited for them to land and then shot, clubbed, or netted them.[56] Some tribes did not consider turkeys enough of a challenge or delicacy to warrant the attention of experienced hunters, but they encouraged children to hunt them.[57] They did so in various ways, an unusual one being a dart blown through a nine-foot-long reed. Some youngsters became proficient enough to kill a turkey at thirty feet.[58] Another description has survived of Cherokee children using a "sarbacan, or hollow cane" to blow a small dart into the turkey's eye. They seldom missed.[59]

2

THE GLOBE-TROTTING TURKEY; OR, HOW THE TURKEY CONQUERED EUROPE

Fifteenth-century Europe consisted of a patchwork of small kingdoms, duchies, and nominal empires. Spain was on its way to unification after the marriage of Ferdinand and Isabella and the resulting union of Aragon and Castile. The re-conquest of Moorish areas of the Iberian Peninsula was a costly venture, and the Spanish needed funds to pay for the war. At that time, a major way of generating revenue was to trade spices. Many desirable ones, such as pepper and nutmeg, originated in India and the Spice Islands (now Indonesia). Spices were transported to Europe either by overland caravan to the Mediterranean or by ship to the Red Sea and then overland to the Mediterranean. Arabs and Italian city-states such as Venice controlled much of the spice trade, which meant that consumers in Northern and Western Europe paid a hefty markup to many middlemen.

Many Europeans wondered if it were possible to find other ways to reach the spices of Asia, thereby establishing a lucrative trade and making a large profit. The Portuguese hoped to open a direct trading link with Asia by circumnavigating Africa. Alternately, Christopher Columbus proposed to travel west across the Atlantic and establish a direct trade connection with the Indies. Others had no problem with the spherical notion of the world, which Columbus's proposed route assumed, but concluded that the world's circumference was much greater than he projected and that his proposed trip would greatly exceed the distance that ships of the day could travel. But Columbus had many supporters, among them Alessandro Geraldini, a cleric who encouraged the Spanish monarchy to fund his expedition, which they did in 1492. Columbus was, of course, thousands of miles off in his calculations, but his voyage changed the world forever. In the following decades, hundreds of ships traversed the Atlantic in search of riches, spices, souls, conquest, glory, and knowledge.

Early Spanish explorers of the New World encountered a multiplicity of unfamiliar birds such as curassows, crested guans, horned guans, and chachalacas. Indigenous people had tamed many and kept them in cages. Confusion is endemic to early European accounts of these birds, which is not surprising. Explorers were not trained naturalists, and at the time there was no common nomenclature to describe the physical characteristics or habits of birds. Explorers recorded their findings as they pleased and bestowed similar names on different birds or gave different names to the same birds.[1] Without a description or illustration it is impossible to identify particular referents mentioned in early accounts. This has led to extensive confusion about when Europeans first saw the turkey and when it was introduced into Europe.

The first European known to have visited lands where domesticated turkeys may have been kept was Pedro Alonso Niño, who in 1499 landed somewhere along the Caribbean coast of present-day Nicaragua, Costa Rica, or Panama. No evidence has surfaced, however, that Niño saw or acquired turkeys. The following year Vincente Yánez Pinzón visited the Gulf of Paria (today in Venezuela), where indigenous people gave him "a great multitude of theyr peacockes, both cockes and hennes" and provisions "to carry them to Spagne for encrease." Off to the side in the margin, Richard Eden, the English translator of Pinzón's voyage, claims that the peacocks were really "Turkye cockes." When the English version was published in 1555, the Spanish did indeed refer to turkeys as peacocks, but Pinzón had not described these birds in his original manuscript, and no evidence has surfaced to indicate that turkeys were in fact raised in Venezuela at the time of Pinzón's visit.[2] Another European credited with the "discovery" of domesticated turkeys was none other than Christopher Columbus, who on his fourth voyage landed on a group of islands off the coast of Honduras and then anchored at Point Caxinas (Cabo do Honduras). The natives brought him *gallinas de la tierra* (land hens) that Columbus proclaimed were better than those of Spain.[3] Unfortunately, he didn't describe or illustrate the birds. They might have been turkeys, but they also could have been any one of a dozen other fowl common to the area.

Other Spanish explorers may have acquired domesticated turkeys and brought them back to Spain. If so, the records for their voyages and cargoes have been lost. A frequently cited document dated October 1511 has led many writers to conclude that there were domesticated turkeys in Spain. In it the Bishop of Valencia requires that each ship returning from the West Indies bring back ten birds—five males and five females.[4] It seems unlikely that he was referring to turkeys, however, because in 1511 few Spanish ships visited Central America, and no evidence for turkey raising in the West Indies before 1520 has surfaced. Even if it were the turkey, no primary source offers evidence that the bishop's decree was followed or, if it was, that any turkeys were raised in Spain as a result.

The first generally accepted reference to the turkey appears in an account of the Spanish expedition led by Juan de Grijalva, who departed from Cuba to explore the coast of Yucatán and Mexico in 1518.[5] The following year Hernán Cortés followed a similar route but landed with an expedition in Mexico, where the conquistadores found an abundance of both domesticated and wild turkeys.[6] Again, neither Grijalva nor Cortés appear to have been familiar with the turkey, suggesting that the birds were not raised in the Caribbean or Europe before 1518.

Shortly after Cortés's landing in Mexico, turkeys appeared in the West Indies. Alessandro Geraldini, who, it will be recalled, supported Columbus on his first voyage in 1492, was appointed bishop of the island of Hispañola (Haiti and the Dominican Republic). In 1520 he sent two turkeys to Lorenzo Pucci, the Florentine cardinal who lived in Rome. Geraldini instructed Pucci to admire the birds but not eat them, which suggests that they were extremely precious at the time.[7]

Another early observation of the turkey in the Caribbean was written by Gonzalo Fernández de Oviedo y Valdés, who migrated to Hispañola in 1514 and later became governor of the island. In 1535 he published his observations about early Spanish explorations in *Historia general y natural de las Indias,* which reports that turkeys were brought from New Spain (Mexico) and that Christians raised them in the Caribbean. He claimed that "the flesh of these peacocks [turkeys] is very good, and incomparably better and more tender than that of the peacocks [real peacocks] of Spain."[8]

Turkeys were raised in Spain during the 1520s and quickly became an important food for the upper class. An early European depiction of the turkey appears in the corner of an illuminated Spanish *responsorial* (collection of responses to be repeated by a congregation during religious ceremonies). The manuscript has been dated to the 1530s, which suggests that the turkey was common in Spain by that time.[9] Despite the bird's early arrival, the first located recipes, such as ones for roast turkey, a sauce, and turkey marinated in wine and spices, published in Spain appear in Diego Granado's *Libro del arte de cocina* (1599).[10] The absence of earlier recipes likely reflects the fact that turkeys were prepared in a manner similar to peafowl, many recipes for which appeared in Spanish cookbooks during the sixteenth century.

Linguistic Confusion

The first Spanish name for turkey was *pavo* (peafowl) or *pavón de las Indias* (peafowl of the Indies). The turkey's association with the peafowl was important, for peafowl was by far the most prestigious food bird in Europe. Peafowl (*Pavo cristatus*), members of the pheasant family *Phasianidae,* which originated in India, were domesticated in prehistoric times and brought into the ancient Mediterranean basin through the Persian empire. They are very large birds and have long and beautiful tail feathers, which they display during their mating season. Peafowl were difficult to raise and thus a status symbol in Europe. Some Romans believed that peafowl flesh was incorruptible, a story St. Augustine picked up in *The City of God* to symbolize immortality. Other writers also praised the peafowl, and the birds retained their special culinary status right up to the Renaissance.[11]

During the early Renaissance, some who wrote about diet and health condemned peafowl flesh as difficult to digest.[12] In addition, it didn't taste very good, according to many writers, yet nothing compared with the spectacle of the cock's long, colorful tail feathers. During the Middle Ages the plumage was removed while the bird was roasted. The feathers were then sewn back into the cooked bird, and cooks and servants paraded their handiwork before the dinner guests. The feathers were then removed and the peacock was carved at the table and served. Alternately, a more tasty variation was to chop the peacock's flesh and place it in a pie. Just before serving, the head was stuck into one end of the dish and tail feathers were placed at the other end. Either way, it was an impressive entertainment.

Adding to the linguistic and zoological imbroglio with the peacock and the turkey, the guinea fowl (*Numida meleagris*) was also called *pavo* by the Spanish and *gallo* or *galle d'India* (chicken of India) by Italians. The bird originated in Africa but was raised in the ancient Mediterranean, where the Greeks named it *Meleagris.* For unknown reasons it disappeared from Western Europe and was reintroduced during the fourteenth and fifteenth centuries by Arab or Turkish traders or perhaps by Portuguese explorers of West Africa. Not as large as the peacock, a guinea cock's tail feathers are not as spectacular, either. But guinea fowl were easier to raise, they tasted better, and their small eggs were considered delicacies. Guinea fowl quickly became common barnyard poultry in Europe and later in America, where their popularity continued well into the nineteenth century.

That the Spanish, Italians, and most other Europeans assumed that the turkey came from India can be partly blamed on Columbus, who set out to find a shorter route to India and claimed he had done so after his return from the Caribbean, which he called "the Indies." When it became obvious that he had not landed in Asia, the name was changed to "West Indies" as opposed to the East Indies, which then meant the fabled Spice Islands. To make matters still more confusing, the terms *cock of India, chicken of India,* and *turkey* were used in Europe before 1492 and therefore, in their initial usages, could not have referred to the bird from the Americas. The generic terms meant unfamiliar or showy birds. It is unclear precisely when the terms changed from a generic reference to one that specifically meant the turkey, which is what occurred by the mid-sixteenth century.

It is also not surprising that Europeans confused the turkey, peafowl, and guinea fowl. All three large birds are remotely related through the avian family tree, and their similar physical characteristics meant they were described in similar ways. Without familiarity with all three it would have been difficult for sixteenth-century naturalists to distinguish among them based solely on confusing descriptions. At the time of the initial European encounter with the turkey, world geography was only dimly understood; animals and plants arrived in Europe in massive numbers and without provenance. Then again, all three birds were prepared in similar ways; from a culinary standpoint it didn't matter which was available. Chefs did not begin to distinguish among the three until the end of the sixteenth century.

The Italian Tacchino

Turkeys were sent to Italy by 1520 from the Caribbean and by 1531 were offered as presents among the nobility of Italy.[13] By 1557 they were so common that the magistrates of Venice passed a sumptuary ordinance repressing turkey consumption, but the law does not seem to have had much of an effect.[14] As the turkey became more numerous in Italy, its use spread to the middle and lower classes, who changed the name for the bird to *tacchino.* According to Nicola Zingarelli's *Vocabolario della lingua italiana,* the word is onomatopoetic. It refers to sounds made by a turkey—in much the same way that the word *gobbler* has come to mean a turkey cock in English.[15]

A fast adoption in Italy is not surprising. Italians were interested in the natural sciences. They were among the first Europeans to establish botanic gardens for unusual plants and menageries of exotic animals from distant places. In the sixteenth century, kingdoms in Italy were part of the Spanish empire and would have had easy access to New World finds arriving in Europe.

Italian cooks readily adopted the turkey into their cookery, and the first known recipes for it appeared in Italian cookbooks. Bartolomeo Scappi, Pope Pius V's chef, may have been from a town near Lake Garda. His *Opera dell'arte del cucinare* (1570), likely published after Scappi's death, was one of the most original and influential cookbooks of the Renaissance. Scappi stressed taste rather than just spectacle.[16] He presents instructions on raising turkeys and offers many recipes with turkey as an ingredient. There is, for example, spit-roasted turkey; turkey meat made into *paupiettes,* or little poached quenelles; stuffed turkey; a whole bird baked in a coarse crust, the bird's head left exposed; and ones for turkey gizzards and livers. Scappi proclaims that a turkey is best slaughtered by hanging it upside down and cutting its throat so the bird bleeds to death—a practice still followed today that prevents blood from settling in the meat. Scappi also offers advice on how to dress the freshly killed bird. For effect, at the time of serving he advises leaving head, snood, wattles, and neck attached.[17]

Scappi recommends larding the bird, a process encouraged by many other cookbook authors up to the twentieth century. Larding places fat under or over the skin. The most common way of larding is through the use of a long, hollow needle into which lard (sometimes bacon) is placed. It is then threaded onto the skin or injected into the flesh. Larding helps keep turkey flesh from drying out, particularly white breast meat; flavors the lean flesh; and prevents meat from burning. It also contributes to crispy, golden-brown skin. The browning is a result of the "Maillard effect"—carbohydrates being heated in a hot, dry environment. When lard fell from favor in the twentieth century, commercial turkey producers injected water into the flesh to keep the bird juicy.

The German Indianischen Hanen

Scappi's recipes were lifted by others without attribution. Marx Rumpolt featured several in his *Ein New Kochbuch* (1581). Rumpolt claimed in the preface that he was Hungarian by birth, having been born in Transylvania (now Romania) but that his family was forced out by a Turkish invasion. He found work as a chef in several countries, where he encountered and learned to prepare various recipes. Turkeys most likely arrived in Germany by 1530 and quickly became an important food.[18] Rumpolt devoted one section of his cookbook to *Indianischen Hanen,* the German term for turkey.[19]

Rumpolt's turkey recipes were relatively simple. His "Turkey Dumplings" are basically meatballs made from turkey breast meat. He also refers to a recipe for "turkey broth" and forty more "that are not small." He urges the cook not to throw anything away; the gizzard, liver, intestines, and blood are all useful. The menus Rumpolt presents for banquets for noblemen are ordered from the higher to the lower ranking, but all recommend a turkey dish, which suggests that by 1581 turkeys were plentiful in Germany.[20]

Perhaps the most unusual aspect of Rumpolt's cookbook is its illustration of a turkey. The image was engraved by a German printmaker named Virgil Solis, who worked for the Frankfurt publisher Feyerabend in the 1550s.[21] Feyerabend continued to publish the picture long after Solis's death, making it the first turkey depiction to appear in any cookbook.

The French Dinde

In France, the phrase *poules d'Indes* (Indian fowl) first appeared about 1485 and was likely a generic term for exotic birds thought to originate in Asia. The term was applied to the turkey when it arrived in the sixteenth century and later shortened to *dinde* for the hen and *dindon* for the turkey cock. The turkey arrived in France shortly after being introduced into Europe.[22] Culinary historian Barbara Ketcham Wheaton located mention of it in 1528.[23] It is believed that the first published French reference to the turkey (*coq d'Inde*) appeared the following year.[24]

By the late 1540s the turkey was an important bird in France. In 1549 Catherine de Medici hosted a banquet in Paris and served seventy turkeys. At the time, turkeys were cheaper than peacocks, herons, pheasants, bustards, cranes, and swans, so it seems likely that turkeys were widely raised in France well before this date and served to the queen due to their taste rather than rarity.[25] For similar reasons the magistrates of Amiens presented twelve turkeys to Charles IX when he passed through that city in 1566.[26] When he married Elisabeth of Austria four years later, turkeys were served at the wedding banquet.[27]

Not everyone in France was enthralled with the turkey. The famous agricultural writer Charles Estienne, author of the influential *L'agriculture et la maison rustique* (1578), believed that "while it is true that his flesh is fine and delicate, but without taste and of hard digestion. And this is the cause why men use to powder them, lard them much, and season them with spices."[28] But Estienne was the exception; most observers praised the turkey's culinary qualities.

Despite the importance of the turkey in sixteenth-century France, it did not appear as an ingredient in French cookbooks until François Pierre de la Varenne's *Le cuisinier françois* (1651; published in English as *The French Cook* in 1653) offered several recipes. La Varenne systematized French cookery and also greatly influenced culinary matters throughout Europe.[29]

In 1667 Cardinal Jacques Davey du Perron wrote, "The turkey is a bird which has increased wonderfully in a short time. It has been a very good asset, people driving them from Languedoc to Spain in flocks like sheep."[30] By the eighteenth century the turkey had largely displaced the goose as the large bird of choice.[31] The turkey has continued to be an important bird in France; by the mid-nineteenth century the consumption in Paris alone amounted to half a million turkeys annually.[32]

The late eighteenth century and early nineteenth century French gastronome Jean Anthelme Brillat-Savarin proclaimed the turkey to be the most savory domestic poultry that was enjoyed by every class of society:

> When our farmers and winegrowers regale themselves on a winter's evening, what do we see roasting before the kitchen fire, close to which the white-clothed table is set? A turkey. When the useful tradesman, or the hard-worked artist, invites a few friends to an occasional treat, what dish is he expected to set before them? A nice roast turkey stuffed with sausage meat and Lyons chestnuts. And in our highest gastronomical society, when politics are obliged to give way to dissertations on matters of taste, what is desired, what is looked out for at the second course? A truffled turkey.[33]

Artistic and Literary Depictions

An indicator of the importance of the turkey in sixteenth-century Europe is the extent to which it so rapidly appeared in literary and artistic works. A depiction of a turkey was frescoed into a vault at the Villa Madama in Rome by 1523.[34] At the Château Fontainebleau in France, one appears in a decoration surrounding the "L'ignorance chassée" (Ignorance Defeated), completed in 1537.[35] The second edition of François Rabelais's *Pantagruel* (1548) mentions turkey cocks, hens, and poults (*coqs, poulles et poulletz d'Inde*), which were served at the fictional feast of the "Gastrolaters."[36] In 1557, Flemish artist Pieter Brueghel the Elder included a slain turkey in *Fortitude,* which was part of his "Seven Virtues" series; he also drew a strutting turkey in the foreground of his engraving *Envy* in the "Seven Deadly Sins" series.[37] Pieter Brueghel's second son, Jan Brueghel, drew turkeys in his *Birds of Paradise.*[38] About 1590 the Venetian Jacopo Bassano painted two white turkeys in his *Animals Entering the Ark.*[39] Vincenzo Campi, whose works consist principally of portraits and still-lifes, incorporated a turkey in *The Poulterer* (ca. 1580).[40] Done about 1600, *The Cook* by Bernardo Strozzi depicts slaughtered turkeys ready for plucking in a kitchen.[41]

Perhaps the most intriguing early representation of the bird was accomplished by the Flemish-Italian sculptor Giambologna, who sculpted a bronze turkey. Giambologna was the sculptor to the Medici in Florence, and Cosimo de Medici likely maintained turkeys in his menagerie. In the 1560s he ordered Giambologna to sculpt a life-sized turkey for his grotto at the Villa di Castello outside Florence.[42] Charles Avery, an expert on Giambologna, proclaims it a "tour de force." The turkey's "ridiculous pomposity," observes Avery, "lampoons—no doubt deliberately—a human figure clad in a formal ruff and heavy robes of state."[43]

European artists depicted the turkey in a variety of other art forms. Giovanni da Udine, for instance, included that in the vault at the Villa Madama, and Angelo Bronzino stitched a turkey into his tapestry *Abundance,* thought to have been completed about 1545, as did Brussels artist Willem Pannemaker (in his *Tapestry with Garden*) and yet another Brussels artist sometime between 1570 and 1600.[44] About the same time, Maerten de Vos included a white turkey in his *Garden of Eden.*[45] In the following centuries the turkey frequently appeared in drawings, paintings, and other works of art.

How to Carve a Turkey

During the Middle Ages, carving meat was considered an art, and it was an honor to be a carver. The art form is traced to Don Enrique de Aragon, who compiled a manuscript on carving in 1423. The art of carving, it says, was only worthy of those of noble birth. That art was exported to Naples, where Robert de Nola, cook to Ferdinand of Aragon and the King of Naples, described the ritual in his *Libro de cocina,* compiled in the 1490s. The Italian Vincenzo Cervio picked up the art form and expanded it. He had been in the service to the Duke of Urbino and later to Cardinal Farnese in Rome. In his book *Il trinciante* (1593), Cervio proclaimed that a carver should be a well-dressed gentleman of handsome presence. Carving was designed to be a spectacle that entertained and astonished diners. One way of causing such excitement was "carving in the air," where the carver demonstrated his proficiency by literally picking up the whole turkey and carving it in the air while slices of meat fell onto a plate.[46] This Italian carving manual includes a chapter titled "come si trincia un . . . gallo d'India" (how to carve a turkey). So there is no doubt about the intended fowl, the chapter is illustrated with a turkey.[47] The style of carving turkeys changed over the years. In the seventeenth century a French book wisely announced that they did not have to be carved in the air but could be on a plate. Rather than broad thin slices of turkey, however, the author recommends square strips.[48]

The custom of carving meat was reserved for the senior male or occasionally to a person of royal birth. Subsequent manuals and cookbooks gave elaborate instructions on how to carve turkeys. The custom extended well into the nineteenth century, when public displays of carving declined, at least on the Continent.

Scientific Naming

The first scientific description of a turkey appeared in a work written by Pierre Gilles, who translated a work by a writer of ancient Rome and added his own comments in 1533. He called the bird the *Gallo peregrino.* Although he was French, Gilles likely saw turkeys in Venice and believed that the bird had originated in the New World.[49] The first published depictions of the turkey appeared in the Pierre Belon's *L'histoire de la nature des oyseaux* and Swiss naturalist Conrad Gesner's *Historiæ animalium,* both of which were published in

1555.[50] Gesner used the term *gallopavo* (*gallus*, "cock" and *pavo*, "chickenlike"). He concluded that the turkey and the guinea fowl were identical, which suggests that he had not seen a turkey at the time. The same mistake as to geographic origin was repeated in 1599 by the Italian naturalist Ulysse Aldrovandi, who did catch some of the descriptive errors that appeared in earlier works.[51]

By the mid-seventeenth century it was commonly understood that the peacock, guinea fowl, and turkey originated in widely separated geographical locations. There was no reasonable explanation why the eighteenth-century Swedish botanist Carl von Linne (more commonly known by his Latinized name, Linnaeus) bestowed on the turkey the generic name of *Meleagris*, the Greco-Roman name for "guinea fowl." For the species name, Linnaeus selected *gallopavo*, presumably derived from Gesner. It is clear that Linnaeus knew the turkey originated in America because he stated so in his description of its habitat. His reason for selecting the name, however, has long puzzled scientists and turkey lovers.

Global Expansion

From Spain, Italy, France, and Germany, turkeys were rapidly disseminated throughout the world. They were raised in England before 1541 and in Scandinavia by the 1550s.[52] At the same time they were becoming known in Europe they were sent to other parts of the world. The Turks, who probably acquired their birds from Italy, called them the *hinde*, perpetuating the reference to India.[53] The Armenians likely first introduced the turkey into Persia, where it was called the "elephant bird."[54]

From Persia the turkey was brought into India, but it might also have been introduced into the subcontinent by this time by the Portuguese. The Hindi word for the turkey, *peru*, is likely derived from the Portuguese, who also call the turkey "peru."[55] Why that is the case is unclear. Most likely, given that the Portuguese acquired the turkey from the Spanish, the word *peru* is a corruption of the Spanish word *pavo*. The Portuguese established colonies in India, such as Calicut (now Kozhikode) and Goa, and Portuguese colonists probably brought turkeys with them. The Indians then adopted the Portuguese word for the new birds.

Seafaring explorers and traders also caused turkeys to be used throughout the islands and land bordering the oceans. Turkeys could easily be stowed in small cages onboard, and, as they ate virtually anything, special provisions were unnecessary. Adult hens were extremely hardy, making them ideal food sources when traveling. Early explorers intentionally introduced animals and plants into new environments, particularly into places with little human food. They hoped that such animals and plants would thrive and help future mariners and colonists survive in these new places. Hence, Thomas Cavandish spotted turkeys in 1588 on the uninhabited St. Helena in the Atlantic Ocean, where they had likely been introduced by the Portuguese.[56] The Dutch probably brought the turkey into what is now Indonesia in the seventeenth century, although the Portuguese may have shipped birds there at an earlier date.[57] From the west coast of the Americas, turkeys were shipped to South America, the Pacific Islands, the Philippines, and Southeast Asia, but the bird did not thrive in the tropics and never became an important food in tropical regions.

Common wisdom has it that it took hundreds of years to integrate New World foods into the Old World. Indeed, hundreds of years lapsed before Europeans adopted now-common New World food such as tomatoes, potatoes, and corn. That was not true of the turkey, which was accepted from its initial arrival in Europe. Of course, the turkey was similar to fowl already integrated into European cookery, whereas other New World foods with no Old World counterparts were seen for centuries as alien. The turkey was larger than the chicken and thus supplied much more meat. It was smaller than the peacock and lacked its impressive plumage, but the turkey's flesh tasted better and virtually any farmer could raise them. It was readily adopted as better-flavored and less likely to cause indigestion, and it could still could be served with flourish.

As flocks multiplied, prices dropped, and by the mid-sixteenth century turkeys cost less than chickens. Preparation was easy using existing fowl recipes and techniques, so adopting the turkey required no new cooking equipment or special knowledge. Turkey flesh was generally found to be "tender, delicate, nutritive, and restorative, of excellent flavour, and more dense and substantial than that of the chicken."[58]

The turkey's arrival and diffusion was an important event in Europe. Five centuries ago European civilization was on the brink of a major food shortage. Following centuries of traditional agricultural practices, European farmers had exhausted large tracts of arable land. Agricultural production was increasing marginally, although the population of Europe was growing rapidly. Europe was on the verge of widespread undernourishment and potential starvation. Too useful to remain the province of wealthy aristocrats, the turkey quickly became a widely available food for all but the poorest of the poor. In protein-starved sixteenth-century Europe, bigger was better.[59]

3

THE ENGLISH TURKEY; OR, HOW THE TURKEY COOKED THE CHRISTMAS GOOSE

Only English-speaking countries use the word *turkey* to refer to the *Meleagris gallopavo.* Many explanations, most of them fanciful, have been offered for its origin. Some have proposed an onomatopoetic derivation, claiming that the turkey named itself because it makes a "turk, turk" sound, but neither wild nor domesticated bird does that.[1] Others claim that the turkey's head looks like a fez.[2] The fez, however, was introduced into Turkey in 1826 to replace the turban and therefore could not have been the source for a sixteenth-century word. Still others maintain that the name derived from the Hindi or Tamil word *toka* (or *taus*), which means "peacock." That evolved into *tukki* (*taūs,* or *tarnegol hodu*), a Hebrew word that means "peacock" or "big hen." Jewish merchants from Spain then brought the bird (and the word) to England. There the word was initially spelled *turky,* which eventually became *turkey.*[3] Unfortunately for this tale, however, Spain expelled the Jews in 1492 before Christopher Columbus left for the New World.

This story was then revised to proclaim that Jewish "turkey merchants," engaged in trade between the eastern Mediterranean (then controlled by Turkey) and England, stopped off in Spain and picked up turkeys before proceeding to England. According to the *Oxford English Dictionary,* however, the term *turkey merchant* originated in the seventeenth century—long after the turkey had acquired its English name—and even then the term referred to those who raised, drove, and sold the birds in England. It had nothing to do with the nation of Turkey or with Jewish merchants.[4] Still others have speculated that the bird's name came about because the cock's peculiar gait resembles the proud "Turkish strut."[5] Yet few in sixteenth-century England had ever seen a Turk, so that, too, is an unlikely explanation for how the bird acquired its English name.

To make matters more complicated, the word *turkey* was used in England before the arrival of *Meleagris gallopavo* in Europe. Like other Europeans, the English confused the turkey with guinea fowl and other birds. The word *turkey* likely referred to the guinea fowl at first, when the term meant "strange" or "exotic." The word became part of the name for other edibles as well, for example, turkey corn (maize from the Americas). Whatever its initial referent, when the New World turkey became commercially dominant among fowl in England it retained the name *turkey* and other birds acquired other names.

Precisely when the turkey arrived in England has been endlessly debated. Some maintain that British explorers along the North American coast acquired wild turkeys and were the first to introduce them into England. No evidence has surfaced suggesting that is true, but even if it were, the introduction would have made little difference. Eastern North America only had wild turkeys at that time, and they did not reproduce in captivity.

The first generally accepted reference to the turkey in England is dated 1541, when Thomas Cranmer, Henry VIII's archbishop of Canterbury, proclaimed that only one large fish or fowl such "as Crane, Swan, Turkeycocke" should be served at meals for ecclesiastics.[6] Turkeys must have been relatively common in England by that date, and perhaps the clergy was a little too well-fed. There is no evidence indicating that anyone obeyed Cranmer's injunction, for turkeys flourished thereafter in England and the clergy seems to have eaten their share.

Turkeys were relatively easy to raise in England, and turkey farms proliferated. By the 1570s, large flocks were being raised in Norfolk, which had vast resources of grains and buckwheat.[7] Turkeys are eclectic in their eating habits. Although they will consume many things not otherwise eaten on farms, such as acorns, and substances considered harmful, such as insects, worms, and weeds, they also can destroy agricultural crops. Hugh Plat discussed this in his cookbook *Jewell House of Art and Nature* (1594). If turkeys were not penned, Plat reported, they ate and trampled crops and were prone to wandering off into the woods or to a neighbor's farm. To avoid that, Plat recommended that turkeys be kept in "coopes" that were "so straight and narrowe as that the hen or capon may onely feed himselfe and roost therein, not being able to turn his bodie, thereby perswading themselves that wanting motion and exercise he wil soon growe to be fat and of greace."[8] Thus, the "modern" industrial mode of raising turkeys was already underway by the late sixteenth century.

In London's public markets by 1559, turkey cocks sold for a little less than swans, cranes, and bustards (Old World land birds of the family *Otididae* that are also native to Australia). The smaller, less attractive hens sold for about a third of the price of gobblers. By the 1560s, P. E. Jones notes, laws were passed to prevent poulterers from letting their turkeys wander the streets, where they created a "common anoyance." As turkeys became more plentiful in England, Jones adds, they became more affordable. By the 1570s the price of both the turkey cock and hen had dropped by 50 percent, whereas the prices of other birds remained constant. In 1572 capons cost more than turkeys. Prices, of course, were based on supply, and those for turkeys dropped sharply at the high point of availability in the late summer and early fall.[9] In 1573 Thomas Tusser reported that turkeys were common fare among farmers.[10]

Sixteenth-century Turkey Cookery

The first located English recipes specifically designated for turkeys—one for baking them and the other for a sauce to serve with them—appeared in *A Booke of Cookrye* (1584), written by the otherwise unidentified "A.W." The former recipe splits the turkey in two, a common technique that permits baking the bird faster and more evenly.[11] Baking in the sixteenth century often resulted in tough meat, which helps explain the presence of the accompanying sauce.

A more sophisticated recipe appears in Thomas Dawson's *The Good Huswives Iewell* (1587). "To bake a Turkie," Dawson advised, required boning the bird, then boiling it. After boiling, lard was placed under the skin to keep the flesh moist. The bird was then enclosed in a "coffin," a raised pastry crust, which was baked.[12] Until almost the twentieth century boiling was the most common way of preparing turkeys. The method had several advantages. Water boils at a constant temperature, so the bird cooks evenly, inside and out. Boiling also yields juicier meat than baking and was the only recommended method of preparing turkeys older than a year. The flavorful stock provides a base for soups, sauces, and gravies. Of course, the skin of a boiled turkey is not browned, but it will be if, as many cookbook writers suggest, the bird is roasted for a short time after being boiled.

Roasting was the second most common method of cooking turkeys. At the time, roasting meant placing the turkey on a heavy metal grate set over hot coals, if prepared outdoors. Indoors, the bird would be roasted in front of an open fire or, later, in a reflector oven. Turkeys were also roasted on spits, which required turning to ensure uniform cooking and prevent scorching. Although mechanical turners (operated by weights and gears, like a clock) were used in wealthy homes, spit-roasting usually required a servant or a child to crank the spit. To keep melting fat from flaring as it dripped onto the hot coals, the spit was placed in front of the fire rather than over it. Under the turkey, a pan caught the drippings that were later converted into gravy. Like baking, roasting often resulted in dry, tough meat, especially if the turkey was a year old or more.

Dawson's recipe mentions "boning" the turkey, a process that left the bird smaller and more manageable so it fit more easily into a kettle for boiling; it also cooked faster and was far easier to carve. If the bones were removed skillfully, the turkey would retain a semblance of its original shape, although the boned bird could also be molded into various forms. For a classic gallantine, a boned turkey would be filled with stuffing so it resembled an entire bird when presented at the table, and its carved slices would include both stuffing and meat. For significant feasts during the Renaissance, and foreshadowing today's "turducken," pigeons, ducks, geese, chickens, and smaller fowl were boned, boiled separately, and then stuffed one inside the other and finally into the largest fowl.

In England as on the Continent, all parts of the turkey were consumed. Giblets were cut up and added to the gravy and stuffing; livers became a specialty; and the neck, carcass, and bones were made into soup. Some parts of the turkey took on special favor. The rump or tail (the uropygial gland) since the sixteenth century has been called the "pope's nose" and later the "bishop's nose." It was (and is) considered succulent and an epicurean morsel by some and abhorred by others.[13]

Seventeenth-century Turkey Cookery

It was Gervase Markham who expanded turkey cookery in England. Markham, a prodigious writer, published numerous books, most of them compilations or translations without attribution of original sources. His *Cheape and Good Husbandry,* first published in 1614, gave recommendations for fattening a turkey: "sodden Barly is excellent, or sodden oats for the first fortnight, and then for another fortnight cram them in all sorts, as you cram your Capon, and they will be fat beyond measure." That advice was repeated in works on husbandry and cookery for the next two centuries.[14] Although turkeys were not generally sold by weight, fatter birds were obviously more appealing to buyers and therefore in greater demand.

Markham's popular cookbook *The English Hus-wife* (1615) noted that turkeys were served at both "great feasts" and "more humble feasts," reinforcing the view that by 1615 turkeys were common yet still considered special fare in England.[15] One recipe called for a turkey "carbonated," which meant broiled over hot coals, a process Markham said originated in France. In "carbonating," meats were usually slashed and scored before being grilled or broiled on a gridiron. Many recipes for carbonated meats appeared in cookbooks during the following centuries.[16] By the nineteenth century the word had changed meaning; the English author Eneas S. Dallas wrote that *carbonade* had degenerated in France into meaning a stew.[17] By the late nineteenth century the word no longer had any meaning in English and was replaced by terms such as *grilled* and *barbecued*.

Markham's *The English Hus-wife* also offered recipes for sauces to be served with turkey. One made from onions, bread crumbs, pepper, claret, orange juice, and lemon peel is for stewing pieces of turkey; another is a gravy thickened with grated bread; and the third, made from white wine, sugar, and cinnamon, is to be served in saucers alongside the turkey. He also featured a recipe for turkey pie, to "be baked in a good white crust, somewhat thick."[18]

Turkey pies were part of a broader European tradition and were extremely important in England (as they later would be in America). Pieter Claesz's painting *Laid Table with a Turkey Pie* (1627) shows a pie in an earthenware pot; projected from the top of the pie are a turkey's head and feathers, which give the pie the appearance of an actual bird.[19] Thomas Dawson's turkey pie was to be "baked in a good white crust, somewhat thick." In Dawson's recipe, the turkey was first boiled and then baked in pastry. Turkey leftovers helped fill meat pies. Another advantage was that the turkey could be boiled a day ahead of time and the pie assembled and baked on the day it would be served. As an economy measure the meat in the pie could be "stretched" with fillers.

In 1653 the second edition of François Pierre de la Varenne's *Le cuisinier françois* was published in English as *The French Cook.* His ten turkey recipes included "Potage of Turkies farced," "Turkie with ragoust," "Abatis or Purtenances of Giblets, of Turkie," "Turkie and Raspis" (turkeys and raspberries), and "Turkie after Daube" (turkey à la daube). According to the culinary historian Karen Hess, "à la daube" recipes in France are rustic dishes composed of braised meat, usually beef, with pork rind layered between the meat for flavoring. The dish is then cooked in wine and seasonings.[20] La Varenne's recipes would be copied and revised in England for almost half a century.

Two recipes for "Jacobins Pottage" appeared in La Varenne's cookbook, although turkey was not an ingredient in either.[21] Other such recipes, like the one in W.M.'s *The Queen's Closet Opened* (1655), did include turkey as an ingredient. In these recipes "Jacobins" means members of the Dominican religious order. The name became associated politically with French radicals during the Revolution of 1789, when they met in a former Dominican monastery. Jacobin pottage is a thick soup or stew composed of minced turkey, grated Parmesan cheese, spices, chicken and mutton broth, and chunks of squash topped with orange juice. W.M. also published "To boyl a Pudding after the French Fashion" in which a turkey is boned, larded, spiced, and then encased in a covered pot with wine that is permitted to stew above a gentle fire for several hours.[22]

Other recipes arrived from outside England and brought new dimensions to turkey cookery. Sir Kenelme Digby was a true Renaissance man—a soldier, sailor, philosopher, diplomat, scientist, mathematician, and alchemist. He was also a good cook, and the recipes he collected on his travels were published anonymously after he died. The two interesting turkey recipes in the collection reflect his contact with foreign cuisines as well as the time he spent at sea. Both are for "pickling" turkeys. Although pickled meat may sound odd now, pickling vegetables and fish—variously called caveach, escabeache, or scapece, depending upon the language—was common at a time when food was preserved without refrigeration and chemical preservatives. In Digby's first recipe, "To Souce Turkes," a boned turkey is boiled in a mixture of wine and vinegar and seasoned with salt. It is then placed into an earthen pot and covered with more vinegar and stored for a month. In the second recipe, which resembles corned beef, the turkey is salted for ten days, then pickled with mace and nutmeg; Digby suggests adding garlic, if liked.[23]

This last ingredient is somewhat surprising because many in England did not view garlic favorably at the time. Digby's contemporary John Evelyn, author of *Acetaria, a Discourse of Sallets,* observed that Spaniards and Italians consumed garlic "with almost everything," but he opposed its use "by reason of its intolerable Rankness, and which made it so detested of old; that the eating of it was (as we read) part of the Punishment for such as had committed the horrid'st Crimes."[24]

One grand tradition of cookbook writing is that of "borrowing" recipes from other works, usually without attribution. That is as true today as it was in the seventeenth century. Many recipes from Kenelme Digby's cookbook were borrowed by others. The English herbalist William Salmon, an outspoken critic of Catholicism, borrowed both of Digby's turkey recipes and published them without attribution in *Family-Dictionary; or, Household Companion* (1705) along with five other turkey recipes lifted from other sources.[25] An otherwise anonymous "T. Hall" incorporated forty of Digby's recipes into his pseudonymous *The Queen's Royal Cookery* (1709). Although Hall claimed to reveal the secrets of Queen Anne's royal kitchens, the "secret" revelations, such as the one for "Turkey-Pye," were similar to previously published recipes.[26]

Another of Digby's contemporaries, Robert May, was trained in France and served as chef to noble Catholic families in England. He left England during the English Civil War. In 1685, shortly after the restoration of Charles II as king, May's *The Accomplished Cook* was published. It contained many turkey recipes, among them one for a "Stofado" that was probably of Spanish origin. The turkey was to be browned in lard and seasoned with nutmeg and pepper, then steeped in wine and vinegar seasoned with cloves, pepper, ginger, nutmegs, mace, salt, lemon, and mutton broth. The mixture was served over French bread, which May suggested buying from a baker.[27]

May also offered a recipe for dressing turkeys "in the French mode or to eat cold, called a la doode." This consisted of boned and larded turkey filled with bacon and seasoned with parsley, pepper, cloves, mace, and nutmegs. The bird was marinated overnight in white wine before being baked in a covered pot. Stuffing was served in saucers, with rosemary, bay leafs, mustard, and sugar; the turkey was laid "on a napkin folded square, and the turkey laid corner-ways."[28] Recipes for turkey à la daube and à la mode—methods that differed mainly in presentation—were published regularly until the late nineteenth century.[29]

Another Restoration cookbook author was William Rabisha, who left England during the civil war and interregnum. His *Whole Body of Cookery Dissected* (1661) begins with a series of menus, and those for many "flesh" days (as opposed to meatless or fast days) include turkey. A roast turkey is presented in the "Bill of Fare for an Extraordinary Feast, on a Flesh-day in the Spring" in the first course, and "a dish of young Turkey larded" is incorporated into the second.[30]

Rabisha presented a number of unusual turkey recipes. "How to congeal a Turkey or Capon" called for separating and mincing white and dark meat and mixing them separately with onion, horseradish, thyme, mace, nutmeg, bacon, and salt. The mixture was layered into a pot along with wine anchovies and other seasonings. This was then boiled and "served at a feast." After the pot cooled it was broken and the turkey mixture was sliced and served.[31] Recipes using minced or hashed turkey flesh were common in British cookbooks before the twentieth century. Chopping turkey flesh allowed the cook to combine lean breast meat with fattier dark meat and skin so the minced turkey would stay moist when cooked. When cost was an issue, cheaper ingredients such as root vegetables could be used as fillers.

In Rabisha's recipe for the "Flesh Sallet of a Capon or Turkey," white and dark meat was separated, minced, and each was mixed with chives, tarragon, spearmint, lettuce, cabbage, parsley, pepper, salt, nutmeg, and horseradish. Both were then layered into a dish, and olive oil and vinegar were poured on top. Rabisha adds a diced lemon as an accompaniment and encourages garnishes "at your pleasure."[32]

At the time, composed salads were frequently made with a mixture of vegetables, fruits, and cooked meat or poultry. Salads had been part of formal English cookery since at least the fourteenth century.[33] Despite numerous salad recipes published in English cookbooks, few incorporated turkey as an ingredient before the mid-nineteenth century.

Turkey Drives

By the mid-seventeenth century turkey-raising had become an important commercial business. In general, birds were kept in enclosures on farms. Most turkey farms were located in East Anglia, which was far from London, so the problem was how to move birds from farm to market. Wagons would not carry many, and before refrigeration turkeys could not be slaughtered until they reached the market. The solution was simple. Like cattle and sheep at the time, turkeys were walked to the cities. To prevent them from flying away, one wing was cut. Those who drove the turkeys were called "turkey merchants."[34]

While touring England in 1724, the English novelist Daniel Defoe, famous for *Robinson Crusoe,* observed that turkeys filled the roads from East Anglia to London in the autumn. The journey took a week, and in one season as many as three hundred droves passed over a single Stratford Bridge. Defoe noted that droves contained from three hundred to a thousand birds each, so he estimated that between ninety and three hundred thousand birds crossed that one bridge in a single year. This was only one of several routes from East Anglia to London, so the market for turkeys would have been tremendous.[35]

The birds' destination was the shops in Poultr, a section of London that dates to Roman times. As turkey drives became larger and more frequent, reported Defoe, "the markets were moved to other sites, including Leadenhall which is still the place where City gentlemen buy their Christmas turkey."[36] Farmers continued to drive turkeys to market until the mid-nineteenth century, when railroads became the main transportation.[37]

Eighteenth-century Turkey Cookery

By the eighteenth century, virtually all English cookbooks provided turkey recipes. An unusual one, "To make a Cold Hash, or Salad-Magundy," first appeared in the second edition of Mary Kettilby's *A Collection of above Three Hundred Receipts* (1719).[38] Salmagundi, a composed salad, was thought to have originated in either France or Italy in the sixteenth century; a reference to *salmigondin* is found in a French text dated 1546.[39] In 1674 Thomas Blount wrote that it was an Italian "dish of meat made of cold Turkey and other ingredients."[40] Recipes for salmagundi continued to appear in cookbooks well into the nineteenth century, although turkey was not always an ingredient.[41] Kettilby also presented a recipe "To Souse a Turkey, in Imitation of Sturgeon," which had been borrowed from Kenelme Digby. According to Kettilby, soused turkey was a much more delicate dish than pickled sturgeon.[42]

Charles Carter's *The Complete Practical Cook* (1730) featured many new recipes: turkey and celery; turkeys served "a la Dobe"; turkey served with a capon and a goose (called "A la Mode de Blois"); one for "la Castrole (or dressed in Embers)"; a turkey "Sattoot" (forced in pastry) and a similar one called "Turkeys Definator"; a "Rockampuff" (hashed turkey in a puff paste); and two for turkey "Ramkins" (small quantities of cheese with breadcrumbs and eggs, baked in a small pan).[43]

Two cookbooks published in England were important in North America: E. Smith's *Compleat Housewife* (1727), which in 1742 was the first cookbook published in North America, and Hannah Glasse's *Art of Cookery Made Plain and Easy* (1747). Smith's turkey recipes included ones for making pie and a sauce and how to chose, stew, and roast the birds.[44] Although Glasse's cookbook would not be published in America until the early nineteenth century, colonists brought numerous copies with them, and it was reportedly the most common cookbook in the Colonies. The *Art of Cookery,* also one of the most influential cookbooks published in England during the century, incorporates seventeen recipes for preparing, stuffing, and serving turkey. The generic recipes for unnamed fowl became standard "turkey" recipes in subsequent cookbooks.[45]

Stuffing a Turkey

The turkey's large body cavities presented unique opportunities for the creative cook. Since the early days of cooking turkeys in Europe the birds were usually filled with some sort of stuffing, often forcemeat. The sixteenth-century Italian chef and cookbook writer Bartolomeo Scappi suggested a stuffing consisting of chopped liver, prunes, cherries (or other berries), and lard, seasoned with mint, marjoram, parsley, egg yolks, pepper, cloves, and nutmeg plus grated cheese, garlic, and fried onions.[46] Robert May directed the cook to "mince some beef-suet and a little veal very fine, some sweet herbs, grated nutmeg, pepper, salt, two or three raw yolks of eggs, some boil'd skirrets or pieces of artichokes, grapes, or gooseberries."[47]

Vincent LaChapelle's *The Modern Cook* (1733) includes "green truffles" in a "turkey stuffing" recipe. Truffles aren't green, so he perhaps meant "fresh," or the reference might have been to some other fungus or root vegetable.[48] Whether intentional or not, the recommended use of truffles in turkey stuffing reverberates in cookbooks down to the twentieth century. Then as now, however, they have never been cultivated. Truffles grow only in southwestern Europe at the roots of oak trees and are not easy to locate and extremely expensive. "As it takes nearly two or three pounds of truffles to stuff a turkey well," the English writer Eneas Dallas noted in 1877, "and as truffles are worth twelve to fifteen shillings a pound, it is not every one who can afford such a luxury."[49] Some American recipes recommended four pounds of truffles, which suggests that the recipes were either "for show" and not intended to be made or that something else or an adulterated product was being sold as truffles. When the price of truffles went up during the early twentieth century they were no longer added to turkey stuffing.

Oysters are a classic part of stuffing, and Carter's *The Complete Practical Cook* incorporates them into several turkey recipes, mainly as an ingredient in stuffing. Other cookbooks offer recipes for oyster sauce to serve with turkey.[50] Initially, oysters were one of few foods in England (and later in America) that both the poor and the rich avidly consumed. They were so numerous in the beds around England and America that almost anyone could dredge them up. Until the beds gave out due to pollution and over-harvesting the oysters were generally cheap as well. When their price went up during the twentieth century they became a delicacy and were used less frequently, although oyster stuffing remains a traditional holiday favorite with many families.

Chestnut trees were common, so recipes for chestnut stuffing proliferated throughout England and the United States and continue to be popular. Susannah Carter's *The Frugal Housewife,* first published in London in 1765, advised pounding chestnuts, turkey liver, ham, and spices to make stuffing.[51] The recipe was included in Carter's cookbook that was first published in Boston in 1772, thus becoming the first chestnut stuffing recipe published in America.

Hannah Glasse offered an interesting recipe for "A Yorkshire Christmas-Pye," which has boned turkey, goose, fowl (i.e., a chicken), and pigeon. Although the directions do not specify placing the smaller birds inside larger ones, they do direct that only the turkey be visible.[52] Subsequent recipes such as the one for "Yorkshire Pye" in Elizabeth Raffald's *The Experienced English Housewife,* first published in 1769, explicitly state that the birds should be placed inside one another.[53] This was common practice in Europe during the Renaissance. The recipe survives in various forms, the most famous of which is the turducken (or "turkducken"), which was created in Louisiana. A turducken consists of a boned chicken stuffed inside a boned duck stuffed inside a boned turkey; dressing is layered between each bird. The dish was made famous by the celebrity chef Paul Prudhomme, who served it beginning in the 1960s at his family's restaurant, K-Paul's, in New Orleans. For some years it was a tradition for John Madden, who coached the Oakland Raiders football team, to pick up a turducken in New Orleans and serve it to the team on Thanksgiving Day.[54]

English Turkey Cookery in the Nineteenth Century

By the early nineteenth century many customs involving turkeys were changing. A pseudonymous food philosopher, "Launcelot Sturgeon," advised in 1822 to never acknowledge mistakes should one be forced to carve at table. He recited the incident of a man of "high fashion" who was telling a story while carving and accidently dropped a whole turkey into a woman's lap. He completed the story and then said, "Madam, I'll thank you for that turkey."[55] Presumably the account was apocryphal. It is difficult to imagine anyone with a turkey in their lap not saying something until a story ends.

The way of serving food changed during the late nineteenth century in Europe. Since the Middle Ages the banqueting style was *service à la française,* in which each course consisted of a large number of dishes presented simultaneously on the table at the same time. *Service à la Russe* meant that dishes were brought out sequentially. In Continental Europe, serving dinners à la Russe meant that servants cut the meat in the kitchen or on sideboards and served it to guests. Service à la Russe became the main mode of presenting food in England, except for carving. Isabella Beeton's *Book of Household Management* (1861), the most popular British cookbook in the late nineteenth century, maintains the old values with regard to carving: "we can hardly imagine an object of greater envy than is presented by a respected portly paterfamilias" at the table carving "his own fat turkey, and carving it well." The tradition of carving a turkey at the table has continued in England and America.[56]

At the same time, boiled and roasted turkeys began to lose favor with the upper class. Launcelot Sturgeon reported that there existed in Paris a "Constitutional Association" whose main interest was to promote good cooking. When boiled and roasted turkeys were served to the association on four alternative days the members complained and demanded a change. The president of the association announced that a prize would be offered for "the best essay on a new mode of dressing turkey." An artist named "Monsieur Le Gacque" proposed that the turkey be braised—browned on the outside by heating it in fat and then completing the cooking process by slow simmering in an enclosed pan. The maître d'hôtel strenuously opposed this as a "dangerous innovation," for "no turkey was ever so treated before." The president decided to experiment. Three turkeys would be prepared: one boiled, one roasted, and one braised. A committee would be selected, and its members would eat all three turkeys and make their decision, which was in favor of La Gacque's braising technique. According to Sturgeon, this was the beginning of braising turkeys, and recipes for doing so did appear subsequently in British and American cookbooks.[57] Entered into the minutes of the association was the following doggerel:

Turkey boil'd
Is turkey spoil'd,
And turkey roast
Is turkey lost;—
But, for turkey braised,
The Lord be praised!

Below it someone scrawled a note that the exception to this was a roasted turkey "stuffed with truffles."[58]

The Festive Holiday Bird

By 1573 Thomas Tusser noted that turkeys were commonly served at English Christmas dinners.[59] During the same period the Protestant reformation in England challenged the very notion of Christmas. Puritans, for instance, believed the day to be a "Popish holiday" and therefore not to be celebrated at all. Another strike against Christmas was that it was then frequently celebrated not with a family dinner and presents but with drunken revelry, which gave the holy day further bad repute. During the Restoration, however, Christmas again returned to England, and the Christmas turkey returned to English tables. John Gay noted in a poem in *Fables* (1792) that the turkey reigned supreme at Christmas dinner: "From the low peasant to the lord, / The Turkey smokes on every board."[60]

By the late eighteenth century the custom of giving turkeys to employees for Christmas dinner was well established.[61] The gift Charles Dickens received in 1839 from his lawyer, Charles Smithson, may have inspired him to write the scene in *A Christmas Carol* (1843) in which the miserly Scrooge gives a "prize Turkey" to his employee Bob Cratchit on Christmas.[62] (Dickens's wife, Catherine, had several recipes for turkey in her menu books—for roasting and broiling and for boiling older birds. The turkey was a popular part of Catherine Dickens's menus. She served drumsticks for family meals of two or three persons, but turkey legs were awkward to eat, as her husband noted in *Bleak House*.[63]) As many authors have pointed out, Dickens's novella greatly influenced the English celebration of Christmas, and the turkey was enshrined as the centerpiece of the dinner. Isabella Beeton proclaimed in 1861 that "a Christmas dinner, with the middle classes of this empire, would scarcely be a Christmas dinner without its turkey." [64] It remains so today.

4

THE CALL OF THE WILD TURKEY; OR, HOW THE WILD TURKEY CAME TO A FOWL ENDING

Many European expeditions explored what is today the United States during the sixteenth century. Some charted the coastline of eastern North America, others established settlements in the New World. In 1562 Jean Ribault, a French captain, explored the coast of southeastern North America. The French established a fort at La Carocine in what is now Jacksonville, Florida. Simultaneously, the Spanish built a fort at St. Augustine to protect the northern sea lanes traversed by their galleons bearing New World treasure back to Spain. The Spanish believed that the French colony threatened their hold on the region, and they destroyed it. But before they did, Jacques Le Moyne recorded life in drawings that have survived. Wild turkeys are visible in one, the first known drawing of the bird in America.[1]

Wild turkeys were generally unknown to most Europeans, but domesticated birds were already an important food source in Western Europe by the 1580s. George Peckham recommended that future English colonists headed for North America take male and female turkeys along on the journey.[2] Evidently, Peckham was unaware that eastern North America teemed with wild turkeys that were much larger than domesticated ones.

In all the European colonies in eastern North America, wild turkeys were highly valued. They didn't need to be penned or fed or cared for; they were there for the taking. In 1630 Thomas Wentworth Higginson, the first minister in the Massachusetts Bay Colony, wrote, "Here are likewise aboundance of Turkies often killed in the Woods, farre greater then our English Turkies, and exceeding fat, sweet, and fleshy."[3] In fact, some colonists did not even need to hunt wild turkeys in the woods. Thomas Morton of Massachusetts would go out onto his porch and watch "great flocks" of turkeys sail by. When dinner was wanted all he had to do was shoot a few.[4]

The actual weight of wild turkeys was much discussed in colonial times. Adriaen van der Donck, a Dutchman who lived in New Amsterdam (now New York) from 1641 to 1645, reported they were "large, heavy, fat and fine, weighing from twenty to thirty pounds each, and I have heard of one that weighed thirty-two pounds."[5] William Byrd of Virginia caught a turkey that weighed thirty-four pounds.[6] John Lawson, a Londoner who surveyed North Carolina beginning in 1700, told of wild turkeys weighing forty pounds, as did John Brickell.[7] Morton in Massachusetts reported that he killed turkeys that "weighed forty eight pound a peece," as did Richard Blome in Virginia.[8] A visitor to Maryland shot a turkey that weighed at "neere forty-nine pounds."[9] John Clayton, the rector at Jamestown, Virginia, reported, "There be wild Turkies extream large; they talk of Turkies that have been kill'd, that have weighed betwixt fifty and sixty Pound weight."[10] The same talk of sixty-pound turkeys was heard by John Josselyn, who chronicled mid-seventeenth-century New England.[11] Yet another observer was told of a sixty-three-pound bird.[12] Many other observers pointed out that some turkeys were so big that they had difficulty flying. Along the Allegheny River in western Pennsylvania, Christian Schultz reported in 1807 that many turkeys were "so overburdened with fat that they fly with difficulty."[13] Along the Mississippi River, James Adair noted that turkeys grew "so fat in March, that they cannot fly farther than three or four hundred yards; and not being able soon to take wing again, we speedily run them down with our horses and hunting mastiffs."[14]

Of course, scales were unusual in those days and the extremely high figures were likely exaggerations, but wild turkeys were very large—much larger than domesticated turkeys of the time. If they weighed so much in the past, why do they rarely weigh more than thirty pounds today? Heavy turkeys had great difficulty flying and were much easier to catch with hunting dogs and horses. Then again, larger turkeys made easier targets and were also prized because they provided more meat. Extremely large wild turkeys did not survive the onslaught, but smaller, more nimble ones did and reproduced.

In addition to weighing more, the abundance of turkeys was found virtually everywhere in great numbers throughout eastern North America. In Massachusetts, William Wood wrote of the turkey: "Of these sometimes there will be forty, threescore, and a hundred of a flocke."[15] John Josselyn claimed that he saw sixty broods of young turkeys, several hundred individuals, "on the side of a Marsh, sunning themselves in a morning betimes."[16] Adriaen van der Donck noted that wild turkeys were found in large flocks, "from twenty to forty in a flock."[17] Along the Great Lakes, the French explorer Pierre Esprit Radisson claimed that "there are so many Tourkeys that the boys throws stoanes att them for their recreation."[18] The English traveler John F. D. Smyth reported that turkeys on the upper Ohio River were "beyond number, sometimes five thousand in a flock."[19] An early traveler to Michigan reported that he had found "numerous flocks of wild turkies."[20] In 1727 a French Jesuit, Father Sébastien Rasles, wrote that in Illinois, "We can hardly travel a league without meeting a prodigious multitude of Turkeys, which go in troops, sometimes to the number of two hundred."[21] Along the Mississippi River, the French explorer René-Robert-Cavelier, Sieur de la Salle, found "plenty of wild Fowl, and particularly Turkeys, whereof we killed many."[22] Georges-Henri-Victor Collot, who surveyed the Mississippi, Ohio, Missouri, and other rivers, found "a multitude of wild turkies and in such numbers that the trees were literally rendered grey."[23] A visitor to Maryland in the early eighteenth century saw "mighty gangs of these Turkies" in "varst numbers."[24] Robert Beverly of Virginia just noted that there were "an infinite quantity of turkies."[25]

Farther west across the Mississippi, wild turkeys were even more numerous. An Oklahoman claimed he had seen flocks "countless in numbers" containing three thousand turkeys each.[26] In Kansas, Richard M. Wright saw flocks of turkeys on the prairies numbering in the thousands: "I have seen thousands of turkeys in a flock, coming to roost in the North Fork and the main Canadian and its timbered branches. Several times, at a distance, we mistook them for large herds of buffalo. They literally covered the prairie for miles, with these immense flocks, and, more than once we saddled our horses to make a run for them, thinking they were buffalo."[27] Texas was particularly well suited for wild turkeys, given its high grass, many river bottoms, and extensive sources for food such as pecans and mast. An observer found wild turkeys "in vast numbers" up the Nueces River.[28] In Frio County, Texas, H. L. Bingham saw "over a thousand turkeys" in one roost.[29] Another Texan didn't even attempt to estimate "how many thousands or millions of turkeys" there were in ten or twelve acres of dense growth of shrubby trees.[30]

The exact number of wild turkeys in America before the arrival of Europeans is impossible to know, but A. W. Schorger, a turkey specialist, estimated the density of the birds per acre in different habitats and conservatively put the wild turkey population at the time of European contact at ten million at least.[31]

Wild Turkeys as Food

Wild turkeys were eaten in every European settlement from the Atlantic Coast to the American Southwest. They inhabited the North Carolina coast, where the first English settlement in America was formed at Roanoke in 1586.[32] When William Strachey arrived at Jamestown in 1610 he reported a "great store" of wild turkeys in the woods. He considered them "an excellent fowle, and so passing good meat, as I maye saie, yt is the best of any kind of flesh which I have ever eaten there."[33] William Byrd believed that turkeys were "a splendid dish, boiled or roasted. The wild ones have commonly a finger's thickness of fat on their back, which one uses for cakes and garden cooking, because it is sweet and far better than the best butter, as I myself have discovered."[34] In 1773 Joseph and Samuel Martin "lived for two or three months altogether on boiled turkies, which were eaten without salt" while their corn crop matured in what is today West Virginia.[35] In 1797 John Heckewelder, a Moravian evangelist in Ohio, fried wild turkey fat as a substitute for butter and lard.[36]

Throughout the rural parts of the South and the West, wild turkey remained a staple for generations. In western Pennsylvania and Virginia, settlers in the late eighteenth century dried turkey breast and called it bread.[37] So did Texans. Settlers in Colquitt County, Georgia, described how this bread was made. They dried "the 'white meat' of wild turkey-breasts, after which they cut it up and beat it into a kind of flour, and kneaded it for bread."[39]

In addition to providing basic sustenance, wild turkeys were also considered gourmet fare. Jean Anthelme Brillat-Savarin spent two years in exile in the United States after the French Revolution in 1789. He was delighted with the turkey, which he proclaimed "certainly one of the most delightful presents which the New World has made to the Old." He ate wild turkey as well as domesticated turkey, writing that wild turkey flesh was "darker and with a stronger flavor than that of the domestic bird." He recorded in his classic *Physiology of Taste* that while visiting Hartford, Connecticut, he was invited to hunt on the land of a local farmer, where he had the "good luck" to kill a wild turkey. Evidently he was the only one to do so, and it was quite by accident. Back in Hartford, Brillat-Savarin roasted the turkey and wrote that it was "flattering to the sense of smell, and delicious to the taste. And as the last morsel of it disappeared, there arose from the whole table the words: 'Very good! Exceedingly good! Oh! Dear sir, what a glorious bit!'"[40] Unfortunately, Brillat-Savarin does not tell how he prepared the bird on this occasion, but he loved truffled turkeys. In his concluding essay he imagines Adam and Eve and asks what would they not have "given for a truffled turkey hen[.]" As they didn't have one, his response was, "I weep for you."[41]

Brillat-Savarin was not alone in his devotion to the wild turkey. John James Audubon wrote that it was "a delicate and highly prized article of food" and "of excellent flavor, being more delicate and juicy" than the domesticated turkey.[42] Todd S. Goodholme, the editor of the *Domestic Cyclopedia of Practical Information,* proclaimed the flesh of wild turkey to be "more succulent, and at the same time more delicate than that of any other game bird."[43] Gilbert du Montier, better known in America as the Marquis de Lafayette, appreciated them to such an extent that when he visited the United States in 1824 he asked John Hartwell Cocke of Virginia to send a flock to his estate in France so he could release them. Cocke sent seven turkeys hatched from wild turkey eggs. In gratitude for the shipment, the Marquis sent Cocke a bell for his barn, which evidently still rings on occasion.[44]

Wild turkey was on the menus of America's best restaurants such as the City Hotel in New York, where it was often served stuffed with truffles.[45] At Delmonico's in New York, wild turkeys were served in a variety of ways, such as in a soup ("Purée of Wild Turkey à la Sartiges") or roasted and stuffed ("Wild Turkey à la Delagrange-stuffed"). Charles Ranhofer, the nineteenth-century Delmonico's chef, believed that the flesh of the wild turkey was "far more delicate and succulent than that of the domestic turkey."[46] Even frozen wild turkeys were considered so tasty that they also shipped by steamer to Europe, where they were "accounted a great delicacy."[47]

Not everyone agreed with these positive assessments. According to one nineteenth-century observer, the superior taste of the wild turkey was created only in the "imagination."[48] Others found its flavor very distasteful. There are a few explanations for these negative comments. Old turkeys, domesticated or wild, do not taste as good as young ones. Domesticated turkeys are slaughtered when fairly young, but a turkey shot in the wild may be years old. As wild turkeys disappeared from eastern North America they were brought from increasingly longer distances, and before the advent of refrigerated train cars, slaughtered turkeys degraded in the weeks it might take them to reach market.

They could only be shipped in extremely cold weather, which meant they were frozen. Weather frequently changed, so they might freeze, thaw, and freeze again before they finally reached the consumer. Finally, the taste of a wild turkey depends upon what it eats. Those, for example, that feed on chinaberries, which are bitter, are inedible.[49]

Naturalists and Ornithologists

The portrait painter and naturalist Charles Willson Peale (1741–1827) created America's first museum of specimens in Independence Hall, Philadelphia. Among the exhibits was a strutting wild turkey, posed to showcase its colorful feathers. Peale was very proud of the turkey, which he placed just inside the museum's entrance. Shortly before his death at age eighty-one he painted *The Artist in His Museum,* a self-portrait posed at the entrance to his museum. A stuffed wild turkey stands in the foreground of the painting.[50]

Peale's museum attracted visitors from around the world, one of whom, Alexander Wilson, had emigrated from Scotland in 1794. He moved to Philadelphia, where he befriended Charles Peale and the naturalist William Bartram, who encouraged Wilson to study ornithology. Wilson began roaming the Pennsylvania countryside, studying and drawing birds. Around 1803 he decided to publish his findings and drawings in book form. The first volume of *Ornithology* was published in 1808, but the eighth volume was not published until after Wilson's death in 1813. For that monumental work with 357 engravings of American birds, Wilson is called the "Father of American Ornithology."[51]

Perhaps the most enthusiastic admirer of the wild turkey was one John James Audubon, born in 1785 in the French colony of St. Domingue, now the nation of Haiti. Audubon was the illegitimate son of a French naval officer and his Creole mistress. After Audubon's mother died during a slave uprising, his father and stepmother brought him up in France. In Paris, he spent some time studying under the French painter Jacques-Louis David. To avoid conscription into Napoleon's army, in 1803 his father sent him to a small plantation, Mill Grove, in Pennsylvania. During the voyage, Audubon contracted yellow fever, and when he arrived in Philadelphia he was placed in a Quaker boardinghouse near the city to recover. While convalescing he began studying, drawing, and painting birds—a calling he would follow for the rest of his life.[52]

First, Audubon went into business in Pennsylvania and then in Kentucky. When his business ventures ended in bankruptcy in 1819 he decided to devote himself solely to painting America's birds. Audubon's descriptions and watercolors were remarkable by any standard. An avid hunter, he roamed throughout the then sparsely settled country in search of birds and their natural habitats. In order to create the most accurate likeness, Audubon shot the birds and then posed them hanging from strings, like marionettes, in naturalistic positions. In 1824 he was introduced to twenty-one-year-old Lucien Jules Laurent Bonaparte, the illegitimate son of Lucien Bonaparte, brother of Napoleon Bonaparte, the former emperor of France. Lucien, a naturalist himself, was very much impressed with Audubon's paintings and tried to find a publisher for them. Those efforts failed, but Audubon continued to paint birds. He was particularly enthralled with the wild turkey, which he had studied in a variety of settings. It was, he wrote, "one of the most interesting of the birds indigenous to the United States of America."[53]

Audubon continued to communicate with his friend Lucien, who was by then lecturing and writing about American birds. When Lucien decided to publish a book, he asked Audubon for his notes on the wild turkey, which Audubon supplied. Making only minor revisions to Audubon's notes, Lucien incorporated them without attribution into *American Ornithology* (1825). That destroyed their friendship.

Audubon began producing his monumental four-volume *Birds of America* in 1827, the first plate of which depicts a wild turkey. He went on to write a five-volume series of "bird biographies": *Ornithological Biography; or, An Account of the Habits of the Birds of the United States of America.* The two works were then combined and published as a seven-volume work, *The Birds of America* (1840–44).[54] In the section on the wild turkey he commented caustically, "A long account of the habits of this remarkable bird has already been given in Bonaparte's American Ornithology, vol i. As that account was in a great measure derived from notes furnished by myself, you need not be surprised, good reader, to find it often in accordance with the above."[55]

In fact, Audubon's record of the habits and lifestyle of the wild turkey was unsurpassed in breadth and depth. He reported that the birds began to assemble in October "in flocks, and gradually move towards the rich bottom lands of the Ohio and Mississippi." The males associated in parties from ten to a hundred and foraged for food separate from females, who were still with their young brood. When wild turkeys came upon a river they remained a day or two. Males would gobble and strut about, and the females and young would "assume something of the same pompous demeanour, spread out their tails, and run round each other, purring loudly, and performing extravagant leaps." At this time the birds mounted to the tops of the highest trees, and the flock flew to the opposite shore. The older ones easily traversed the rivers, "but the younger and less robust frequently fall into the water." There "they bring their wings close to their body, spread out their tail as a support, stretch forward their neck, and, striking out their legs with great vigour, proceed rapidly towards the shore."[56]

Audubon reported that when mast was abundant in mid-November turkeys separated into smaller flocks and devoured "all before them." When winter set in and food was scarce, wild turkeys in search of food approached farmhouses, congregated with domesticated fowl, and ate any food they could find. In mid-February the mating season begins; males and females separate into groups but remain in close proximity. The males gobble, and when a female utters a particular sound the gobblers return it. They then fly toward the female, spread their tails, draw back their shoulders, depress their wings, and strut "pompously about, emitting at the same time a succession of puffs from the lungs, and stopping now and then to listen and look. But whether they spy the female or not, they continue to puff and strut."[57] The hen responds by strutting and gobbling, and she "suddenly opens her wings, throws herself towards him, as if to put a stop to his idle delay, lays herself down, and receives his dilatory caresses." If more than one gobbler locates the same female, the males engage in fierce combat. The two can hold each other with their beaks and move backward and forward, "their wings drooping, their tails partly raised, their body-feathers ruined, and their heads covered with blood." If one loses hold, the other knocks him down and strikes him violently with his spurs and wings until the opponent is dead.[58] Turkeys are polygamous, and the surviving male usually mates with multiple hens.

In mid-April the hens separate from the gobblers and begin to look for a place to lay eggs. They frequently nest in driftwood on isolated islands or in well-concealed thickets. The nest, consisting of leaves, rests on the ground "in a hollow scooped out, by the side of a log, or in the fallen top of a dry leafy tree, under a thicket of sumach or briars, or a few feet within the edge of a cane-brake, but always in a dry place," reports Audubon. The nest needs to be well camouflaged and concealed from crows, which will eat the eggs. Audubon observed that a hen usually lays about ten to fifteen eggs, which are cream-colored and sprinkled with red dots. Hens rarely abandon their nest even when discovered; sometimes two deposit their eggs in the same nest and rear their broods together. One always watches the common nest, the other leaving only for brief periods to eat, drink, and defecate. Audubon watched the chicks hatching and saw the hen help remove the shells from the young "and with her bill caress and dry the young birds, that already stood tottering and attempting to make their way out the nest."[59] Chicks begin to tumble, roll, and push each other a few moments after emerging from their shells. Before leaving the nest with her young brood, the hen checks for predators and spreads her wings a little as she walks to protect the chicks, who stay close by.[60]

Chicks are particularly vulnerable to rain and cold during their first two months, but after that they are extremely hardy and can survive even freezing temperatures for short periods. On the ground, they roll themselves in dust "to clear their growing feathers of the loose scales, and prevent ticks and other vermin from attacking them." About two weeks after hatching the young birds begin to roost in the low branches of trees, "where they place themselves under the deeply curved wings of their kind and careful parent, dividing themselves for that purpose into two nearly equal parties."[61]

Audubon and others recorded the turkey's natural enemies as crows, eagles, owls, hawks, racoons, wolves, foxes, cougars, panthers, opossums, skunks, wildcats, and lynxes. In addition, snakes, skunks, foxes, racoons, and other animals eat turkey eggs. By August the young poults can easily leap into the branches of high trees to protect themselves from some predators. As a protection against ground predators, wild turkeys frequently prefer to roost in trees over swampy terrain.

Wild Turkey Recipes

Few recipes specifically for wild turkey appeared in nineteenth-century cookbooks, and most were similar to those for preparing domesticated turkeys. For cookbook author Eliza Leslie, wild turkey was an alternative ingredient in "A Raised French Pie."[62] The French-born chef and cookbook author Pierre Blot added trimmings and used the bones of wild turkeys to make a "hunter's Soup."[63] Marion Harland incorporated a wild turkey recipe into her popular *Common Sense in the Household* (1871).[64] Marion Cabell Tyree's *Housekeeping in Old Virginia* (1879) contained recipes for "Wild Turkey" and "A Simpler Way to Prepare Wild Turkey."[65] Lafcadio Hearn's *La Cuisine Creole* (1885) offered a recipe for "Wild Turkey."[66] By the early twentieth century the population of wild turkeys was diminished, and such recipes disappeared from mainstream American cookbooks.[67]

Although wild turkeys can generally be cooked in the same ways as domesticated birds, there are some differences. Domesticated turkeys are fed a consistent diet and are of a fairly uniform age and size when slaughtered. With a wild turkey, it's the luck of the hunt. Because wild turkey may be old, tough, and stringy, some authors recommended boiling before roasting them or using the meat in stews or soups rather than roasting it. Wild turkey has a greater proportion of dark meat, which some consider more flavorful but others find unpleasantly strong and gamey. Wild birds were most prized during the fall or early winter when they would have been feeding on mast and other food abundant during that season. At other times of the year they could be very lean, requiring larding or basting. Feed is usually withheld from domesticated turkeys for about twelve hours before they are killed so their crops empty of undigested food. Wild turkeys, however, often have rank-smelling, partially digested food in their crops. All in all, preparing a wild turkey was a chancier proposition than cooking a domesticated turkey.

One unusual way of roasting wild turkeys was tried in Texas. A pit was dug and rocks placed in it, then a fire was constructed in the pit. The coals were removed when the ground was heated. The turkey, feathers and all, was placed in the pit and covered in such a way as to prevent it from touching dirt. Then the pit was covered with earth, another fire was built over it, and the turkey was heated underground for several hours. When it was unearthed, feathers and skin would fall off, thus saving the trouble of removing them before cooking.[68]

Hunting the Wild Turkey

It was best to hunt turkeys during the fall and early winter, when food was abundant and birds were their heaviest. During the coldest months, when other game was not easily found, wild turkeys often became a main source of food for colonists and frontier settlers. Unlike smaller birds and animals, they were large enough to make it worth a rifleman's trouble "to expend a bullet and a whole charge of powder."[69] With the invention of the Kentucky rifle in the eighteenth century it became easier and cheaper to hunt wild turkeys.

Native Americans often traded wild turkeys to European settlers and also taught colonists how to trap, capture, and hunt them. Although the colonists found it easier to use hunting dogs to find, kill, and retrieve turkeys, Adriaen van der Donck observed that the greatest number were shot from their roosts at night. Frequently they stay in the same tree, and "when a sleeping place is discovered, then two or three gunners go to the place together at night, when they shoot the fowls, and in such cases frequently bring in a dozen or more."[70] Turkeys were also easy to track on snow-covered ground. In 1634 William Wood advised, "Such as love Turkye hunting most follow it in winter after a new-fallen Snow, when hee may followe them by their tracks; some have killed ten or a dozen in half a day; if they can be found towards evening and watch where they perch, if one come about ten or eleven of the clock, he may shoote as often as he will, they will sit."[71]

Still others trapped wild turkeys. In eighteenth-century Virginia, Robert Beverly wrote that a friend had "invented a great trap, wherein he at times caught many turkeys, and particularly seventeen at one time; but he could not contrive it so as to let others in, after he had entrapped the first flock, until they were taken out."[72] Sometimes entire flocks were driven into log-pen traps. In 1708 John Oldmixon reported that "the Virginians have several ingenious Devices to take them; among others, a Trap, wherein sixteen or seventeen have been caught at a time."[73] Circular hunts were organized in which beaters would ring an area of several square miles and slowly drive the turkeys toward a group of hunters. Colonists and early Americans perfected the method, and one such hunt could net hundreds of birds.[74]

Audubon provided one of the best descriptions of turkey trapping. The most common means of doing so, he reported, was to construct pens where wild turkeys were known to roost and then bait the birds into the pens. Traps were built by cutting logs twelve to fourteen feet long and four or five inches in diameter and placing the logs at right angles to a height of about four feet. A trench was dug under one side of the cage, and a quantity of corn was placed in the trap and in the trench. Sometimes kernels of corn were also strewn in the woods around the trap. When turkeys discovered the corn, they would eat it, following the bait, Audubon said, until they "come upon the trench, which they follow, squeezing themselves one after another through the passage under the bridge. In this manner the whole flock sometimes enters." Those inside, "having gorged themselves, raise their heads, and try to force their way through the top or sides of the pen." Rarely did the turkeys find their way out. Audubon heard of eighteen being caught in a single trap at one time. One winter he kept an account of the yield of each pen and found that seventy-six birds were caught in two months. There were sometimes so many that the pen builders grew "satiated with their flesh."[75]

Hunters became expert at luring wild turkeys into the open by mimicking turkey sounds. Turkeys were called, Audubon said, "by drawing the air in a particular way through one of the second joint bones of a wing of that bird, which produces a sound resembling the voice of the female." Unfortunately, it had to be done perfectly because gobblers were "quick in distinguishing counterfeit sounds, and when half civilized are very wary and cunning."[76] Instruments to reproduce turkey sounds can also be made from leafs placed in the mouth or clay pipes, but historically the most common was made from a turkey's wing bone. Then as now, such instruments required great skill because false notes frighten turkeys away.

The Disappearing Wild Turkey

Even during the seventeenth century, Americans began to recognize that wild turkeys were disappearing from some areas. In 1672 John Josselyn reported that New England colonists and Indians had "destroyed the breed, so that 'tis very rare to meet with a wild Turkie in the Woods."[77] By the 1730s, wild turkeys had almost become extinct east of the Connecticut River, although they still throve in upstate New York, eastern Pennsylvania, most of the South, and all of the West. By the late eighteenth century the Virginian Joseph Doddridge recorded that "the wild *Turkeys,* which used to be so abundant as to supply no inconsiderable portion of provision for the first settlers, are now rarely seen."[78]

When Audubon began looking for wild turkeys during the early nineteenth century he reported that the "unsettled parts of the States of Ohio, Kentucky, Illinois and Indiana" were "most abundantly supplied with this magnificent bird." It was "less plentiful in Georgia and the Carolinas" and "scarcer in Virginia and Pennsylvania." When he visited Long Island, which once had supported a huge population of wild turkeys, he found none. By 1828 he reported that turkeys could be found in the Allegheny Mountains, but the birds had "become so wary as to be approached only with extreme difficulty."[79]

The disappearance of the wild turkey from many areas of original habitat did not diminish the wholesale slaughter of those that survived. The last one in Connecticut was seen in 1813; the last records of wild turkeys in Vermont date to 1842, and in New York to 1844. In Massachusetts, the last wild turkey was killed on Mount Tom on November 1, 1847, and the specimen was preserved at Yale University in New Haven for decades.[80] As wild turkeys disappeared from the East Coast they continued to be hunted in western states and sent east in the winter when cold weather helped preserve them.[81]

By the mid-nineteenth century observers were noting the decline of wild turkeys everywhere there was human settlement. Writing about the wild turkey in 1864, the husbandry expert Roger Jennings reported that "in the Western and Southwestern States they are still numerous, though constantly diminishing before the extending and increasing settlements."[82] In 1876 the Philadelphia Women's Centennial Committee published *The National Cookery Book,* which explains that in western states the wild turkey was "still a familiar dish, but it is seldom seen in the cities of the Atlantic coast; here they are only to be obtained in the severe winter weather, when they are brought in a frozen condition many hundreds of miles."[83] By 1876, however, wild turkey populations had dwindled in many western states as well. They were last seen in Kansas in 1871 and disappeared from South Dakota by 1875 and from Ohio and Nebraska by 1880, from Wisconsin in 1881, Michigan in 1897, the Province of Ontario in 1902, Illinois in 1903, Indiana in 1906, and from Iowa in 1907. Although still common in remote areas of the South, turkey populations were declining there as well.

With scarcity came being even more prized as a delicacy, and restaurants reserved wild turkeys for special occasions. When Charles Dickens visited the United States in 1842, for instance, he was served "Roast Wild Turkies Stuffed with Truffles."[84] As wild turkeys became ever more rare in New England they also became a subject for artists. Charles Hayden painted *Wild Turkeys* late in the nineteenth century when the birds had almost been exterminated in New England, and in 1895 he received the Jordan Prize of $1,500 for *The Turkey Pasture,* which was later presented to the Museum of Fine Arts in Boston.

Wild turkeys so quickly vanished from North America that in 1884 Gaston Fay predicted they would soon become "as extinct as the dodo." (Reflecting the times, Fay, a southerner, inaccurately blamed African Americans for the disappearance of the wild turkey. They had, he claimed, "an affinity" for the fowl "from the earliest days of slavery.")[85] During the following decade George Enty, a wild turkey enthusiast, also lamented their disappearance: "It will not be many years before they become almost as much of a rarity as a wild buffalo ranging his Western prairies."[86] A twentieth-century writer in the *New York Times* proclaimed that the wild turkey "was already joining the ranks of extinct species and may, in the times to come, be classed with the dodo."[87] Even with those dramatic warnings, few paid any attention, and wild turkey populations continued to decline.

Of course, hunting contributed to much of the loss, but it was not the only cause. Loggers destroyed the wild turkey's habitat on a grand scale, and farmers did so as well by chopping down forests and filling in swampland. Moreover, turkeys ate and trampled crops, so farmers came to consider them as pests and killed as many as they could—or encouraged their dogs to do so. The market price rose as numbers declined, so professional hunters avidly sought out and killed any they could find.

The final reason for the disappearance of the wild turkey was the destruction of their important food sources. As farmers chopped down oak trees to clear land for crops, once-abundant acorns—a favorite of wild turkeys—became scarce. But that was minor compared with the loss of the American chestnut (*Castanea dentata*), once one of the most common trees in the United States east of the Mississippi. The American chestnut had virtually no natural enemies in the New World, and it grew to tremendous size. Its flavorful nuts provided food for turkeys and other wild animals. In 1904, however, the Bronx Zoological Park imported Japanese and Chinese chestnut trees that were infected with a blight (*Cryphonectria parasitica*). American chestnuts were not immune to the fungus, which spread with lightning speed throughout the United States, and by 1940 the American chestnut tree had all but disappeared.

With farmers and loggers destroying the wild turkey's habitat, hunters killing the birds in vast numbers, and a tree blight destroying one of their most important food sources it appeared that the dire predictions of Gaston Fay and George Enty would come true. By the 1920s the wild turkey had virtually disappeared from twenty of thirty-nine states of its original range.[88] By the late 1930s only pockets of the species survived in isolated and inaccessible locations.[89] In 1941 Harold Blakley, a wildlife conservationist, called the wild turkey the "vanishing American." According to Blakley, in the South only one small flock was left in East Texas, the bird was "a rarity in Eastern Oklahoma," and it survived in Georgia only in private preserves along the state's southern border. Blakley projected that the species would soon be exterminated in southern and southeastern states.[90] Estimates vary as to the number of wild turkeys at that time, but some claim that at one point as few as thirty thousand birds were left in the United States.[91] The high estimate was a hundred thousand.[92]

The fall in numbers of wild turkeys parallels the demise of other North American wildlife. It all seemed so limitless when Europeans first arrived. An estimated sixty million buffalo (*Bison bison*) roamed throughout much of eastern North America in pre-Columbian times. During the eighteenth and nineteenth centuries, however, hunters and sportsmen killed vast herds, and farmers and ranchers fenced the areas where the buffalo once roamed. By 1900 only a few thousand buffalo survived. A similar fate confronted many wildfowl. Large birds such as North American cranes and swans were so prized that they had largely disappeared from the East Coast by 1750. Brants almost disappeared by the 1880s, and the canvasback duck became nearly extinct. The passenger pigeon numbered an estimated five billion before European contact but were slaughtered to such an extent that by 1909 only two remained alive. Five years later the breed was extinct. It appeared that the turkey was soon to follow.

5

THE WELL-DRESSED TURKEY; OR, HOW THE TURKEY TROTTED ONTO AMERICA'S TABLE

The disappearance of wildfowl did not present a problem for European colonists, who had imported domesticated poultry—particularly chickens, turkeys, ducks, geese, and guinea fowl—shortly after colonization. Domesticated fowl generally foraged for themselves in the barnyard, and their diet was supplemented with kitchen scraps and grain. They needed protection from marauding predators, so most farmers constructed coops to protect them at night. But little else was necessary.

Domesticated turkeys were reportedly raised in Jamestown by 1614, but they were evidently still rare in 1623 because a law was passed imposing the death penalty for the theft of turkeys if valued at more than 12 pence.[1] Within a decade, however, tables were filled with turkeys at Jamestown.[2] Likewise, domesticated turkeys were sent to Massachusetts Bay by 1629 if not earlier.[3]

During the early years wild turkeys were numerous and easy to acquire. Domesticated turkeys were smaller than wild ones and known to destroy crops and cause other damage if not controlled; some farmers considered domesticated turkeys so mischievous that they were judged uneconomical to raise in large numbers. To further complicate turkey-keeping, cocks had to be separated from hens, especially when the hens laid eggs in the spring.

Because raising turkeys was a marginal activity for most farmers, little attention was directed toward breeding them. Free-range domesticated turkeys mated with wild turkeys, however, and produced new breeds, one of which was the Blue Virginia. Larger than the European turkey, it was therefore more valuable as a food source. Turkey flocks increased to such an extent that by 1744 they were being exported from southern colonies to the West Indies.[4] This export business expanded, and by the following century American turkey growers were sending thousands of turkeys abroad. Two in Massachusetts, for instance, sent a total of 1,300 live birds to London during one month in 1833.[5]

Tobacco Turkeys

Domesticated turkeys had other attractions in addition to meat. Their feathers, for instance, were used for various purposes. The French colonists in Louisiana, according to French historian Le Page du Pratz, joined four turkey tails together to produce umbrellas.[6] In New England, turkey feathers were used to make hearth brushes.[7] Turkey feathers continued to be used for making dusters, quills, corsets, and whips until the end of the nineteenth century.[8] Up to the mid-twentieth century artificial flowers, hats, and clothes were manufactured from turkey feathers.[9] They were also used to stuff mattresses and pillows.

By far the most important reason for the growth of the domesticated turkey population in America, particularly in Virginia and Maryland, was tobacco. Colonists were lured to the southern colonies, where conditions for that crop were ideal. Tobacco was America's first agribusiness and the preeminent colonial export.

A major challenge in growing the crop was to control tobacco hornworms (*Sphinx carolina*), which infested fields in the South from June to August.[10] In a time before pesticides and other deterrents, planters were helpless to fight hornworm infestation other than by sending numbers of slaves through fields to hand-pick the worms from tobacco leaves. Even then, half of a crop could be lost to the voracious creatures. To the rescue came the turkey, an omnivore that loves to feast on insects and bugs and finds the large and meaty tobacco worm irresistible. By the mid-eighteenth century planters were sending turkeys into their tobacco fields to eat the worms. In 1784 John F. D. Smyth, a British traveler, reported that turkeys were particularly dexterous at finding hornworms. A tobacco grower would keep a "flock of turkeys, which he has driven into the tobacco grounds every day by a little negroe that can do nothing else," reported Smyth. "These keep his tobacco more clear from horn worms, than all the hands he has got could do, were they employed solely for that end."[11]

One turkey could eat worms from an estimated thousand plants, but fifty turkeys could handle an estimated hundred thousand if properly managed. Flocks were slowly driven by slaves over tobacco fields each day. After the tobacco leaves were picked, the turkeys were placed in a fodder house or hog pen "until about Christmas—when a fat hen turkey and a ham of bacon make a very tolerable dinner," reported a farmer in 1822.[12] The practice of using turkeys to rid tobacco of the hornworm was noteworthy enough for James Fenimore Cooper to mention it in *The Spy* in 1821: "If I had you on a Virginia plantation for a quarter of an hour, I'd teach you to worm the tobacco with the turkeys."[13]

Insects consumed by turkeys were not limited to tobacco hornworms, and the practice of using them as insect-control agents continued well after the Civil War.[14] In Norwich, Connecticut, W. A. Browning raised the birds "to eat the bugs, worms, grasshoppers, &c." Because the turkeys could then be eaten, Browning was converting "pests of earth into good nourishing food."[15] Another farmer proclaimed that an age-old enemy, grasshoppers, could become a profit center as the turkeys that ate them were then sold.[16] When tomatoes became a popular food, the tomato hornworm, a close relative of the tobacco hornworm, ate large swaths of tomato plants. Again, turkeys were called upon to rid the plants of these pests.

Turkey Drives

Turkey drives were common in the United States for the same reasons they were employed in England (chapter 3). Roads were not in great condition, and wagons held few birds. There were no refrigerated trucks until the twentieth century, so turkeys could not be easily slaughtered on the farm and transported to the city. Driving them along roads to markets became the norm throughout America.

Driving turkeys was a difficult task. In Pennsylvania, "armies" of turkeys were driven along "less frequented highways" between Lancaster and Philadelphia. Julius F. Sachse noted that the great danger was that turkeys "were apt to crowd together and trample each other to death." To prevent this, drivers divided the flock into sections of fifty or a hundred turkeys. "Shooers," armed with long poles, tended each section. These armies at best averaged a mile an hour, and their speed decreased toward nightfall when the birds began to roost in orchards or copses. The day's journey ended for the turkeys, but drivers still had plenty of work to do. They watched the flock through the night and prevented the birds from roaming into local farms or "being raided by evilly disposed persons." A covered wagon carried feed and permitted some drivers to sleep while others remained on guard.[17]

Others commented on the problems particular to nightfall. As a Salem, New Hampshire, observer reported, "When the shades of evening had reached a certain degree of density, suddenly the whole drove with one accord rose from the road and sought a perch in the neighboring trees. The experienced drover just drew up his wagon beside the road, where he passed the night."[18] The turkeys scattered if they were not immediately brought under control in the early morning, and it was virtually impossible to re-form them in groups.[19]

Turkeys were usually herded short distances to markets or railheads, but some were driven great distances. One drive went from Ohio to Missouri.[20] On another occasion two boys drove five hundred turkeys from Iowa to Denver, accompanied by a wagon loaded with shelled corn. As they traveled across the prairie the birds foraged on grasshoppers. There were few trees, so at night some birds roosted on the wagon and others on the ground.[21]

Turkey drives were also common in California, where domesticated birds had been introduced by Franciscan missionaries.[22] During and after the Gold Rush turkeys were dear; gobblers sold in Sacramento at $7 each in 1854, and breeding pairs cost three to four times that.[23] By 1866, however, birds were plentiful enough in Placerville for Henry C. Hooker to buy five hundred and drive them over the Sierra Mountains to Nevada, where he sold them at a great profit to silver miners.[24] Drives also occurred in southern California. An article in *Atlantic Monthly* described ones of five hundred to three thousand turkeys, usually controlled by a man on horseback with the assistance of a sheep dog. One man cleared "three thousand dollars a year in the business," a large amount by the standards of the day. Californians may have considered a turkey driver low on the social scale, "but when he comes to town at Christmas with his cribs of fat gobblers at sixteen cents a pound, no true Californian will refuse him respect."[25] The drives continued well into the 1930s. They were finally discontinued because turkeys lost too much weight during the drive and other means of transportation became more convenient and less costly.[26]

American Turkey Cookery

Despite the diversity of people who came to North America in colonial times, English colonists were most numerous, and English institutions, practices, and customs predominated. No where was that more obvious than in the early American kitchen, where English culinary practices were dominant until almost the mid-nineteenth century. British colonists brought cookery manuscripts with them to the New World, and English cookbooks were also shipped regularly to the Colonies. They were republished in America, and most, such as E. Smith's *The Compleat Housewife* (1742), contained turkey recipes (chapter 3). Few families owned the cookbooks, but turkey recipes still found their way into cookery manuscripts. A "D. Petre" kept a manuscript recipe book, dated 1705, that included "To make a grand sallet," which begins with directions to roast two turkeys and shred the meat.[27] In Massachusetts, Mrs. Gardiner, who began her cookery manuscript in 1763, had recipes for "A Gravy Sauce for Turkey, Fowl or Ragoo," "Mock Oyster Sauce either for boiled Turkies or boiled Fowl," "Celleri Sauce, for Turkies and all other white Fowls boiled," "Mushroom Sauce, for a boiled Turkey &c," and two recipes for a "Gravy Sauce for a boiled Turkey."[28] These were taken from various editions of English cookbooks, including Hannah Glasse's *Art of Cookery Made Plain and Easy* and Elizabeth Raffald's *The Experienced English Housewife.*

Despite the political split with England, the newly independent United States remained faithful to British culinary traditions long after the War for Independence. British cookbooks continued to be published in the United States, often with "American" titles, and American cookbook writers borrowed heavily from English sources. The first cookbook written by an American, Amelia Simmons's *American Cookery* (1796), contained five turkey recipes similar to those published in English cookbooks.[29] Subsequent American cookbooks published many additional recipes. Generally, the instructions fell into five categories: how to select a turkey for the tables; how to roast, boil, fry, steam, or bake the bird; how to stuff it; dishes or condiments to accompany turkey; and what to do with leftovers.

Several cookbooks published during the 1820s and 1830s demonstrated a real American cookery. As Karen Hess has pointed out, Mary Randolph's *Virginia House-wife* (1824) made a notable break from British practices. Based upon Randolph's experiences managing a boardinghouse, the cookbook featured many original recipes, including "To Boil a Turkey with Oyster Sauce." In addition to these simplified European recipes, there was an "A-La-Daube" recipe from the West Indies that was likely introduced to Virginia by slaves.[30] Similar recipes were published in other cookbooks. N. K. M. Lee's *The Cook's Own Book* (1832) copied the encyclopedic A-to-Z approach and the recipes of the British author Richard Dolby. *The Cook's Own Book,* essentially a compendium of simplified recipes compiled from diverse British and American sources, featured white sauce, celery sauce, sausage stuffing, mushroom stuffing, and unusual ones for "Hashed Turkey," and "Turkey Custard."[31]

Another important pre–Civil War cookbook author was Philadelphia-born Eliza Leslie, whose *Domestic French Cookery* (1832) contained recipes for "Stewed Turkey or Turkey en Daub" and an unusual one for "Turkey Puddings."[32] Her *Directions for Cookery* (1837) featured a recipe for "Boned-Turkey Jelly."[33] Leslie's influence was so great that when Sophia Hawthorne, the wife of the American writer Nathaniel Hawthorne, cooked a five-pound turkey she did so "sentence for sentence" from that cookbook.[34]

As turkey became ubiquitous on the American table, particularly in the fall, many visitors remarked on them. The Englishman Thomas Hamilton ate dinner in Philadelphia in the early 1830s and concluded, "No man can say a harsh thing with his mouth full of turkey, and disputants forget their differences in unity of enjoyment."[35] Others were less enthusiastic about the quantity of turkey served in America. Adam Hodgson, also English, visited the United States in the fall of 1819. From the time he set foot on the American soil until he left Virginia, he wrote, he did "not recollect to have dined a single day without a turkey on the table." In "gentlemen's houses" he often saw two turkeys at a single dinner, and at other dinners there were "four or five turkeys on the table." Dinner was followed by tea with a "profusion of meat, fowls, turkey legs &c." In Norfolk, Virginia, six thousand turkeys were on the market for Christmas, claimed Hodgson.[36] An American who reviewed Hodgson's book, surprised by this last statistic, sarcastically countered, "Now if the marshal's returns are to be credited, and there is any truth in arithmetic, this would make two thirds of a turkey for every individual, man, woman, and child, master and servant, in that happy town."[37] Whatever the number of turkeys in Norfolk, turkey appeared on America's table in prodigious quantities, particularly where tobacco was king.

Turkey Eggs

Americans consumed turkey eggs in addition to its flesh. The eggs are about half again as large as chicken eggs and have a stronger flavor. They are also proportionally much higher in fat and cholesterol and richer in vitamin E. Of course, Americans were not the first to eat turkey eggs. Native Americans "sought after and relished" them, and Europeans had also done so as well.[38] The sixteenth-century French writer Charles Estienne, however, was not enthralled: "The housewife shall not make any great account of Turkie egs: at least he that loveth his health, shall not esteeme of them for to use them: for phisitions hold, that egs of Turkies engender gravell, and minister cause to breede the leprosie."[39] Gervase Markham, a seventeenth-century

English cookbook author, appreciated turkey eggs, which were "exceeding wholesome to eate, and restore nature decayed wonderfully."[40] During the following century the English agricultural experts John Mortimer and others heralded turkey eggs to be "very wholsome, and a great Restorer of Nature."[41] In the mid-nineteenth century, Alexis Soyer, a French chef who lived most of his professional life in England, proclaimed, "Turkey eggs are good boiled, and are preferred to those of hens for pastry; mixing them with common eggs makes an omelette more delicate."[42]

In America, European colonists, particularly those on the frontier, also ate wild turkey eggs, generally substituting them for chicken eggs in recipes.[43] In 1791 Israel Donalson, a New Jersey native who became a Kentucky pioneer, made meals of wild turkey eggs while fleeing from Indians.[44] In 1797 the Pennsylvania missionary John Heckewelder reported that turkey eggs were more "palatable than wild goose or wild duck eggs."[45] Sarah Brewer-Bonebright, an early settler in Iowa, agreed. Turkey eggs, she noted, were "more palatable than those of wild goose or wild duck eggs."[46] Charles Ranhofer, the haute-cuisine chef at Delmonico's, believed turkey eggs to be "much liked either boiled or cooked in an omelet."[47] As long as wild turkey eggs could be found, Americans continued to eat them.[48]

Turkey eggs were rarely sold in nineteenth-century markets and were scarcely mentioned in twentieth-century cookbooks.[49] That is because domesticated turkey hens laid only about a hundred annually, depending upon the breed and conditions of the hatchery.[50] By comparison, a laying chicken hen can produce almost three hundred eggs per year. In addition, turkey hens take longer to mature before they are ready to lay, so more costs are incurred in feeding hens. Virtually all turkey eggs are used for production of more turkeys, and breeders are not usually licensed to sell the eggs as food.

The Rise and Fall of Haute American Turkey Cookery

By the mid-nineteenth century turkey cookery began to take off, largely due to immigrant chefs who introduced European cooking techniques and practices to America. The art of braising turkeys, which was invented in France and adopted in England, for example, became part of American cuisine at this time. A recipe for braised turkey appears in the American edition of Alexis Soyer's *Modern Housewife or Méagère* (1850).[51] Cookbook writers in the United States picked up the concept and published additional recipes for braising turkeys by

1857.[52] By the early 1860s birds were frequently served *à la braise,* but the technique was "one of the most momentous operations of the kitchen" and rarely done properly one anonymous observer reported.[53]

That changed after the Civil War, mainly because of the influx of French chefs into the United States. Turkey cookery achieved its highest degree of excellence in America during the late nineteenth and early twentieth centuries, in general because of a rapid growth in the popularity of international fare served in haute-cuisine restaurants. Charles Ranhofer, for example, born in France in 1836 and apprenticed to a pastrymaker at the age of twelve, immigrated to the United States at the age of twenty. In 1862 he was hired as a chef at Delmonico's, where he remained for most of his professional life. At the time, the restaurant, which catered to those engaged in conspicuous consumption, was the spot to publicly display personal wealth during the Gilded Age. Ranhofer flattered diners by occasionally naming dishes after them, making him among the first chefs in the United States to designate dishes after living people. He was also among the first American chefs to achieve international acclaim. When he retired in 1894 he produced his masterpiece, *The Epicurean.* Thirty-six of Ranhofer's recipes have the word *turkey* in their title, and many more incorporate turkey as an ingredient. Many of the titles are intriguing, for example, "Turkey à la Chipolata—stuffed" (with small sausages), "Turkey with Cèpes," "Turkey Truffled and Garnished with Black Olives," and "Turkey—Grenades—à la Jules Verne" (named for the French science fiction author).[54]

Despite the importance of the turkey at Delmonico's and a few other restaurants that catered to the wealthy, turkey flesh was largely considered a common food. Rather than recipes for truffled turkeys, most cookbooks provided inexpensive means of preparation. Whenever turkey was served leftovers were sure to follow, and among the recipes for post-turkey-dinner dishes in American cookbooks were suggestions for turkey salads and sandwiches.

Recipes entitled "turkey salad" were unusual before the mid-nineteenth century, but those for chicken salad often advise substituting turkey. The first located published reference to "turkey salad" appears in Elizabeth Ellicott Lea's *The Domestic Cookery* (1853), a recipe composed of chopped white turkey meat seasoned with "butter, mustard, pepper, salt, and celery, chopped very fine, and a little vinegar."[55] Pierre Blot's recipe for turkey salad, which appears in his *Hand-Book of Practical Cookery* (1869), directs making it "exactly the same as a salad of chicken," that is, covering the cold turkey meat in freshly made mayonnaise.[56] By this date, turkey salads were quite popular and served at balls, parties, and afternoon teas.[57] Two recipes entitled "Turkey Salad" appeared in Marion Cabell Tyree's *Housekeeping in Old Virginia* (1877). One involved minced turkey meat combined with celery; the dressing was a sauce made from the mashed yolks of hardboiled eggs along with butter, vinegar, and celery seed. The other recipe used minced turkey, ham, celery, apples, and pickles in a similar dressing.[58] Turkey salads have thrived in America ever since, although it has always taken second place to chicken salad.

Nineteenth-century turkey sandwiches were basically turkey salad served between two pieces of toast, condiments added. Although early recipes for sandwiches frequently mention poultry, turkey was not specified as an ingredient until the late nineteenth century. Theodore Francis Garrett, editor of the massive seven-volume *Encyclopædia of Practical Cookery* (1890), published the first located recipe for a turkey sandwich.[59] Perhaps turkey sandwich recipes did not appear earlier because they were so easy to make. Anyone could substitute turkey for chicken. As Mrs. Alexander Orr Bradley wrote in her *Beverages and Sandwiches for Your Husband's Friends by One Who Knows* (1893), why bother to include a recipe for turkey sandwiches when it was so obvious how to make them?[60] By this date, commercial companies were manufacturing sandwich meat made from turkey, which made it even easier to make turkey sandwiches without preparing a bird.[61] Commercial turkey spreads for use in making sandwiches were sold in grocery stores by 1893.[62]

Sarah Tyson Rorer, director of the Philadelphia Cooking School and a prolific cookbook writer, had no qualms about giving a recipe for turkey sandwiches in *Sandwiches* (1894), the first book totally devoted to the art of sandwich making. She also published the first known recipe for the club sandwich, describing it as being made in a number of ways but always served warm on toasted bread. Her recipe calls for thin layers of ham, pickles, cold roasted chicken or turkey, and lettuce with mayonnaise dressing.[63]

The hot turkey sandwich emerged from upper-class hotel restaurants; the first located recipe for it appears in *Vachon's Book of Economical Soups and Entrees* (1903).[64] Since then, turkey sandwiches are a regular part of English and American cookbooks. In the twentieth century they began to be served in delis, sandwich shops, and fast food restaurants, where their reasonable fat content is often featured.

The Turkey Shoot

Mary L. Booth, a historian, reports that in Dutch New Amsterdam on Christmas Day "the young men repaired to the 'commons' or 'Beekman's swamp' to shoot at turkeys which were set up for a target. Each man paid a few stuyvers for a shot, and he who succeeded in hitting the bird took it off as a prize."[65] Whether that accurately represents events in Dutch New Amsterdam, the turkey shoot was an important Christmas tradition in America during the nineteenth century. David Sturges Copeland described one such event in Clarendon, New York, where turkeys were tied in a meadow and shooters would "blaze away at the poor turkey's head."[66] Samuel H. Hammond described a slightly different event in which the shooters gave money to the proprietor, and "a plank was placed at some five and twenty rods distance, with a hole in it, through which was thrust the head of the turkey, while his body was secured behind it. At this mark the sportsmen fired. If blood was drawn, the marksman was entitled to the turkey."[67]

Descriptions of a turkey shoot also appeared in novels.[68] In *The Pioneers* (1823), James Fenimore Cooper devoted an entire chapter to "the ancient amusement of shooting the Christmas turkey," which was "one of the few sports that the settlers of a new country seldom or never neglect to observe."[69] According to Cooper, the bird was "fastened by a string to the stump of a large pine . . . its body was entirely hid by the surrounding snow, nothing being visible but its red swelling head and its long neck." Shooters stood a hundred yards away and took turns shooting at the bird. The first to hit a visible feather took the turkey home.[70]

Turkey shoots were so memorable that painters frequently depicted them. Around 1837 Charles Deas painted *Turkey Shoot,* which "was so graphically delineated as at once to hit the fancy of a genuine Knickerbocker whose ancestors were among the early colonists, who became its purchaser."[71] In 1856 William Walcutt painted the same scene, as did Tompkins H. Matteson in 1857 and John Whetten Ehninger in 1879.[72] Other artists have subsequently done so as well.[73]

The idea of the turkey shoot came under fire after the Civil War. In 1866 a writer in *Harper's Weekly* refused to describe the event because it was "cruel and unworthy of Christian men."[74] That the practice of shooting at a captive turkey went out of fashion was thanks in part to the efforts of Henry Bergh, who in 1866 founded the American Society for the Prevention of Cruelty to Animals (ASPCA), which was modeled on the Royal Society for the Prevention of Cruelty to Animals in England. Bergh believed that the practice was villainous and insisted "on the substitution of a dummy target for the living animal." An article on turkey shooting in *Poultry World* reported in 1879 that in most places, "the occupation of these turkey manglers" had already disappeared.[75] Some turkey shoots converted to clay pigeons or standing targets shaped and painted to look like turkeys. Successful marksmen would then receive a turkey as a prize, and occasionally the event raised funds for charity. Live turkey shoots continue to be held, although they are usually clandestine and not associated with Christmas.[76]

The Turkey Raffle

Turkeys were also raffled at Christmas and Thanksgiving, although some participants were less interested in acquiring the turkey and more interested in gambling. A nineteenth-century raffle in New York set the value of a live turkey at four shillings (about 48 cents). Each participant bought a chance at throwing twelve pennies that had been placed and shaken in a hat. The one who threw the largest number of heads won the turkey, but many just took the four shillings instead. This went on through the evening without anyone actually taking the prize.[77]

Frank Leslie's Illustrated Newspaper described a different type of turkey raffle in 1872. Signs inscribed "Turkeys to be Raffled Thanksgiving Eve" were posted in bars and restaurants a few weeks before the holiday. Participants contributed 50 cents or a dollar and then threw dice three times. The person who had the largest cumulative score won a live turkey. The article's author noted that the person who really won was the bartender, who sold a considerable amount of liquor during the event.[78]

Raffles were also conducted by or for the poor. In one described in *The Living Age* in 1885, individuals put money into a hat; the winner of the raffle bought a turkey with proceedings and also assumed the responsibility of running the next raffle.[79] An 1874 lithograph in *Harper's Weekly* portrays an African American family gathered around a small turkey won at a Christmas raffle. The caption reads, "De breed am small, but de flavor am delicious."[80]

The Christmas Turkey Dinner

The original purpose of a turkey shoot and raffle was to take a bird home for the family dinner. European colonists brought the tradition of serving turkey at Christmas dinner to America, a custom followed wherever the holiday was celebrated in Colonial America. In Dutch New Amsterdam, for instance, Christmas was celebrated, and turkeys were an important part of the celebration.[81] Episcopalians who settled in the southern colonies also celebrated Christmas, and a turkey was part of their feast. On August 8, 1770, Martha Goosley of York, Virginia, sent two birds to John Norton, then living in London, so he might celebrate Christmas as if he were in Virginia.[82] In Philadelphia, roast turkey was served at a Christmas dinner in 1777.[83] Ten years later it was the main dish for Christmas dinner in Ohio.[84] By the early nineteenth century, turkey was served at Christmas dinners in New England.[85]

Numerous descriptions and references to turkey dinners served at Christmas have survived from the nineteenth century. In her short story "Snow-balling" (1838), Eliza Leslie describes such a dinner, with a turkey as the main course.[86] Leslie was the first American cookbook writer to include turkey in her Christmas dinner menus: boiled turkey with oyster sauce, roasted turkey with cranberry sauce, and boiled turkey with celery sauce.[87] Subsequent cookbook writers followed Leslie's example and proposed turkey-centered meals for the holidays.[88]

Fresh turkeys were also an important dish for Christmas celebrations during the Civil War.[89] Indeed, they were a significant part of the troops' diets. To feed the Union Army, contracts were let to canners whose goods were shipped by train to distant outposts. For many of the troops, it was the first exposure to canned goods, chief among which was canned turkey. Soldiers thought about Christmas turkeys when they mused on the holiday celebrations they were missing. As John Faller, serving with the Pennsylvania Reserves, wrote home five days before Christmas in 1861, "So when you are all eating your big Christmas turkey just think of me standing guard out in the cold." He closed by wishing "all a happy Christmas and a merry new year, a big turkey and lots of good things to eat."[90]

The turkey remained an important part of Christmas celebrations after the war. In 1873 a turkey-raiser reported that "It is very fast becoming the fashion that every family, from the millionaire to the pauper, or even the state prison convicts, must have a roast turkey" for Christmas.[91] Hotels such as Louisville's Galt House served "wild turkey with cranberry sauce" on the holiday.[92] In 1915 Caroline Hunt of the Bureau of Home Economics, U.S. Department of Agriculture, reported that a turkey stuffed with bread and chestnuts was the ideal main dish for a balanced Christmas dinner, and the pronouncement was important enough to be recorded in the *New York Times.*[93]

Although the turkey still remains common at Christmas, the tradition of a turkey dinner declined in the United States, mainly because of the increasing prominence of Thanksgiving. Many Americans were reluctant, after eating a turkey at Thanksgiving and the leftovers for a week after the holiday, to confront more turkey a few weeks later at Christmas. Thanksgiving became the main holiday at which turkey was served.

delas aues fo. 57

especial quando se enojan, es
punto: tienen vn pico de carne
que le cuelga sobre el pico, hosa
hinchase, o erizase.

Los que quieren mal a otros
dan les a comer o a beuer, aquel
pico de carne, y blanduxo que
tienen sobre el pico, paraque
no pueda armar el miembro
gentil

tome, xixiaoa, xelhoaçe, el
metze: ciciotcaio, quechveiac
quechoocaio, cozque, quechta
tapachtic, quaxoxoctic, qua
toltic, quatolle, ixquatolli
mimiltic, ixquatol popoçac
tic: iacatolli, iacaciuitle: mo
xittomoniani, motomoniani,
tepan tlhol: moxittomonia,
motomonia: quitetecuitza,
quicocomotza iniaco: teque
queça, teicça, tepantholoa:
iniiacatol, atultic, cuetlax
tic, cuetlaxiuhqui, iamaqui,
iaia maztic. In tecocoliani; ca
caoatl, molli ipan quitequal
tia, quitetololtia: quilictetla
mictilia: njc vivitla, njcahavits
ana, njccuitlapilhuivitla,
njccaccollaça, njctencopina.
tetlamjctilia intotoli yiaca
cuitl: njcacon vitequj, njca
contlapana, njcxixiapachoa.
Injtlaqual tonacaiutl; tlax
calli, tamalli, tlaolio, tlaolli.

Turkey illustration from Bernardino de Sahagún, author of the *Historia General de las Cosas de la Nueva España* (General History of the Things of New Spain). (Author's Collection)

"Shooting the Christmas Turkey" (date unknown). (Author's Collection)

Thanksgiving-Day among the Puritan Fathers in New England, Harper's Weekly (1870). (Author's Collection)

J. W. Ehninger, *Thanksgiving—a Thanksgiving Dinner among the Puritans, Harper's Weekly* (1867). (Author's Collection)

W. S. L. Jewett, *Thanksgiving—a Thanksgiving Dinner among Their Descendants, Harper's Weekly* (1867). (Author's Collection)

Uncle Sam's Thanksgiving Dinner by Thomas Nast, *Harper's Weekly* 13 (1869). (Author's Collection)

J. W. Ehninger, *Preparing for Thanksgiving, Harper's Weekly* (1868). (Author's Collection)

Trap for Wild Turkeys from *Turkeys and How to Grow Them* edited by Herbert Myrick (1897). (Author's Collection)

"Calling" Wild Turkeys from *Turkeys and How to Grow Them* edited by Herbert Myrick (1897). (Author's Collection)

The Prize Bronze Turkey from *Turkeys and How to Grow Them* edited by Herbert Myrick (1897). (Author's Collection)

Narragansett Turkeys from *Turkeys and How to Grow Them* edited by Herbert Myrick (1897). (Author's Collection)

Buff Turkey Cock from *Turkeys and How to Grow Them* edited by Herbert Myrick (1897). (Author's Collection)

Turkeys and the Pilgrims appeared on postcards around 1900.

Thanksgiving Day
RULER · OF · THE · DAY

Some postcards incorporated patriotic symbols, including the American flag, the stars and stripes, and Uncle Sam (ca. 1900). (Author's Collection)

A holiday warning, around 1905. (Author's Collection)

Another postcard equating the American eagle with the symbol of Thanksgiving (ca. 1905). (Author's Collection)

Thanksgiving Dinner at the Five Points Ladies' Home Mission of the Methodist Episcopal Church, Harper's Weekly (1865). (Author's Collection)

Ornithology from the presidential campaign of 1852 that pitted the Whig Winfield Scott against the Democrat Franklin Pierce. (Library of Congress Prints and Photographs Division)

6

HALE'S TURKEY TALE; OR, THE INVENTION OF TURKEY DAY

The Separatists, a small splinter group of Puritanism, followed John Calvin's teachings. Separatists believed that Scripture was the only guide to all matters of faith and that individuals had the right to interpret the meaning of Scripture. Each Separatist congregation selected its own pastor, whose responsibilities were limited to the jurisdiction of that single church. When the English Parliament banished those who refused to join in common prayer, many Separatists left England for Amsterdam. One group formed a church in Leyden, but in 1619 some decided to sail for North America. After leaving Holland, they stopped for repairs and provisions in Plymouth, England, and one vessel, the *Mayflower,* set sail for Virginia in 1620.

Whether by accident or design, the ship came ashore in present-day Massachusetts, where the settlers established what they called Plimoth Plantation. With the help of local American Indians, the Wampanoags, they barely survived the challenges of their new life in America. The leaders of the small band knew that additional settlers would be needed if the struggling colony were to survive. Two—William Bradford and Edward Winslow—wrote reports of the wonders of America to encourage others to follow them, and many Puritans did leave England for America. Some reinforced Plimoth Plantation, and others established new communities in Massachusetts and other locations in New England.

Throughout the seventeenth and eighteenth centuries thousands of Thanksgiving days were proclaimed by ministers and governors in various locations throughout the European colonies in North America. Observances were usually organized in response to specific events such as a military victory, a good harvest, or a providential rainfall, but no specific day of thanksgiving was observed on an annual basis.[1] A Puritan thanksgiving was a solemn religious day celebrated in church, praying to God.

Not much is known about early Thanksgiving dinners in New England—if there were any—and of all the hundreds of Thanksgiving days observed there in the seventeenth century, only one church record in 1636 suggests the possibility of a feast. This account reports that after church services there was "making merry to the creatures, the poorer sort being invited of the richer." Unfortunately, no description of the "making merry" has survived, but the presumption is that it included food of some sort. Similar events were likely conducted on October 12, 1637, and December 11, 1639.[2] No further references have been located for the next 150 years in New England, although fall festivals and feasts were typically English traditions.[3] The absence of references does not imply that there were no Thanksgiving dinners during this period, but it is surprising that more records have not been found.

Days of thanksgiving were celebrated in all colonies, and in the American South there is evidence of dinners. In November 1732, for example, there was a thanksgiving at the first settlement in the Colony of Georgia, and a "plentiful Dinner" with "eight Turkeys" and other food was provided after the ceremony. On July 7, 1733, the town of Savannah gave thanks with a "very substantial dinner."[4] What's interesting about these incidents is that those who marked the events with a dinner came directly from England and were not from existing American colonies.

Even from the eighteenth century, only a few other descriptions of Thanksgiving dinners have been unearthed. During the Revolutionary War, the Continental Congress declared December 18, 1777, a day of thanksgiving in honor of the American military victory at Saratoga. One soldier, Joseph Plumb Martin, noted in his journal that "each man was given half a gill of rice and a tablespoonful of vinegar."[5] A more sumptuous feast dates to 1784, but the description is not very precise. It mentions drinking and eating in general and then comments, "What a sight of pigs and geese and turkeys and fowls and sheep must be slaughtered to gratify the voraciousness of a single day," suggesting that all these meats were served.[6] Two years later, Boston's *Continental Journal* encouraged everyone to "furnish their Thanksgiving day tables with "Turkies."[7] By 1792 a newspaper editor in Norwich, Connecticut, estimated that 85,694 turkeys and geese were eaten on Thanksgiving.[8] By the beginning of the nineteenth century, turkeys played an extremely important role in the Thanksgiving dinner; one newspaper account in 1801 estimated that 125,000 turkeys and geese were consumed at Thanksgiving in New England that year.[9]

The feast that emerged in the early nineteenth century was in some ways a New England substitute for traditional English autumn holidays, none of which the Puritans observed. Guy Fawkes Day, for instance, celebrated the foiling of the Gunpowder Plot in 1605, when Catholic conspirators attempted to blow up the British Parliament. The plot was uncovered, and the plotters, led by Guy Fawkes, were executed. Thereafter, November 5 was celebrated as a "public thanksgiving to Almighty God," and it is still celebrated with bonfires and fireworks. Then there was the traditional British Harvest Home Festival, usually celebrated in October or early November, that dated back to Druid and Roman times. Harvest Home was celebrated with queens robed in white who rode on carts or were carried through villages. The Puritans considered that idol worship and refused to partake.[10] For religious reasons the Puritans condemned the traditional holidays celebrated by the Church of England and the Catholic church, such as All Saints Day (November 1) and Christmas (December 25). The fact that many fall holidays were celebrated with gluttony, drunkenness, lewdness, and frivolity also led to Puritan condemnation.

The American Thanksgiving celebration may have derived from traditional English holidays, but it evolved in a unique way. Thanksgiving, for example, was to be a day when the extended family gathered, and it culminated in a grand dinner. As the event became more important during the late eighteenth century, specific culinary traditions arose around the meal that were not associated with traditional English autumn feasts, for example, the special role of New World bounty—turkeys, pumpkin pies, sweet potatoes, succotash, and cranberries.

In contrast to the eighteenth century, a large number of descriptions of sumptuous Thanksgiving dinners date to the nineteenth century. William Bentley, the Harvard University–educated pastor of the East Church in Salem, Massachusetts, made several notations about Thanksgiving in a copious diary he began in 1784 and continued until his death in 1819. It was not until 1803, however, that he made his first mention of Thanksgiving dinner—a report on the price of turkeys at that time. Two years later he mentioned that Thanksgiving had created a great demand for poultry, and in 1806 Bentley observed that "a Thanksgiving is not complete without a turkey. It is rare to find any other dishes but such as turkies & fowls afford before the pastry on such days & puddings are much less used than formerly."[11] Bentley's description suggests that a two-course meal—the first consisting of turkey and perhaps other meat dishes and the second of dessert. That pattern was common during the early nineteenth century, and these traditions were long maintained.

Of course, not every Thanksgiving dinner featured a turkey, but those that did not were exceptions. At first turkey was served with main dishes such as venison and other wild game, but as the nineteenth century progressed game largely disappeared from American tables. Next came the domesticated goose, which had been the main course for the traditional English Christmas. Because Christmas was not celebrated in early New England, goose was an excellent choice for celebrating Thanksgiving, and it continued to be served throughout the nineteenth century. Beef was occasionally mentioned in descriptions of Thanksgiving dinners; it was an important meat source in New England and frequently cheaper per pound than poultry. But by far the closest challenger to the turkey as the centerpiece of the dinner was chicken pie, a traditional English savory dish. These alternatives to turkey were generally of secondary importance and did not completely disappear from the menu until the end of the nineteenth century.

Thanksgiving Dinners

Edward Everett Hale, the American author and Unitarian minister, remembered that the Thanksgiving dinners of his childhood would commence with chicken pie and roast turkey, then proceed to several different types of pies, tarts, and puddings, and end with dried fruit.[12] A New Hampshire Thanksgiving dinner of the same era began with a ham and a large roasted turkey that were followed by chicken, duck, celery, plum pudding, pies, and fruit and by coffee and tea.[13] A dinner in Geneva, New York, in 1831 featured turkey, beef, duck, ham, sausage, potatoes, yams, succotash, pickles, nuts, raisins, pears, peaches, pie, tarts, creams, custards, jellies, floating islands, sweetbreads, wines, rum, brandy, egg-nog, and punch.[14] In 1837 Joseph Porter Dwinnell enjoyed Thanksgiving in Massachusetts at "a Table loaded with a Turkey." He made no mention of any other food.[15] In the mid-nineteenth century Carol King, a resident of Salem, reported that Thanksgiving dinners were "always the same": chicken pie and boiled turkey and oyster sauce.[16] In Portsmouth, New Hampshire, Sarah Rice Goodwin recalled that "the dinner began with a ham, handsomely decorated, at one end of the table and a large roast turkey at the other. Chickens and ducks followed, with celery dressed and undressed."[17] Harriet Beecher Stowe, born in 1811, remembered her childhood Thanksgiving celebrations in Litchfield, Connecticut, as elaborate meals that took a week to prepare and included turkey, chicken, chicken pies, plum puddings, and four types of pie.[18]

Numerous observers have recorded that by the mid-nineteenth century most Americans would have found it difficult to contemplate a Thanksgiving dinner without turkey.[19] The Swedish visitor Frederika Bremer, for example, concluded that roast turkeys and "pumpkin pudding" were indispensable in the late 1840s.[20] Thomas Mackay, an Englishman who visited the United States in 1857, stated that shops were closed on Thanksgiving Day, and Americans pursued the great event: dinner and "the piece de rigueur," the roast turkey.[21]

Many influences helped transform Thanksgiving dinner from a regional New England celebration into a national holiday. One major factor was migration. New England soil was not the best for farming, and many New Englanders moved to other parts of the country in search of better farmland. New York's central valley, for instance, was largely settled by New Englanders, as was much of the Midwest. They kept the observance alive in their new homes and urged their newly adopted communities to celebrate it as well.

Thanksgiving also became part of popular culture. Poems, for example, were common fare throughout the nineteenth century. A newspaper in 1801 published "A Merry Ode for Thanksgiving," which announced that turkeys were carved "in heaps" on that day.[22] Perhaps the most famous holiday poem was written by Lydia Maria Child, author of *The American Frugal Housewife,* whose "The New-England Boys Song about Thanksgiving" was better known to most Americans by its first line, "Over the river and thro' the wood."[23] No mention of turkeys appears in the poem, but many other Thanksgiving poems did mention them.

The Pilgrims and Thanksgiving, Part 1

None of the previously mentioned Thanksgiving proclamations, poems, or descriptions of feasts mentioned a "First Thanksgiving" or even Pilgrims. Those connections sprang from a different tradition. In 1769 members of the Old Colony Club met in Plymouth on December 22 to celebrate the landing of the *Mayflower* in Plymouth. They enjoyed a dinner of whortleberry pudding, succotash, clams, oysters, codfish, venison, seafowl, frost fish, eels, apple pie, cranberry tarts, and cheese—no turkey. The event was commemorated as "Forefathers' Day," which the club observed until 1774, when members were divided by different loyalties during the Revolutionary War. Forefathers' Day continued to be celebrated off and on in Plymouth, however, and it gained enough support in Boston such that in 1799 the local "Sons of the Pilgrims" sent out an invitation to a Forefathers' Day dinner. Their message contained the first located use of the word *Pilgrim* applied to the first settlers of Massachusetts.[24] In 1820, on the bicentennial of the establishment of Plimoth Plantation, Daniel Webster visited Plymouth. In his speech, entitled "First Settlement of New England," he paid homage to "our Pilgrim Fathers" but made no mention of any First Thanksgiving, turkeys, or of any dinner associated with it.[25]

Not everyone was happy with the newly resurrected Pilgrims or the celebration of Forefathers' Day. Many Native Americans, for instance, did not believe that Pilgrims or "forefathers" should be honored. In 1836 William Apess, a Methodist minister of Pequot Indian descent and the first major Native American writer, urged that "the children of Pilgrims blush" at their forefather's treatment of Native Americans and asked that "every man of color wrap himself in mourning, for the 22d of December," for it was a day "of mourning and not of joy."[26]

Few paid attention to Apess at the time, but his writings and concerns received visibility in the following century when some Native Americans began observing "A National Day of Mourning" on Thanksgiving Day. When the 350th anniversary of the Pilgrims' arrival in Massachusetts was celebrated in 1970, Frank James, a Wampanoag leader, was invited to speak at the ceremonies. Before he delivered his pro-American Indian perspective, however, its text was leaked to the press and his invitation to speak was rescinded. On Thanksgiving Day, James, along with hundreds of other Native Americans and their supporters, gathered at Coles Hill, which overlooks Plymouth Rock, and declared a national day of mourning. Every year since the United American Indians of New England has sponsored similar days. James died in 2001, but his son has carried on the tradition.

The first association between the Pilgrims and Thanksgiving appeared in print in 1841, when Alexander Young published a copy of a letter written by Edward Winslow, which was dated December 11, 1621, to a friend in England. It described a three-day event, the dates of which were not given. The letter was published the following year in England but was forgotten until the 1820s:

> Our harvest being gotten in, our Governor sent four men on fowling, that so we might after a more special manner re[j]oice together, after we had gathered the fruit of our labours. They four in one day k[i]lled as much fowl as, with a little help besides, served the Company almost a week. At which time, amongst other recreations, we exercised our arms, many of the Indians coming amongst us, and amongst the rest their greatest king, Massasoit with some ninety men, whom for three days we entertained and feasted. And they went out and killed five deer which they brought to the plantation and bestowed on our Governor and upon the Captain and others.[27]

In a footnote to the letter Young claimed that the event Winslow described "was the first thanksgiving, the harvest festival of New England. On this occasion they no doubt feasted on the wild turkey as well as venison."[28] In the same 1841 volume, Young also cited Governor William Bradford's 1650 manuscript, "Of Plymouth Plantation," which had been lost for decades and was not published in its entirety until 1856.[29] Bradford told of Plimoth Plantation from 1620 to 1647 but made no mention of the event described by Winslow. He did, however, report that in the fall of 1621 "a great store of wild turkeys," venison, cod, bass, waterfowl, and corn was available at the colony.[30] Neither Winslow nor Bradford used the word *thanksgiving* to describe this or any event in the fall of 1621.

Whatever happened in the autumn at this event, the Puritans made no subsequent mention of it, and no evidence has surfaced suggesting that it was remembered or observed in later years. Winslow makes no mention of prayer at the feast, and his description does include many secular elements. Puritans would not have considered it a day of thanksgiving, a distinction well-understood by New Englanders in the mid-nineteenth century. *Gleason's Pictorial Drawing Room Companion,* for instance, published an engraving in 1852 that illustrated the traditional Puritan Thanksgiving, which was observed in church, and compared it with the way Thanksgiving was then celebrated, as a large family get-together.[31]

The idea that the 1621 event Winslow described was the "First Thanksgiving" was picked up by others who wrote about the Pilgrims, and it was generally believed in New England that the Pilgrims had started the Thanksgiving dinner tradition.[32] That claim was rarely cited until after the Civil War.

There was good reason for not repeating the claim nationally. Jamestown, settled fourteen years before Plymouth, observed many days of thanksgiving before the arrival of the Pilgrims in Massachusetts and had a much better claim to have observed the First Thanksgiving than did Plimoth Plantation. Today, there is a plaque in Jamestown marking the purported site of the real First Thanksgiving. In addition, other observers have made specific claims for different First Thanksgivings celebrated by other Europeans in what is now the United States, and some predate the arrival of English colonists in Jamestown.

Sarah Josepha Hale's Tale

The driving force behind making Thanksgiving a national holiday was Sarah Josepha Hale, who was born in 1788 in Newport, New Hampshire. After running a school for five years she married David Hale, a lawyer, who died in 1822, leaving her with five children to support. She turned to writing to generate money and published her first book of poetry in 1823. (It is for one of her poems that she is mainly remembered: "Mary Had a Little Lamb.") In 1827 Hale published a two-volume novel, *Northwood; or, A Tale of New England,* which compared life there with life in the South. The book made her one of the first American women to publish a novel; she was also one of the first Americans, male or female, to write a novel that raised the problem of slavery. Hale moderately opposed slavery, a position that was not popular even then in New England. An entire chapter of *Northwood* describes Thanksgiving dinner in New England. Of the turkey, she writes that it "took precedence on this occasion, being placed at the head of the table; and well did it become its lordly station, sending forth the rich odour of its savoury stuffing, and finely covered with the froth of the basting."[33]

The publication of *Northwood* brought Hale fame, and she became the editor of *American Ladies Magazine,* a small magazine published in Boston. Louis A. Godey, who had launched *Godey's Book* in 1830, purchased the *American Ladies Magazine* in 1836 and asked Hale to edit the combined magazine, renamed *Godey's Lady's Book.* Under Hale's management the newly named magazine went from selling ten thousand copies annually in 1837 to 150,000 copies by 1860.[34]

At the time, only two national holidays were celebrated in the United States. One was Washington's Birthday (February 22), and the other was Independence Day (July 4). Hale believed that America needed an autumn holiday and that holiday should be named Thanksgiving. Hale commenced her campaign to create a national Thanksgiving holiday in 1846. For the next seventeen years she wrote annually to members of Congress, prominent individuals, and the governors of every state and territory, requesting each to proclaim the last Thursday in November as Thanksgiving Day. She also wrote editorials in *Godey's Lady's Book* to promote Thanksgiving and noted each year how many states had agreed to celebrate the holiday and which had not. In an age before word processors, typewriters, or the mass media, the campaign was a daunting task.

Hale appealed to other editors to campaign on behalf of Thanksgiving, and whether in response to her request or because of the increasing popularity of the holiday, many magazines did publish Thanksgiving-related stories, poems, and illustrations, although few advocated for a national holiday. During the 1850s, for instance, *Harper's Weekly* published several Thanksgiving-related engravings drawn by Winslow Homer.[35]

Thanksgiving and the Civil War

Sarah Josepha Hale believed that Thanksgiving could pull the United States together even as sectional differences, economic self-interest, and political bickering pulled the nation apart. Slavery was the main issue. In 1852 Harriet Beecher Stowe's novel *Uncle Tom's Cabin* inflamed the public, North and South. Six months after its publication, Hale revised and republished *Northwood* with a new subtitle: *Life North and South; Showing the True Character of Both*. In the preface, she argued for national harmony.

Hale still hoped that giving thanks would serve as a national symbol to help bind all Americans together and prevent the dissolution of the nation.[36] Her campaign nearly achieved success in 1859. Americans, she reported proudly, had celebrated Thanksgiving on the last Thursday in November in thirty states and three territories. "If every state would join in union thanks-giving on the twenty-fourth of this month," she asked, "would it not be a renewed pledge of love and loyalty to the Constitution of the United States which guarantees peace, prosperity, progress, and perpetuity to our great Republic?" Thanksgiving, she proclaimed, was America's national festival.[37]

Despite her declaration and hopes, the nation split apart in April 1861 and the Civil War commenced. With the Union Army's military defeat at the Battle of Bull Run, many Northerners believed that there was not much to be thankful for in November 1861. Sarah Josepha Hale, however, was undeterred. If Americans were not in a celebratory mood, then she urged them to perform benevolent actions such as sending gifts to the poor or observing the holiday as a fast day rather than a feast.[38] In September 1862 the Union Army repulsed Southern forces at the Battle of Antietam, and the mood in the North was more sanguine. Thanksgiving was again celebrated throughout the Northern states.[39]

Hale redoubled her efforts to make the day a national holiday. Her problem was that every year she had to begin the campaign anew and seek support from every state and territory, and during the war she was unable to communicate with many Southern states. Hale tried a different strategy. She wrote privately to William Seward, Abraham Lincoln's secretary of state and a former senator from New York, to request that the president declare Thanksgiving a national holiday.[40] She also wrote directly to Lincoln and may have met with him. A few months after the North's military victories at Gettysburg and Vicksburg in the summer of 1863, he declared the last Thursday in November a national day of thanksgiving.[41]

The Civil War Turkey

As the war dragged on, collections were taken in the North to buy turkeys for holiday dinners for war widows and their families.[42] Northern prisoners of war occasionally ate turkey for Thanksgiving, and Northern officers in one prisoner-of-war camp in Texas were paroled to seek turkeys among the local population for a Thanksgiving dinner. They only found an old chicken, which they brought back to camp to share with fourteen fellow prisoners.[43]

Turkeys were also an important gift from civilian populations to soldiers in the field. The practice appears to have begun in the North for Thanksgiving and then continued over for Christmas. In December 25, 1863, the *New York Herald* reported that some Union soldiers were lucky enough to eat turkeys at Christmas.[44] When the Army of the Potomac was severely tried while besieging Richmond (the capitol of the Confederacy) a plot was hatched in New York to lift the soldiers' and sailors' spirits. In October 1864 George W. Blunt, a hydrographer living in New York, asked New Yorkers to send "Thanksgiving dinner to the soldiers and sailors."[45] The Union League Club of New York responded to his appeal by asking everyone to help make Thanksgiving 1864 a show of support for the Union forces: "We desire that on the twenty-fourth day of November there shall be no soldier in the Army of the Potomac, the James, the Shenandoah, and no sailor in the North Atlantic Squadron who does not receive tangible evidence that those for whom he is periling his life, remember him." They asked for "donations of cooked poultry and other proper meats, as well as for mince pies, sausages and fruits," but financial contributions were welcome. The club agreed to cook poultry donations and send them to the Union Army and Navy. In three weeks the club collected more than $56,566 toward the purchase of 146,586 pounds of poultry. An additional 225,000 pounds were received as contributions, along with enormous quantities of other Thanksgiving dinner accouterments.[46]

Delmonico's also contributed the services of its chefs to roast and stuff thousands of turkeys, pack them, and send them by train all the way down to Virginia.[47] As a result, many troops in the field and onboard ships at sea had turkey on Thanksgiving. Captain George F. Noyes reported that "the want of proper appliances compelled most of the men to broil or stew their turkeys, but everyone seemed fully satisfied, and appreciated the significance of this sympathetic thank-offering from the loyal North. One soldier said to me, 'It isn't the turkey, but the *idea* that we care for,' and he thus struck the key-note of the whole festival."[48]

Not everyone was happy with their Thanksgiving dinners. The cooked turkeys and other dinner accouterments were sent by various means, but generally government transport was involved. That meant disrupting the normal supply system for the Union Army. The Ohio general and future president Rutherford B. Hayes noted that the "overcoats, stockings, shirts, etc.," which were greatly needed, "couldn't come because all the transportation was required to haul up the turkeys and Thanksgiving dinner!" Later, however, he proclaimed that "the turkeys, etc., sent from the Christian land [have arrived] and everyone is happy and jolly."[49]

Harper's Weekly published a major story, illustrated with engravings by Winslow Homer, about how the military celebrated Thanksgiving in 1864. One illustration showed soldiers with bloated bellies. The caption read, "Bellycose Appearance of Our Brave Boys after Thanksgiving."[50] No Thanksgiving turkeys were sent to General William Sherman's army, which had left Atlanta, but plans were made to supply his soldiers with birds when they finally reached the sea.[51] His troops, however, liberated turkeys from Southern farms as they marched through Georgia, so shipments from the North were unnecessary.

By comparison, conditions in the South were much harder. The Union naval blockade declared during the first few months of the war prevented foodstuffs from being easily imported into the Confederacy. As the war dragged on the blockade became more effective. Turkeys were raised throughout the South and wild ones were still common in some forests, so the blockade did not initially affect the supply. But even turkeys became scarce as hunters joined the army and the domesticated birds were consumed. In 1863 Richmond's *Southern Illustrated News* pictured very scrawny turkeys with the caption: "Poultry for the Times."[52] In Mobile, turkeys sold for $15 apiece in November 1863.[53] On January 25, 1864, a Southerner in Richmond commented in his diary that wild turkeys commanded "enormous prices."[54] The *Charleston Mercury* encouraged Southerners to follow the "Yankee" example and send fat turkeys to soldiers in the field, but few did so.[55]

The Postwar Thanksgiving Turkey

As the turkey was the centerpiece for the Thanksgiving dinner it also became an object of humor. *Harper's Weekly* illustrated two birds talking to each other:

> *Mr Gobbler.—.—"Ain't you going to et any thing?"*
> *Mrs Gobbler.—.—"No. I ain't going to fatten myself up for other people's benefit!"*[56]

Since then similar poultry-themed gallows humor and jokes have regularly reappeared, usually around Thanksgiving.[57] In 1872 the *Harper's Weekly Supplement* provided a satirical engraving by F. S. Church, *The Turkeys' Revolt against Thanksgiving,* in which the birds proclaim "We Are Bitterly Opposed to the Enforcement of President Grant's Thanksgiving Proclamation, and will Leave the Country Rather then Submit."[58]

Although Thanksgiving church services continued to be held in the nineteenth century, one writer in *Scribner's Magazine* in 1871 proclaimed that Americans had "almost lost sight of" the religious character of the day. In cities, the author reported, no one considered attending religious services on Thanksgiving a duty, and in the country women and men attended services but attention was really focused on "what has grown to be considered the real event, the raison d'etre of the day, namely, the dinner."[59]

By the nineteenth century's end the meal was an elaborate and abundant display of a family's wealth. At the center of the feast, the turkey reigned supreme. Its price had declined so much by century's end that turkey was less expensive than the alternatives and thus affordable to all but the poorest Americans. Its central role was exemplified by the phrase *Turkey Day,* which became a synonym for Thanksgiving by the 1880s.[60]

By the turn of the twentieth century a Thanksgiving dinner that featured turkey had become enshrined in cookery magazines and cookbooks, which published menus for proper Thanksgiving meals and offered recipes to help the uninitiated prepare traditional dishes.[61] Fannie Farmer, the principal of the Boston Cooking School, offered a Thanksgiving menu of twenty-three dishes in her *Boston Cooking-School Cook Book* (1896); the only meat served was roast turkey.[62] Other menus were more elaborate. The Thanksgiving dinner in *The Picayune's Creole Cook Book* (1900), a New Orleans culinary bible, for instance, featured thirty-three dishes, among them "Baked Red Snapper à la Creole" and "Turkey Stuffed with Chestnuts." This was followed by a supper menu centered on "Cold Turkey, Cranberry Sauce." The book's menu for "A More Economical Thanksgiving Dinner" included only twenty-eight dishes along with extensive suggestions for proper Thanksgiving decorations that would suggest "wild luxuriance and freedom of growth, the spirit of American liberty which gave birth to this day."[63]

The Pilgrims and Thanksgiving, Part 2

Sarah Josepha Hale's pre-1865 letters and editorials promoting Thanksgiving made no mention of the Pilgrims or the First Thanksgiving. Neither did the hundreds of previously published local and state Thanksgiving Day proclamations or newspaper or magazine articles. The first connection Hale made between the Pilgrims and Thanksgiving was in an 1865 editorial in *Godey's Lady's Book,* and it was a passing one: "The Pilgrim Fathers incorporated a yearly Thanksgiving day among the moral influences they sent to the New World." Seven years later she wrote "America's Thanksgiving Hymn," which celebrated the Pilgrims and "their first Thanksgiving Day."[64]

Northern newspapers and magazines began making the connection between the Pilgrims and Thanksgiving dinner after the Civil War. The November 30, 1867, issue of *Harper's Weekly,* for instance, featured *Thanksgiving Dinner among the Puritans,* in which a stern-looking, formal family is seated around a table for their feast, along with an engraving of *A Thanksgiving Dinner among Their Descendants,* which shows an upper-class party.[65] In 1870 *Harper's Weekly* was among the first to illustrate the "first thanksgiving" in an engraving entitled *Thanksgiving Day among the Puritan Fathers of New England.* In it, Pilgrims and American Indians stand by a large table, praying before the meal.[66]

Textbooks were retelling the tale of the first Thanksgiving dinner by 1870, and magazines, newspapers, and books repeated it during the 1870s and 1880s.[67] The linkage was important enough by 1879 for several scholars to write histories of Thanksgiving. Other works followed along similar lines.[68] The Reverend W. DeLoss Love Jr. was more systematic in collecting Thanksgiving proclamations, many of which he published in *The Fast and Thanksgiving Days of New England* (1895), a massive compilation that proved there was no First Thanksgiving. But the popular press already had made the connection, and the reality didn't matter.

By the late 1880s the Pilgrim-centered story of the First Thanksgiving had blossomed in accounts published in magazines, newspapers, and books. One version appeared in Jane G. Austin's *Standish of Standish: A Story of the Pilgrims,* which contained a full chapter on the First Thanksgiving. In this fictional account the Pilgrims, less than a year after arrival in America, celebrate Thanksgiving at a long table, with bowls brimming with hasty pudding topped with butter and treacle, "clam chowder with sea biscuit swimming in a savory broth, while great pieces of cold boiled beef with mustard, flanked by dishes of turnips." Another table, claimed Austin, had held a large pewter bowl full of "plum-porridge with bits of toasted cracker floating upon it," and turkeys were stuffed with beechnuts. Then there were "oysters scalloped in their shells, venison pasties, and the savory stew compounded of all that flies the air." Hunters caught game, and the Pilgrims and American Indians ate "roasts of various kinds, and thin cakes of bread or manchets, and bowls of salad" and "great baskets of grapes, white and purple, and of native plum, so delicious when fully ripe in its three colors of black, white, and red." Of course there were "flagons of ale" and "root beer, well flavored with sassafras." Finally, popcorn was kindly provided by the Native Americans in attendance.[69]

The sad news, reported Austin, was that the Pilgrims had to do without milk and sweet potatoes at the First Thanksgiving, but she assured readers that a few years later cows were imported (which was true), as were sweet potatoes, from the "Carolina colonies" (which was false). Austin fabricated her description of the meal, which she was entitled to do in a work of fiction, but the drama of her account had tremendous appeal to others. As unbelievable as her fictional account of the First Thanksgiving dinner was, it was readily accepted in late-nineteenth-century America and became one of several such fictional accounts that was repeated as fact. These fabrications were then adopted by many elementary and secondary school teachers. Many schools offered special

Thanksgiving dinners based on Austin's fictional vision of life in Plymouth in 1621.[70] Plays were devised celebrating Thanksgiving, with school children reenacting the "First Thanksgiving."[71] The curriculum, in turn, spawned a large children's literature, which still continues, that focused on the Pilgrims, the First Thanksgiving, and the turkey.[72]

By the early twentieth century immigrant children often performed in pageants celebrating the First Thanksgiving.[73] The Pilgrims and the First Thanksgiving became imbedded in the nation's schools, as did the Thanksgiving feast.[74] In 1921 many schools and communities celebrated the three-hundredth anniversary of the First Thanksgiving, and the fictitious dinner was part of that occasion.[75]

Pilgrims and myths about a turkey dinner were enshrined on the covers and inside pages of some of America's most popular magazines, among them *The Saturday Evening Post* and *The Country Gentleman,* as with J. C. Leyendecker's *Pilgrim Stalking Tom Turkey* cover for the November 23, 1907, *Saturday Evening Post.*[76] American painters also contributed to the myth. Jennie Augusta Brownscombe's *The First Thanksgiving,* completed in 1914, appeared in numerous school textbooks, and Jean Louis Gerome Ferris's *First Thanksgiving* portrays a long table, serving dishes, and women decked out in nineteenth-century finery. Artists, books and textbooks have continued these myths ever since.[77]

The reasons for the willing adoption of the Pilgrim/Thanksgiving/turkey myths had less to do with historical fact and more to do with the arrival of hundreds of thousands of immigrants to United States. Previous immigrants had come mainly from the United Kingdom and Ireland, with a smattering from Western and Northern Europe. In the 1880s, however, the immigration pattern changed as people from Southern and Eastern Europe flooded into the United States. The pace of immigration exploded in 1900; nine million people arrived in American cities. Because they came from many lands, the task of America's public education system was to create a common heritage. One curricular need was an easily understood history of America, and the Pilgrims were an ideal symbol for that beginning.

The First Thanksgiving dinner is an origin myth that traces the nation's roots to Plymouth and the Pilgrims. That Jamestown has a better historical claim is complicated by the fact that American slavery began there, which made it an unacceptable location for the mythical birthplace of the nation. Because this origin myth did not become prominent until after the Civil War, the South was in no position to challenge the primacy of the mythical Pilgrims idealized by New England advocates for Thanksgiving. As a result, many Southerners refused to celebrate Thanksgiving long after the war.

Jack Santino, a professor in the Department of Popular Culture at Bowling Green State University, has written that on Thanksgiving Americans act out basic beliefs about national origins: "Within the Thanksgiving meal as we give thanks to the Lord for all his blessings. The blessings are manifest in the food itself: its quantity, its voluminousness. We eat until we can eat no more, and still there is food left to be eaten. The big, round, fat turkey in the center table serves all seated around it, inexhaustibly, and then continues to feed us through the holiday weekend."[78]

Large numbers of immigrants who had not celebrated Thanksgiving in their native lands readily adopted the holiday and the dinner. In the process, they added to and modified the traditional Thanksgiving menu.[79] As James Robertson suggests, "Turkey is consumed at Thanksgiving feasts because it was a native to America, and because it is a symbol of the bounteous richness of the wilderness."[80] Although not every immigrant has retained the turkey as the central feature of the Thanksgiving dinner, Elizabeth Pleck, a historian, has pointed out that in general the turkey "became the symbol of the dominant culture, and the stuffing and side dishes, and desserts the immigrants' contribution."[81]

Thanksgiving and its turkey dinner remains one of America's most important holidays. Retailers, most famously, Macy's, have commercialized the day as the start of the Christmas shopping season, and illustrators, film makers, and television producers have generated new Thanksgiving images. The day's association with the Pilgrims and the centrality of the turkey in the dinner have not faded, however, for those things symbolize a basic truth for most Americans: The nation is a land of abundance, and they owe thanks to God for it.[82]

7

THE WELL-BRED TURKEY; OR, HOW THE TURKEY LOST ITS FLAVOR

Of the six major subspecies of wild turkeys, only two contributed genetically to the modern commercial turkey. The Mexican turkey (*M. g. gallopavo*) is believed to be the progenitor of domesticated turkeys that the Spanish found in Central America.[1] These birds were exported to Europe, where they were bred in different countries. In Spain, the Black Spanish emerged; in Holland, turkey farmers developed a buff-yellow bird with a white topknot; and in Austria, an all-white variety was bred.[2]

These domesticated turkeys were imported into North America shortly after the initial European settlements were established in the seventeenth century. The Dutch introduced their turkeys into New Amsterdam, the French brought theirs to New Orleans and Canada, the Black Spanish variety was introduced into Florida and other Spanish colonies in the Americas, and the British introduced their turkeys into eastern North America. Through trade among these diverse settlements the varieties of domesticated turkeys commingled.

In general, American farmers were little concerned with turkey breeding before the mid-nineteenth century. Most permitted their birds to roam freely about the farm, where they ate insects and plants and mated at will. Domesticated European birds bred with each other and with the wild eastern turkeys (*M. g. silvestris*), creating a true "melting-pot" bird. Crossbreeds were mentioned by John Mortimer, who was English, as early as 1708. He "knew a Gentleman that had a Hen-Turkey of the wild Kind from *Virginia;* of which an *English Cock* he raised a very fine Breed, that bred wild in the Fields." It was much larger than the domesticated turkeys then in England.[3] Likewise, Richard Bradley, a British agricultural writer, reported in 1736 that there was "a Breed in some part of the West of England, between the Turkey and the Virginia Bustard, which produces the largest sort I have yet seen. I have eaten part of one of them, which I judged to excell our common Turkey abundantly in Fineness of Flesh."[4] In 1750 William Ellis, also of England, observed that there were "two sorts of this species, the common *Suffolk* or *Norfolk* turkey and the *Blue Virginia* sort. The first are bred in vast numbers in those counties, from whence *London* is chiefly supplied with these excellent fowls, as appears by the many droves of them, frequently seen on the roads thither."[5] In 1779 breeding turkeys was described in great detail in London's *Farmer's Magazine,* which mentioned White Suffolk and darker Norfolk varieties in Great Britain as well as the Virginia Bronze.[6]

The matter of how to raise turkeys had been a subject of concern dating to their initial arrival in Europe in the sixteenth century. Most agriculture books mentioned turkey husbandry, but the bird itself was of minor importance. In England, the interest in poultry raising was piqued by the translation and publication of a book by a French biologist, René-Antoine Ferchault de Réaumur, *The Art of Hatching and Bringing Up Domestick Fowls* (1750), which laid out the best and most current scientific knowledge on poultry.[7] Raising turkeys became important enough to be included in sections of such works.[8] John Lawrence ("Bonington Moubray"), who was British, summarized what was generally known about the subject in *A Practical Treatise on Breeding, Rearing and Fattening All Kinds of Domestic Poultry* (1816) and urged the creation of incubators and hatcheries. His book went through several editions in England, and copies were sold in the United States.

Many eighteenth- and nineteenth-century cookbooks, newspapers, and books on agriculture also offered advice on raising turkeys. Homemakers, for instance, were urged to plunge newly hatched chicks into cold water and force-feed them with peppercorns, advice repeated for decades.[9] Books also advised how to fatten turkeys by cramming them for two weeks with rice, oats, barley, mashed potatoes, eggs, beans, buckwheat, and milk. Thrice-daily feeding was recommended. A French chef, Alexis Soyer, reported that in Provence, in a practice reminiscent of the gavage of geese and ducks to produce foie gras, turkeys were force-fed walnuts, which Soyer believed gave their flesh a richer, more oily taste.[10]

Hen Fever

In the mid-eighteenth century few American farmers saw the advantage of breeding turkeys. In fact, Americans paid little attention to breeding fowl in general until almost the mid-nineteenth century. The first American to write a book on poultry was Caleb Bement, who did so initially under the appropriate pseudonym Micajah R. Cock. In the *American Poultry Book* (1843), subsequently renamed *The American Poulterer's Companion,* Bement supplied detailed coverage of American poultry breeds, thirty pages of information about wild and domesticated turkeys, and historical facts about the birds as well as directions for raising them. He reported that turkeys were second in importance only to chickens in America.[11]

John C. Bennet, a medical professional who lived in Plymouth, Massachusetts, read Bement's book and thought he'd try his hand at raising poultry. He bought expensive chickens that had recently been imported from Asia and permitted the various breeds to mingle. By sheer accident he produced a new variety, which he dubbed the Plymouth Rock.[12] Never one to be modest, Bennett crowed about his successes in a series of essays on poultry, including one on raising turkeys, and announced his intention to exhibit his own fowl in Boston's Quincy Market, challenging anyone to present a superior strain of fowl at the market for comparison. The resulting Exhibition of the New England Convention of Domestic Fowl Breeders and Fanciers was a success beyond anyone's expectations. Dozens of exhibitors, including Daniel Webster, showed their poultry, and thousands of people attended. Bennett was launched into poultry sales. To promote the new venture he pulled together his essays, revised them slightly, hired an artist to make engravings of the various breeds, and published *The Poultry Book* (1850), which had nineteen pages on the wild and domesticated turkeys.[13] Bennett cited numerous sources, including Lucien Bonaparte, John James Audubon, John Lawrence, and H. D. Richardson, a British poultry-raiser and author of *Domestic Fowl and Ornamental Poultry.* Of the turkey, Bennet concluded that he knew "of no birds more calculated to be profitable to the breeder."[14]

Bennett did not bother to promote his poultry book, which eventually went through three printings. He was too busy making money promoting and selling fancy fowl.[15] "Hen fever," as it was called, quickly infected others in New England and promptly spread to the South and West. The *Massachusetts Ploughman* announced that "the fever of the season" was fowl, and the *Boston Travel-*

ler stated that hen fever was "now raging among our amateur farmers." In 1854 *Northern Farmer* proclaimed, "Never in the history of the world, has there been so deep an interest felt in the gallinaceous races at present in this country."[16]

What drove hen fever was an increase in poultry books and agricultural journals. Bennett's volume wasn't alone; even before its release his close friend George Burnham published *The Poultry Breeder's Text Book* in 1850. Burnham then went on to write *A History of Hen Fever* (1855), and, after the war, an enlarged edition of the poultry book appeared. Edmund Saul Dixon and J. J. Kerr's *A Treatise on the History of Ornamental and Domestic Poultry* was published in 1857, and many others followed.[17]

As a result of hen fever, agricultural magazines began regular coverage of issues relating to poultry during the early 1850s. The *Cultivator,* for instance, ran a monthly column on the topic during 1852; the June issue offered an article on raising turkeys. In 1870 H. H. Stoddard launched *The Poultry Bulletin*. Disagreement with some of the descriptions of fowl in that periodical led William H. Lockwood of Hartford, Connecticut, to launch the *Poultry Standard.* Lockwood and Stoddard later combined their publications under the name *Poultry World,* which was intended for the poultry fancier and those raising poultry for market. Within a few years its subscription base reached five thousand. By 1874 three more poultry journals were published, one each in Minneapolis, Cedar Rapids, and Philadelphia. With such proliferation advertising became common for such poultry-related products as proprietary medicines and special feeds.[18]

An increase in the number of poultry exhibitions throughout the United States also contributed to improved breeding as poultry societies formed around the exhibitions. Hen fever abated during the Civil War, but poultry fanciers continued to raise unusual fowl and interest revived after the war.

Turkey Breeds

In 1865 the Poultry Club of London issued *Standard of Excellence in Exhibition Poultry,* copies of which were also sold in the United States. That created a dilemma because English and American standards for fowl differed. American poultry-raisers embarked on a lengthy effort to create their own standards for birds raised in the United States. In the first issue of *Poultry Standard,* William Lockwood attempted to begin the process. He described the Bronze as a "breed," a term that meant a turkey variety (now called a strain). But the job of developing generally accepted definitions of American fowl was bigger than a single person could accomplish. To meet that goal, the American Poultry Association was formed in Buffalo, New York, in February 1873, and it has defined standards for fancy poultry breeds ever since. In 1874 the association published *The American Standard of Excellence,* which claimed to contain "a complete description of all recognized varieties of fowls."[19] Those for turkeys were the Bronze, Narragansett, Black, Buff, Slate, and White breeds.[20]

The American Bronze turkey had first been described in England in the early eighteenth century. Its foundation stock was likely a combination of imported turkeys from Europe and the wild Eastern turkey (*M. g. silvestris*). This union likely occurred by accident as wild turkeys seeking food visited farms where domesticated turkeys lived and domesticated turkeys roamed into areas where wild ones roosted. There was also a deliberate attempt by some British and American poultry fanciers to increase the size of the domesticated turkey, which was still smaller than the wild bird. Numerous descriptions have survived of poultry enthusiasts locating wild turkey eggs and placing them under domesticated hens to be hatched and reared. The offspring were then interbred with domesticated turkeys. Most such efforts failed, but some produced desirable characteristics, for example, docility, bronze coloring, and larger and heavier bodies.

The Bronze turkey breed was most popular in the United States during the nineteenth and early twentieth centuries. Its large size, hardiness, and the coloring of its feathers made it popular at the market, where it demanded the highest prices. Large Bronze turkeys were noted in the 1830s in Rhode Island, and some were called the Point Judith Bronze. The markings on the domesticated Bronze are similar to those of the eastern wild turkey. Head and throat wattles are red and can change to blue, the feathers are a light metallic bronze, and the beard is black. The feathers of the wings, body, and tail are a combination of black, brown, and bronze-green. In the 1850s R. H. Avery of Wampsville, New York, began development of a larger Bronze turkey, which he exhibited in 1860. Over the years the Bronze turkey continued to be bred for increased weight, and by 1900 Bronze toms commonly weighed thirty-six pounds. By that date, larger versions, the Mammoth Bronze, had been created and weighed forty pounds or more.[21]

The Narragansett turkey was named for the bay that borders Rhode Island and likely originated in that state or in Connecticut. It was probably a cross between the Norfolk Blacks imported from England and the eastern wild turkey. Narragansetts were larger than other turkeys except the Bronze; toms weighed thirty-two pounds, and hens ten pounds less. They were hardy enough to survive the cold New England climate and mainly raised outdoors, where they foraged for their own food. Although colors differed among strains, the Narragansett was a mixture of metallic black and white; in sunshine its striking plumage appeared to be greenish-bronze. Until the early twentieth century the Narragansett was particularly popular in New England, the Midwest, and the mid-Atlantic states.[22]

Black turkeys likely derived from the original Mexican domesticated turkeys imported into Europe in the sixteenth century. They were popular in Spain and later in England. The American Black breed may have derived from the Black Norfolk turkey, which had been standardized in East Anglia, England, and imported into North America during the colonial era. Bred for early maturation and rapid growth, it was a small, fat bird and historically did not have uniform black feathers. By 1874, when it was described in Lockwood's *Standard,* males weighed in at a minimum of twenty pounds, and their feathers had a greenish-black sheen. The Black breed, like most others, has increased in size over the years, reflecting the American consumer's expectation of larger turkeys; by 1895 the weight of Black toms had increased to twenty-seven pounds. Now the bird is defined as uniformly black with no white in its feathers, and males weigh in at thirty-three pounds.[23]

Buff turkeys had white to light-buff wing feathers and white tail feathers with buff tips. The breed may have been a cross between Black and Red domestic fowls. Historically, Buff turkeys were most common in the mid-Atlantic states, specifically Pennsylvania. By 1900 the Buff was fast disappearing, and it was considered so rare by 1915 that it was removed from the *Standard of Perfection.* The breed was revived during the 1940s by the New Jersey Experiment Station, which produced a small- to medium-sized turkey, called appropriately the New Jersey Buff. Commercial interest in it declined with the popularization of Broad-breasted varieties during the 1950s.[24]

The Slate (also called the Blue, Maltese, or Lavender) breed was a cross between the White Holland and the Black breeds. Its plumage was a grayish-blue. The Slate never achieved commercial popularity and was mainly raised by fanciers for exhibition.[25]

During the 1920s, Enoch Carson developed the Royal Palm breed; Carson also raised Blacks, Bronzes, Narragansetts, and wild turkeys in a mixed flock in Florida. When a "palm" pattern appeared in the plumage of some birds he carefully cultivated it until it bred true. A relatively small bird that was popular with exhibitors before World War II, the breed has white feathers with a black band toward the edge of its tail feathers. It is also seen in blue and red colors. The Royal Palm was admitted into the *Standard of Perfection* in 1977.[26]

White turkeys, likely part of the original Mexican stock sent to Europe, were particularly appreciated in Holland and Austria, where White breeds were stabilized. The birds were imported into America during colonial times, but the White turkey (later called the Holland White) that appeared in the American *Standard of Perfection* is thought to have been a genetic mutation among Black turkeys. What relationship European breeds had to the American White is unknown. In 1875 White turkeys were pure white other than the male's beard, which was deep black. The breed was popular in New England and continued to be an important one until the 1950s.[27]

J. F. Barbee is credited for breeding the Bourbon Red in Bourbon County, Kentucky, about 1890, and the turkey was admitted to the *Standard of Perfection* in 1910. The Buff, Bronze, and White Hollands are believed to have been its foundation stock. Barbee initially called the birds "Bourbon Butternuts," but that name, unsurprisingly, didn't stick. Under the name Bourbon Red, the breed took off. Its distinguishing characteristic is a brownish-red body and white tail feathers. The Bourbon Red, an active forager and good market bird, was a commercial success, especially in the Midwest, until the 1940s.[28]

The recognition of poultry breeds by the American Poultry Association encouraged development of poultry shows so fanciers could compete for how well their birds conformed to the association's descriptions. Turkeys were exhibited as well in poultry shows and at state and county fairs. There were also specific turkey shows, the largest of which were the Northwestern Turkey Show in Roseburg, Oregon, the All-American Turkey Show in Grand Forks, North Dakota, and the Northern State Turkey Show in Alexandria, Minnesota. These shows rewarded growers for the excellence of their birds as defined by the American Poultry Association's *Standard of Excellence.* In addition, turkey clubs developed to foster interest in specific breeds. The International Turkey Association was formed in 1927 to encourage participation in shows and improve breeding.[29]

By the 1920s the two most important commercial American breeds were the large Bronze and the medium-sized White Holland. The Bronze could be raised at great distances from population centers, taken to central slaughterhouses, dressed, and frozen for storage or transportation. The White Holland was raised closer to population centers and sold directly to nearby customers.

In 1934 Stanley J. Marsden, employed by the U.S. Department of Agriculture (USDA) at Beltsville, Maryland, crossbred the Holland White with strains of wild turkeys, the Bronze, and others to eventually produce the Beltsville Small White, a compact, meaty turkey designed for families with small ovens.[30] The breed was extremely popular during the 1940s and early 1950s, when an estimated nineteen million were raised, but less popular with restaurants. Due to its small size, it was less profitable than the larger broad-breasted turkeys and lost popularity by 1960.[31] The Beltsville Small White was accepted into the *Standard of Perfection* in 1951.

The Revolutionary Broad-breasted Turkey

The Bronze turkey was described in Lockwood's *Standard* and the *American Standard of Excellence* in 1874 as the largest of the turkey breeds, and by the 1880s it was the preferred breed of commercial growers. In addition to size, the main goal of breeders was to produce specific-colored feathers, so there were Green-, Copper-, and Purple-bronze turkeys.[32] As many observers pointed out, few consumers cared about the color of the feathers, which, of course, were removed by the time consumers received the dressed turkey. The hobby was inspired, however, by formal competitions among growers. In their quest to achieve awards at shows, many breeders purchased birds for $500 just to improve their flock's feather coloring.

During the early twentieth century breeders in western states and Canadian provinces began to concentrate on putting meat on the turkey's frame rather than worrying about the color of its feathers. One such breeder was Jesse Throssel, who had raised Sheffield Bronze turkeys since 1900 on his family's farm in England. In 1926 he moved to Aldergrove in British Columbia, and the next year he imported one tom and two hens from home. From these birds he bred turkeys with increased meat, good hatchibility (the percentage of eggs that hatch), and early maturity. Some of his gobblers weighed forty pounds at nine months of age. These birds put on heavy meat about their breast. When Throssel exhibited his birds at the 1930 Portland International Livestock Show no one in Oregon had ever seen such turkeys, and they created quite a stir.[33]

Throssel sold some of his toms to breeders, who mated them to hens preselected for their meat-producing qualities. The resulting crossbreed had the ability to put on even more heavy flesh on the breast. The new crossbred birds were such a vast improvement on other breeds that they rapidly replaced the older types of turkeys.[34] The turkeys had such wide breasts and short legs that it was difficult for them to mate, so low fertility made artificial insemination necessary. The first practical method of doing so was developed by the USDA in 1934.[35] Artificial insemination also made it possible to control breeding, and it became the standard method of breeding birds by the 1950s.

The new turkeys were given many names. One was "Bronze Mae West" because the birds were "developed frontally," as one observer noted.[36] Despite such creative names, in 1938 a committee unanimously adopted "Broad-breasted Bronze" (BBB) for the new birds, and the new-style turkeys quickly revolutionized the industry.[37] By 1947 the BBB was the standard commercial turkey throughout the United States.[38] During the 1950s researchers at Cornell University and elsewhere crossbred the BBB with the White Holland, which matured earlier and had a cleaner appearance when dressed. The result was a Broad-breasted White, which by the 1960s had become the commercial standard.[39]

The Tasteless Turkey

Virtually all turkeys now consumed in America are strains of Broad-breasted Whites. Many people feel that turkey flesh, particularly breast meat, is bland and tasteless when compared with the taste of the meat on wild turkeys or to traditional turkey breeds. The modern commercial turkey has been bred for various characteristics—docility, early maturity, maximum growth, and color of the carcass. Flavor isn't one of those traits. It would be easy to blame the industry for the commercial turkey's lack of flavor, but it produces what consumers demonstrate they want. Americans consistently choose lower prices and greater quantity in their food, and in many ways the modern commercial turkey reflects that trend.

In the United States white meat is favored for various reasons. Because it has less fat the breast has been considered more healthful, and it is touted as an ideal meat for dieters. Then again, the dark meat on drumsticks is difficult to remove with a knife and fork. It's necessary to pick up a drumstick in order to get all the tasty bits, and that is unacceptable table etiquette on many occasions. It was such a problem in polite society that Isabella Beeton, who wrote cookbooks in nineteenth-century England, advised that drumsticks were to be not eaten at the table but should be sent back to the kitchen, where servants would cut meat away from the bone and serve it in other forms at later meals.[40]

Americans have an obsession with white breast meat, not only that of turkeys but also of chickens and some fish, such as tuna, although white meat is typically less flavorful than dark. Both white and dark meat are mainly muscle tissue. When muscles (such as the legs and thighs of a turkey) are exercised, their oxidative fibers store lipids (fats), their metabolic fuel, which permits extended use of those muscles. This turns the meat darker and juicer than white meat, which is composed of little-used muscle. Hence, the enormous breast of a turkey contains little fat. Moreover, when a bird is roasted in the traditional way the white meat usually cooks faster and is done before the thighs and legs, so breast meat typically becomes dry and overcooked. Although there are ways to prevent this, such as covering the breast, many cooks don't spend the time doing so.

That the modern turkey has less flavor than its forebears seems to be of little interest to most Americans, for consumers usually add flavoring and condiments to make the turkey meat more palatable, for example, gravy, cranberry sauce, stuffing, and salt and pepper. In some ways it is better for the turkey flesh to be relatively bland so the taste of the meat does not interfere with those of the consumer-added flavorings.

8

THE INDUSTRIALIZED TURKEY; OR, HOW THE TURKEY BECAME A PROFIT CENTER

In the midst of the Civil War the U.S. Congress boldly launched two major efforts unrelated to the war: creation of what became the Department of Agriculture and passage of the Land Grant College Act. The latter established agricultural colleges throughout the nation. The Hatch Act twenty-five years later created agricultural experiment stations, which were frequently housed at the land grant colleges. In order to coordinate research at the experiment stations, which issued reports on a wide variety of agricultural matters, the act also launched the Office of Experiment Stations in the Department of Agriculture.[1]

Beginning in 1898, states began to establish agricultural extension services, which were assigned to disseminate the latest and best agricultural information. In 1914 Congress passed the Smith-Lever Act, which created the cooperative agricultural extension service at land grant colleges. Each development influenced American agriculture and the turkey industry.

The experiment stations conducted research into turkey husbandry beginning in the 1890s, and in 1893 the Rhode Island Station released the first publication on turkeys. Others would follow.[2] The problem was how best to keep farmers informed, so women began to be hired as teachers and specialists, given that many growers were boys and women—who raised birds for "pin money." "A boy of ten or twelve years old, with little direction from his father," one nineteenth-century turkey-raiser announced, "will do the taking care to raise a hundred turkeys; he cannot earn so much money in any other way."[3] Another observer noted, "Many a farmer's wife, whose husband does not care to 'bother with poultry,' can earn from fifty to three hundred dollars a year." Before readers could object, the writer quickly noted that this could be done "without seriously impeding the other necessary work which falls to the lot of farmers' wives."[4]

The Automated Turkey

The turkey industry had grown slowly throughout the nineteenth century. Turkey farming was second in importance only to raising chickens, but it was a distant second. Most farmers raised turkeys to feed their families and sold a few birds to make a little extra money. Turkey raising was typified by W. A. Browning, a farmer who had begun keeping the birds during the 1830s in Norwich, Connecticut. With an eye on profit, he developed productive ways of raising, feeding, branding (the turkeys tended to wander to neighboring farms), fattening (he recommended boiled potatoes mixed with corn accompanied by milk and occasionally apples), and finally butchering. According to his records, Browning sold turkeys for $386 in 1869, and feed cost him about $147. Browning was quite satisfied with the $239 net profit. When he retired he wrote and published a small pamphlet describing his success. *A Complete System of Raising Turkeys* (1873) was the first booklet devoted to the topic.[5]

Browning's book was followed fourteen years later by Fanny Field's *Practical Turkey Raising: Turkeys for Market and Turkeys for Profit* (1887). The pseudonymous Field, identified as "the most experienced turkey raiser in America," reported that there was "no branch of poultry farming that pays so well in proportion to the investment of time, labor and capital as raising turkeys for market." She claimed that one year she had raised 150 turkeys in addition to doing all "housework and sewing for a family of five." She grossed $400 from the sale of the birds, two-thirds of which was profit.[6]

The price for turkeys dropped during the following decades. In Texas at the turn of the century, for instance, toms retailed for 75 cents apiece and hens for 50 cents. The main reason for the decline was the ease with which turkeys could be raised and the greatly improved transportation system in America. Then there was also the low price of beef, which many Americans preferred to turkey. Beef production rapidly expanded during the late nineteenth century, and vast shipments were imported from Mexico. In 1897 Congress passed the Dingley Act, which placed a tariff on imported beef, and prices went up. The demand for turkeys increased apace, and so did their prices. Increased profits made raising turkeys a more attractive proposition. In 1905 a grower in Texas,

E. A. Tully, began selling his birds by weight, and other farmers followed suit.[7] The shift from price per turkey to price per pound was one important reason why turkey breeders began to breed bigger birds.

At the beginning of the twentieth century the industry consisted mainly of turkey growers on small farms, local slaughterhouses and processors, and small distributors. Commission men would visit farms with carts—later, trucks—to pick up live birds. The commission men then either transported the turkeys to local butchers or sold them directly to local consumers who did their own butchering.

As fat and heavy turkeys became the market standard, farmers increased the birds' weight by stuffing them with food in the period just before slaughter. In some cases turkeys were force-fed by hand for a few weeks until twelve to eighteen hours before they were to be killed. That emptied the crop (part of the bird's digestive tract) and left the dressed bird with a more pleasant smell.[8]

Just before the beginning of the twentieth century, revolutionary changes in farm-to-market delivery were underway. The first concerned transportation and refrigeration. Before this time, turkeys had to be eaten within a few days of slaughter so most consumers bought locally raised birds. Ice-cooling made it possible to hold turkeys for a few days longer, but the system was still cumbersome and expensive. Ice was bulky and required costly transportation; large, insulated storage facilities; and massive distribution systems consisting of ships and ice wagons. Moreover, ice was only effective when it came in direct contact with turkeys. In rooms or small enclosures it was difficult to lower the temperature of the birds adequately with ice, even when combined with salt. By the 1880s, however, new cooling systems based on absorption and condensation had been developed. Those processes cooled food well below the freezing point without the drawbacks of packing in ice.

The frozen turkey resulted from changes in technology. Then railroads added refrigerated cars, and the frozen turkeys became mobile. Turkeys could be raised, slaughtered, butchered, and stored at one location and then shipped to cities hundreds or thousands of miles away. Freezers also meant that birds could be slaughtered and frozen when prices were low in the fall and sold when prices were high in winter or spring.

Because refrigeration and storage systems required large amounts of capital, industrial poultry operations began to replace turkeys being raised on small farms. Larger operations had bargaining power. They needed greater quantities of feed and so could negotiate for lower prices. Better yet, they could establish their own feed operations. They could buy chicks more cheaply or they could open their own hatcheries. Larger operations could invest in selective-breeding research to produce bigger profits and take advantage of the poultry research from agricultural experimental stations. Moreover, increased efficiency permitted large operations to undersell small turkey farms.

The Caged Turkey

Turkeys, like all fowl, are susceptible to a number of diseases, and at the beginning of the twentieth century one of the most damaging was blackhead. Although best known as a disease of turkeys, the organism infects other birds as well. Chickens, the most resistant, can carry and pass it on but usually do not become ill. The turkey is the most susceptible to the disease, which is usually fatal.

Although researchers did not know the cause of blackhead early in the twentieth century they found it could be prevented by adding potassium permanganate to the birds' water. That solution was partially successful; others were tried but nothing seemed to work well. Researchers determined that blackhead was caused by ingesting a microscopic parasite (*Histomonas meleagridis*) from feed or water contaminated by infected poultry. The blackhead organism cannot live long outside the host, so the first solution was to use large, divided pens. Farmers would move their birds from one section to another every few weeks.[9] That required a large amount of space and was also an imperfect way to combat the disease. It was later found that the main way that the parasite was transmitted was by ingesting infected cecal worm eggs, and the parasite can live for years in the eggs.

The alternate was the cage system, which had been used with mixed results for hundreds of years. Turkeys raised in confinement and no exposure to sunlight, however, develop rickets, a vitamin D deficiency. After the discovery of vitamin D in 1922, rapid progress was made on improving poultry feed. Researchers could calculate the proper balance of protein, vitamins, and other nutrients, and today farmers make it standard practice to use antibiotics to keep caged birds healthy. Caging also made it possible to feed and water the birds, gather eggs, and remove manure mechanically. Those changes led to a doubling of production and a further increase in farm efficiency. By the 1940s large numbers of turkeys were raised in cages.

As selective breeding continued to produce birds with broader, meatier breasts, turkeys' bodies became more disproportionate. It became difficult for them to stand, and even more difficult (and now impossible) for them to mate, so artificial insemination became common in the 1950s. Although most turkey-processing operations have been industrialized, the process of insemination must be done by hand. First, semen is collected by picking up a tom by its legs and one wing and locking it to a bench with rubber clamps, rear facing upward. The copulatory organs are stimulated by stroking the tail feathers and back; the vent is squeezed; and semen is collected with an aspirator, a glass tube that vacuums it in. The semen is then combined with "extenders" that include antibiotics and a saline solution to give more control over the inseminating dose. A syringe is filled, taken to the henhouse, and inserted into the artificial insemination machine. A worker grabs a hen's legs, crosses them, and holds the hen with one hand. With the other hand the worker wipes the hen's backside and pushes up her tail. Pressure is applied to her abdomen, which causes the cloaca to evert and the oviduct to protrude. A tube is inserted into the vent, and the semen is injected.[10]

Incubators were used to hatch poultry in ancient Egypt and have been in use ever since. Advice on how to construct natural incubators was common in poultry and agricultural books during the eighteenth and nineteenth centuries. In the United States, commercial artificial incubators were first advertised in the 1870s, but the first major commercial models were sold by the Cyphers Incubator Company at the end of the nineteenth century. Other companies followed. By 1900 hatcheries used small, three- to four-hundred-egg-capacity models. The size of incubators increased, however, and now manufacturers sell mammoth machines that hatch ten thousand chicks at a time.[11]

Virtually all commercial turkeys today are raised under conditions of intense confinement. Because overcrowding encourages aggression and cannibalism, chicks are routinely debeaked, de-snooded, and de-toed within three to five days of hatching. Debeaking routinely removes one third of the beak with a hot blade, which burns through the beak. It also cauterizes the wound and prevents bleeding. De-snooding (or dubbing) removes the snood, mainly on male chicks, and de-toeing removes three toes (nails) from each foot. Where necessary, the turkey's spurs are also trimmed. Each action is intended to reduce injury that might be caused by pecking and scratching at each other. Chicks are also injected with antibiotics to prevent diseases common to confinement.

The chicks are then sexed because toms and hens are raised for different purposes. Hens are smaller, and their flesh tends to be juicier, so they are usually processed as whole birds that are popular during the fall from Thanksgiving through New Year's. Toms are larger, but their flesh is drier and is more likely to go into ground turkey, turkey bacon, other processed products or become food for dogs and cats. It is difficult to determine the sex of a chick. In the past, the task was performed by well-trained specialists who held chicks upside down and examined the lateral folds in their vents. Because not many people qualified for that job, however, a hatchery might incorrectly classify chicks more than 10 percent of the time. Misclassifications can cost a producer heavily at processing time, so hatcheries' reputations were based on the ability to identify the chicks' sex. Today, turkeys are bred for sex-linked genetic characteristics, and hatchery staff can more easily separate hens from toms. Specialists who sex turkeys are now mainly employed only when hatcheries and breeders produce parent stock.

Newly hatched chicks are held in a brooder, a warm room that is safe from predators. After four weeks chicks are herded into a windowless barn that is illuminated twenty-four hours a day to encourage the chicks to eat more food.[12] Factorylike warehouses hold seven to ten thousand birds that receive high-nutrient food conveyed automatically via feeder chains along small troughs throughout the house. When the birds reach slaughter weight (fifteen to nineteen pounds) in twelve to nineteen weeks they are crated and transported to slaughterhouses.

Until the early twentieth century turkeys were killed by one of several methods. Wringing the bird's neck left a lot of blood inside the carcass, and chopping off a turkey's head soaked its feathers with blood, rendering them unusable, and also left considerable blood in its flesh. As farm and poultry books pointed out, Americans preferred poultry flesh as bloodless as possible, so the most common way of slaughtering turkeys was to bleed them. A string was tied around both legs, and the bird was suspended upside down. That prevented its wings from hitting things and avoided breaking bones and bruising the wing flesh. The turkey's jugular was slit, and the fowl was often "brained" by sticking a knife into its brain to paralyze but not kill the bird. The turkey then bled to death, and its feathers were plucked in such a way as to preserve the skin. This was a difficult task because unsightly tiny pinfeathers had to be removed as well. An easier method of removing feathers was to scald a dead bird. Unfortunately, however, that darkened the skin and dried out the carcass, making it unsightly.[13]

Defeathering was automated by the late 1930s by using an automatic rougher that used rotating rubber "fingers" to remove large feathers; smaller ones were removed by singeing the bird over a flame or dunking it in wax. When the wax hardened it was pealed away, bringing the feathers with it. The few pinfeathers remaining were still plucked by hand. Depending on the weather, carcasses were hung again for a few days or a week in a cool, dry place. The bird was then ready to cook and serve.[14]

Until the mid-twentieth century birds were generally left intact with heads, feet, and entrails. This was called the "New York style" of dressing. A turkey dressed in that manner could be preserved longer than one that had been eviscerated but created more work for the butcher or homemaker who did the processing. During the 1930s commercial processors began to eviscerate turkeys by removing their heads, feet, crops, and entrails. The carcasses were cleaned, and the liver, gizzard, and heart were replaced. These "ready-to-cook" turkeys could either be sold fresh or frozen. New York style went out of style by the 1950s, when virtually all turkeys were eviscerated.[15]

Historically, none of the turkey was wasted. The heads and feet were sold to fish hatcheries, and fat was extracted from the entrails for making chicken soup. In 1943 *Fortune Magazine* reported that the "oil sacs in the tail have medicinal uses. Testicles are regarded as a rare delicacy by city slickers who relish them as 'short fries.' What is left is sent to a rendering plant."[16] Feathers are now generally ground for compost.

Processing turkeys has become more automated since the 1950s. Birds are transported to central slaughterhouses and shackled upside down on an assembly line; then the turkeys are stunned by submerging their heads and necks in a bath of electrified water. In smaller slaughterhouses birds may be stunned by a hand-held gun. Their throats are cut by a mechanical blade or, in smaller slaughterhouses, by hand. The bleeding turkeys are next immersed in a scalding tank to loosen their feathers, which machines remove. Finally, the carcass is dressed for market.

The Year-round Turkey

Most agricultural production greatly declined during the depression, but turkey production remained strong. In 1929, the last year before the depression, America produced eighteen million birds, and by 1940 the number had increased to thirty-two million.[17] The reasons for this increase were obvious. Pound for pound, turkey was the least expensive meat, and virtually anyone with a farm could raise turkeys cheaply. During the depression the federal government began to purchase the birds for public school food service, and turkey products have proliferated in school cafeterias ever since.

The prewar increase in turkey production encouraged the creation of the National Turkey Federation composed of state turkey grower associations. The group's main mission was to lobby Congress for benefits for its members and engage in national promotion efforts. Within two years of its formation the United States was at war, and the federation could provide the industry with a means of relating to the numerous federal agencies that dealt with food production during the war.

Turkey production increased even more during the war. Pork and beef were rationed, so turkey meat became an obvious alternative. The U.S. military also began purchasing large quantities of turkey and turkey feathers, which the army stuffed into mattresses and pillows.[18] Turkey growers, however, made more money selling to civilians. One farmer in 1942, for instance, cleared $46,000, just on his turkeys. Prices skyrocketed, and price controls were imposed in late 1942. Many growers responded with an embargo on sales to the military and sold their birds on the black market. Supplying to the armed forces became mandatory, however, in 1943, and by 1945 forty-five million birds a year were being produced.[19]

As the war neared its end the National Turkey Federation began to plan for the postwar period. The fear, of course, was that peace would bring a collapse in the demand and that production would return to prewar levels. One way to prevent a postwar slump was to encourage Americans to eat more turkey and turkey products. The federation's modest campaign to "Eat More Turkey" in 1944 didn't accomplish much, and production declined to thirty-one million birds by 1948. The campaign went into high gear and employed new advertising gimmicks as the federation and its affiliates expended thousands of dollars on the effort. One promotion involved giving President Harry Truman a Thanksgiving turkey. The U.S. Department of Agriculture supported the federation's efforts by issuing bulletins entitled *Turkey on the Table Year Round,* beginning in 1949 and continuing through the 1950s; targeted toward consumers, the publications were filled with instructions on preparation and cooking methods. Turkey production soared as a result of these activities, hitting forty-one million birds in 1949. In 1951 production surpassed its wartime high with fifty-three million. Sales and profits increased further, and it appeared as if expansion was limitless. In 1961 turkey growers raised 107 million birds, more than twice as many as they had produced a decade before.[20]

Traditionally, the vast majority of commercial turkeys were sold during October, November, and December. That dovetailed perfectly with the natural seasonality of poultry raising. Turkey poults hatched in the spring are ready for market in the fall. As trains and trucks became able to handle frozen foods and freezers grew common in supermarkets, it was possible to supply Americans with frozen turkeys all year. Unfortunately, however, there was little demand other than in the fall. The strong association of the turkey with Thanksgiving—and to a lesser extent, Christmas—made it difficult to sell the birds at other times.

That began to change in the mid-twentieth century. Because turkey is a low-fat, less-expensive alternative to other meats, school lunch programs served turkey throughout the year. Turkey exports rapidly increased during the 1950s, and people in other countries, who did not have the same food pattern as Americans, bought them throughout the year. Exports were encouraged in 1954 by the passage of the Trade Development Act (PL 480).[21]

Another way to keep production high was by developing new commercial products. Among the first was the "split turkey." Because of the breeding efforts of the 1930s and early 1940s, broad-breasted turkeys had become so big that they did not fit into many ovens of the day, so producers split turkeys in two, hoping that doing so would attract more consumers. It was a great idea, but it didn't work because homemakers had no idea how to prepare half of a turkey.[22]

Processors experimented with many more products. Turkey steaks, smoked turkey, canned turkey, turkey sandwich spread, turkey rolls, turkey sausages, and turkey bacon all arrived on the market during the late 1940s and early 1950s.[23] Turkey bacon is made from turkey meat, not fat, and therefore has less fat than traditional bacon, and ground turkey, less than 15 percent fat, has been often recommended as a good substitute for ground beef. Health and other considerations also increased the importance of turkey meat in delis for lunches, and turkey frankfurters were sold commercially by 1951.[24] Turkey burgers and meatballs became common during the 1970s.[25] By the end of the 1980s turkey products were sold year round, although autumn remained the high point in sales due to Thanksgiving, as it still does.

The TV Dinner

Turkey farmers owe a huge debt of gratitude to Carl A. Swanson, who in 1896 migrated at the age of seventeen from Sweden to the United States. He worked on a farm in Blair, Nebraska, and then moved to Omaha, where he worked in a grocery store during the day and at night took accounting courses. While working at the store he met John O. Jerpe, who owned a small commission company. The Jerpe Commission Company acquired eggs and cream from local farmers, processed the eggs, manufactured butter, and sold those products to distributors, charging a commission to the farmers. In 1899 Swanson, who had saved money from his work, became a partner. With Swanson on board the company began to expand, selling chickens, turkeys, and other meat. Swanson did well in the commission business and bought the company in 1928. During the 1940s he renamed it C. A. Swanson and Sons.[26]

In 1935 Birdseye selected the company as its supplier for frozen turkeys, and Swanson leased a large warehouse in Colorado that he converted into a cold-storage facility. He also built a sizable turkey-processing operation. Beginning in February 1936, Swanson guaranteed that he would purchase turkeys at 18 cents a pound in September. It was the depth of the depression, and farmers struggled to keep their land, so Swanson also advanced funds up-front to help pay for feed and other expenses in the spring. That worked well during times of turkey scarcity because Swanson would have a guaranteed supply whereas other processors would have to pay a higher price for their turkeys. He also had a solution for the lean years. In times of plenty he froze turkeys in the fall when the birds were plentiful and then sold them in the spring when supply was limited. By 1942 Swanson was the nation's largest turkey processor, with sales of $9 million. *Fortune* magazine dubbed him the "Turkey King."[27]

During the late 1940s Swanson decided to try to corner the turkey market and began a massive buying campaign from California to Minnesota. That drove up the price of turkeys, which encouraged more farmers to start raising them. In 1950, however, the bubble burst because of the glut of turkeys on the market. Swanson was left with a huge quantity of birds, many more than he could expect to sell the following spring. His storage facilities were filled, and it became necessary to rent cold-storage railroad cars for the overflow. By February 1951, Swanson had more than twenty refrigerated train carloads of frozen turkeys, fifty-two thousand pounds in each car, traversing the country because there was no market for them and cold-storage facilities were unavailable.[28]

At an emergency meeting of the company, senior staff conferred on what to do with the unwanted turkeys. On the way to the meeting, Gerry Thomas, a Swanson's executive, met with one of the company's distributors—a firm that prepared food for Pan-American Airways' overseas flights. Those meals were packed in aluminum trays that could be heated in onboard convection ovens, but the product was not marketed to the general public. Thomas proposed at the meeting that Swanson make a similar meal for postwar consumers, who were interested in faster, more convenient food preparation. He also developed the concept of an aluminum tray divided into three compartments, one for a turkey entrée and two for side dishes. The original meal had giblet gravy and stuffing (in the compartment with the turkey), sweet potatoes, and green peas. The whole was then covered by foil.

Swanson liked the idea and gave permission to test-market what Thomas named the "television dinner," thereby associating his creation with the new and exciting technology just entering mainstream American life. At the time, most frozen food packages were printed in two colors, so the six-color package of the television dinner stood out. A few thousand meals were test-marketed in cities from Omaha to Chicago in the spring of 1951.[29] It was a risky venture because frozen foods were not yet a significant part of the American food supply. During World War II, canned goods, needed for the war effort, were in short supply, and many Americans tried frozen food for the first time. Those made with meat were rationed, but frozen fruits and vegetables became more popular.

When the war ended, new frozen foods—Sara Lee cakes, Quaker Oats waffles, and Birds Eye fish sticks—hit the market, and orange juice followed in 1946. During the late 1940s C. A. Swanson and Company produced frozen chicken and turkey pies. Despite these successes, processing and marketing frozen foods were still uncertain ventures. Food processors did not fully understand the processes needed to manufacture the products, there were few refrigerated trucks to transport frozen products to stores, freezers were not yet common in grocery stores, and not every home had a refrigerator or freezer in which to store frozen food. The packages often thawed and were then refrozen, which wreaked havoc with the quality of the food. There was little consumer enthusiasm for frozen foods in 1951.

Yet the idea of a prepared meal that could be eaten in front of the television set intrigued consumers, and after successful test-marketing Swanson expanded the line to include chicken and beef entrées and varied the side dishes as well. The company also invested extensively in promotion and shortened the name of the product line to "TV dinner."[30]

The concept was so successful that within three years Swanson was selling thirteen million turkey dinners a year. Based on that phenomenal success, the Campbell Soup Company acquired Swanson in 1955.[31] Others were encouraged to jump into the market, and thousands of similar products have been offered. Swanson's TV dinners slowly lost ground to the varied competition, and Pinnacle Foods Corporation acquired Swanson in 2001. The company has celebrated fifty years of the TV dinner, and turkey remains the most popular frozen entrée.

Vertical Integration

Throughout the twentieth century the turkey industry has attempted to maximize profits through improved efficiency. A major way to reduce costs was through vertical integration—combining all the aspects of turkey farming into one operation eliminated middlemen. Hatcheries and turkey feed operations were a logical marriage, so feed mills were built next to hatcheries. The industrial assembly line made it possible for turkeys to be raised in warehouses near hatcheries, and slaughterhouses could be built on or near the same sites. Such changes saved on expenses related to transportation, management, marketing, and record keeping. The changing industry also required extensive research, and discoveries, particularly in genetics, led to even greater efficiency.

The growth of the turkey industry also encouraged geographical shifts. Before 1890 turkey farms were concentrated in New England, but they gradually gave way to growers in the Midwest and South. In 1890 American farmers raised about eleven million birds, and the turkey trade exceeded $12 million annually. The largest turkey-producing state was Illinois, followed closely by Iowa and Missouri. Each of these states produced almost twice as many turkeys as their nearest competitors: Pennsylvania, Ohio, Indiana, New York, Kansas, Kentucky, Texas, Florida, and Virginia.[32]

Turkey raising reached the western United States during the 1920s. California was ranked seventeenth among the states in turkey production in 1900, and by 1935 it had risen to second place. During the same period New York dropped from fourteenth to thirty-third place.[33] In 1939 George and Johnny Nicholas purchased a farm near Vineburg, California, that became the largest turkey enterprise in America. By the 1950s the Nicholas Turkey Breeding Farm had developed the first commercially successful, large, white-feathered bird that became the industry standard.

In Montana, Harriette E. Cushman, an agricultural extension agent, organized a turkey marketing association after Congress passed the Capper-Volstead Act, which empowered farmers to market and sell agricultural products through cooperatives. Other states followed Montana's example, and eight turkey cooperatives in Washington, Oregon, Idaho, Montana, Colorado, and Nevada combined in 1929 to form the Northwestern Turkey Marketing Association.[34] The name was changed to Norbest Growers Association in 1943 and later shortened to Norbest, Inc. Today, Norbest, headquartered in Midvale, Utah, is supplied by approximately 125 independent turkey growers in Utah and Nebraska.[35]

The growers expanded operations during the boom years of the 1950s and anticipated still-greater profits in the following decade. The market became over-extended, however, and supply outstripped demand in 1960. Many growers lost their businesses when the market crashed the following year, and those who remained had to cut costs to survive. Narrow profit margins drove many small farms out of the business, which concentrated the industry in fewer hands. Turkey raising and processing had evolved from a collection of regional businesses to a highly centralized national industry.[36] The industry has continued to centralize since the 1960s. The largest turkey companies today are the Butterball Turkey Company, Carolina Turkeys, Cargill Turkey Products, and Jennie-O Turkey Store.

The Butterball Turkey Company began in 1894 when Peter Eckrich, an immigrant from Germany, opened a meat market in Fort Wayne, Indiana. He opened a second store and then began selling products at wholesale. In 1925 the company was incorporated as Peter Eckrich and Sons, and it established branches in seventeen states.

In 1954 Eckrich introduced Butterball Turkeys, sold with a device (a "bar strap") to keep drumsticks tucked neatly against the bird, which makes skewering or trussing unnecessary. Fourteen years later Eckrich became a wholly owned subsidiary of Beatrice Foods Company, which merged with Swift and Company to create Swift-Eckrich. In the 1970s Butterball pioneered the turkey lifter, which made it easier to raise a hot bird from a roasting pan, and in 1981 the company launched the "Butterball Turkey Talk-Line" to answer consumers' questions. During the first year of operation, 1981, the Talk-Line staff responded to eleven thousand telephone calls, and now there are more than a hundred thousand questions annually.[37] Butterball was also among the first companies to produce "self-basting" or "enhanced" turkeys. Self-basting is a means of injecting chemical solutions of approved additives into a turkey's flesh to increase flavor and juiciness; it can also increase the bird's weight. In 1990 ConAgra Foods acquired Beatrice and merged Eckrich with its Refrigerated Foods Group, which is headquartered in Downers Grove, Illinois.[38] The company sells nearly a hundred different turkey products, such as a 90 percent fat-free turkey bacon, marinated turkey steaks (teriyaki, lemon pepper, barbecue, and Italian), and strips used for fajitas or stir-fry. Butterball is America's third-largest turkey producer.

Carolina Turkeys was created in 1986 when two family-owned businesses, Goldsboro Milling Company and Carroll's Foods, combined operations. Smithfield Foods purchased Carroll's Foods' interest in Carolina Turkeys in May 1999. Based in Mt. Olive, North Carolina, Carolina Turkeys has the world's largest turkey-processing plant along with a fully integrated operation combining diagnostic laboratories, research farms, breeder farms, hatcheries, growing farms, and feed mills.[39]

In 1865 William Wallace Cargill set up a grain storage facility in Conover, Iowa, and over the next several decades the company followed the expansion of the railroad system to gather and process grain. Headquarters were moved to Minneapolis. Cargill began acquiring turkey companies during the 1950s; its operations work under the brand names of Honeysuckle White, Plantation Fiesta, and Black Forest Turkey Ham. All, however, are managed by Cargill Turkey Products, the world's second-largest turkey producer.[40]

Meanwhile, Farmer's Produce Company was launched in 1949 by Earl B. Olson, who operated a small creamery and raised turkeys on the side in Minnesota. In 1953 the company named its eviscerated turkey Jennie-O after Earl and Dorothy Olson's daughter, Jennifer. In 1971 the company changed its name to Jennie-O Foods and began expanding operations and its product line. In 1986 Jennie-O became part of Hormel Foods Corporation.[41]

Wallace Jerome started raising turkeys in 1922 in Barron, Wisconsin, and expanded his operation in 1941, creating a "Home Farm" that processed "New York dressed" turkeys. In 1950 Jerome purchased a small canning company, equipped it to prepare oven-ready turkeys, and named it Badger Turkey Industries. In 1964 the name was changed to Jerome Foods, and twenty years later Jerome began producing turkey products under the Turkey Store brand. The brand was so successful that the company changed its name to the Turkey Store in 1998, and three years later Hormel acquired the company and merged it with its Jennie-O Foods. The new name for the combined companies is Jennie-O Turkey Store, and it is America's largest turkey producer.[42]

Product Diversification

From the turkey industry's perspective, one of the great advantages of Carl Swanson's frozen dinners was that they sold throughout the year. There were other frozen turkey products as well. Swanson sold frozen turkey pot pies before marketing the complete dinners, and in 1949 the Farmer's Produce Company created the "Tur-King," a nine-pound log of raw turkey meat that was compressed in molds, frozen, and then wrapped in foil. It was just what delis, cafeterias, and small restaurants needed. Preparing turkey sandwiches, salads, and dinners was easier when using the Tur-King than when dealing with a whole bird.[43]

Other turkey products were developed and marketed. Norbest featured boneless roasts for both retail and food service; ground turkey; turkey steaks; cooked, roasted, and smoked deli turkey breasts; turkey ham; and a host of other products.[44] Butterball Turkey began selling turkey parts, turkey sausages, ground turkey, sliced turkey for sandwiches, and stuffing and gravy mixes.[45] Jennie-O first marketed turkey hot dogs in 1984 and now makes turkey pastrami, which is supplied in sandwich form to airlines for in-flight meals.

Sausage made of minced turkey meat has been around since the late nineteenth century. Spices of all types are added to the otherwise bland meat. The products make it possible to serve turkey as an alternate breakfast meat that has 80 percent fewer calories than regular pork bacon or sausage. Not mentioned, however, is the fact that most turkey bacon and sausage has double the amount of salt than the other products, and turkey patties, served in hamburger buns, are not far behind.[46]

Supermarkets began selling freshly ground turkey, frequently mixed with ground beef so shoppers would accept it more readily. Turkey rolls and turkey hams, which were pressed into shapes that could be sliced like a boneless roast, came along in the following decades and were perfect for sandwiches.[47] Deli turkey, turkey pastrami, turkey cutlets, turkey tenderloin, and many other turkey-based products are marketed as low-fat, and diet-conscious Americans have flocked to embrace them. Efforts to diversify and promote turkey products have been successful; sales increased, and turkey is now served all year.

Stuffing mix was created as an adjunct to turkey. Around 1916 Sophie Cubbison and her husband opened a small bakery in Los Angeles. Her first commercial success in 1925 was with Zwieback and Melba toast, the latter created by a French chef, Georges Auguste Escoffier, who named it after the Australian opera diva Nellie Melba. In 1948 Cubbison packaged stuffing mix in boxes and promoted it through magazine and newspaper advertising with the slogan "Turkey tastes Better. . . . When stuffed with 'Mrs. Cubbison's All Purpose Dressing and Cornbread Stuffin' mixes." The products were advertised on a Los Angeles radio program hosted by the then-little-known Bob Barker, who became the host of the *Truth or Consequences* game show. During the 1950s Sophie Cubbison became a regular on television cooking shows. She retired in 1955, but her commercial business expanded, and the stuffing mix remains on the market.[48] Many other companies also produced stuffing mixes. Stovetop Stuffing, created in 1971 by Ruth M. Siems, a home economist at General Foods' technical center in White Plains, New York, was marketed the following year.[49] Peppridge Farm, Arnold, and other commercial bakeries offer their own brands as well.

Commercial Turkey Problems

In general, America's turkey industry has prospered since the 1950s. Per-capita sales have increased, and turkey products have diversified such that the industry is no longer totally dependent on the sales of whole birds in the fall. In addition, the price of turkey meat continues to be lower than that of other meat, and the turkey's lower fat content has given growers and producers a competitive advantage.

Competition remains high among producers. Most consumers consider commercial turkeys as generic commodities and usually shop by price, so producers have consistently striven for the lowest possible cost. Commercial operations have remained in business only because they cut costs by expanding operations and increasing efficiency.

Turkey meat has since the middle of the twentieth century been presented as a nutritious, low-calorie alternative to beef and pork. Indeed, skinless turkey has the smallest amount of saturated and unsaturated fat—and the highest percentage of protein—of any available meat. It is also low in cholesterol and a source of iron, zinc, phosphorus, potassium, and B vitamins.

Producers have confronted problems similar to those faced by the rest of the poultry industry. Some observers believe that cost-cutting has lowered standards and created health risks; around 1960 safety concerns over turkey-processing plants began to emerge and voluntary inspection was instituted. Many fell short of sanitation standards, however, and so plant inspections became mandatory. But even mandatory inspections did not resolve the problems.

Since 2001 the Centers for Disease Control (CDC) have regularly reported that at least 13 percent of raw U.S. turkeys carry salmonella, a bacterium that thrives in raw meat and can cause serious health problems if the meat is not properly handled and thoroughly cooked.[50] Salmonella is heat-sensitive and can be destroyed by cooking food to temperatures above 165° F. Fully cooked birds do not normally contain salmonella, but it may occur if they are not properly handled.

Yet another medical problem related to turkeys is bacterial dysentery caused by shigellosis. The bacteria are spread by food handlers who may be symptomless carriers, and food is contaminated by hand contact. Bacterial dysentery is found in turkey salads and other types of cut, diced, or chopped and mixed food. To prevent the occurrence of shigellosis, those preparing the turkey need to cook it properly and maintain high standards of personal hygiene.[51]

A more serious problem is *Listeria monocytogenes* contamination, which can cause death. In December 2000, for instance, the CDC revealed that Cargill turkey products had been contaminated with *Listeria monocytogenes* bacteria, which was believed to be responsible for four deaths and three miscarriages or stillbirths. Cargill recalled some 16.7 million pounds of its cooked products, which had been distributed to grocery stores, restaurants, and other institutions in the United States and other countries.[52] Skeptics remain unconvinced that the industry has cleaned up its act, and critics call for greater monitoring by the U.S. Department of Agriculture to avoid more problems in the future.

9

THE SOCIAL TURKEY; OR, HOW THE TURKEY BECAME A CULTURAL ICON

The turkey was just a big bird to raise, hunt, and consume until the American War for Independence, when it began to acquire symbolic value. The new nation needed to differentiate itself from its English roots, and "American" foods began to take on nationalistic values. A main instigator for this change in the turkey's symbolic shift was Benjamin Franklin, who had numerous turkey connections. First, he liked to eat the bird; indeed, one of the few surviving recipes directly associated with him is one for an oyster sauce for a boiled turkey.[1] Second, the turkey figured in Franklin's scientific experiments. In 1749 Franklin proposed that a turkey "be killed for dinner by the *electrical shock,* and roasted by the *electrical jack,* before a fire kindled by the *electrified bottle.*"[2] That proposed technique did not turn the culinary world on its head.

It is neither for his turkey experiment nor his culinary enjoyment of the bird that Franklin is remembered today. His third and most important contribution to America's turkey lore were his comments regarding the official seal of the United States. In a private letter to his daughter Sarah Bache, dated January 26, 1784, Franklin wrote, "For my part, I wish the Bald Eagle had not been chosen as the Representative of our Country; he is a Bird of bad moral Character. . . . For in truth, the Turk'y is in comparison a much more respectable Bird, and withal a true original Native of America. . . . . It is, [though a little vain and silly, it is true, but not the worse emblem for that,] a Bird of Courage, and would not hesitate to attack a Grenadier of the British Guards, who should presume to invade his Farm Yard with a *red* Coat on."[3] At the time, people believed that the color red upset turkeys and that turkeys would attack anything with red on it.

Some have taken Franklin's statement to mean that he had argued that the turkey should be part of the Great Seal of the United States. In 1776 the Continental Congress appointed a committee to recommend a national seal and Franklin did propose a design jointly with Thomas Jefferson, but it was of a biblical scene—Moses crossing the Red Sea chased by the pharaoh, nary a turkey in sight. Numerous other designs were also proposed, and the committee ended its tenure without recommending one. A second committee followed and was again dissolved without making a recommendation. The third committee finally selected the bald eagle as the national emblem on the seal, and Congress passed that recommendation into law on June 20, 1782. It was that legislation Franklin lamented to his daughter. His letter was made public and has been often quoted, and just as often misinterpreted, ever since.[4]

Yet in many ways the turkey became an *unofficial* national symbol. Turkey hens hatched their young in the spring, and birds were ready for the cooking pot by fall. Autumn in agrarian America was a time of feasting to celebrate a successful harvest and also thin flocks and herds, leaving fewer animals to house and feed over the winter. Turkeys were mainstays of autumn and early winter meals, and because holidays such as Thanksgiving, Christmas, and New Year's were often celebrated with extended family, the birds were also associated with such gatherings. As the turkey became standard fare at Thanksgiving, the bird was imbued with myths surrounding that holiday, specifically within the national origins myth and the myth of a New England where Pilgrims led stoic, quietly heroic lives. Eating turkey on Thanksgiving became a patriotic act that reinforced national pride with every bite.

After the Civil War, turkey iconography frequently built on national and patriotic themes. A Thomas Nast cartoon in *Harper's Weekly,* for example, shows Uncle Sam carving turkey at a large and capacious dinner table surrounded by men, women, and children of different races, religions, and ethnicities.[5] Thanksgiving menus frequently were decorated with American flags or caricatures of Uncle Sam, particularly during the period of nationalistic fervor between the Spanish-American War and World War I.[6]

It was customary for those unable to make it home for Thanksgiving to write to relatives, apologizing and wishing them a wonderful dinner. Beginning around 1880, publishers began printing Thanksgiving postcards that could be sent in place of a formal letter. Thousands of different cards were published, and millions were circulated. Those that survive depict idyllic and nostalgic themes of a rural America that was fast disappearing; others reflected the now-well-established fakelore of Pilgrims celebrating the mythic First Thanksgiving. Most cards had as their central image male turkeys displaying their tail feathers. Some postcards were gently humorous. One, postmarked 1912, offers an antisuffrage perspective—a flamboyantly dressed turkey, with a sign "Votes for Women," encounters a wise old owl that exclaims "Oh, you suffragette." On another, a farmer carts a turkey to slaughter while a skinny bird tells a fat one that is feeding, "Keep it up, they'll have you next." Cards also incorporated patriotic symbols such as the American flag, red-white-and-blue stars and stripes, and Uncle Sam hats and images. When the United States entered World War I, images of Uncle Sam and the flag became even more common. The custom of sending Thanksgiving greeting cards declined after World War I as the Christmas greeting card business became popular. It seemed foolish to send cards at Thanksgiving and then a few weeks later for Christmas.

Turkey iconography continued to evolve after the war, and magazines still printed traditional images of the bird at Thanksgiving. The person who most personified these images during the mid-twentieth century was Norman Rockwell, who was born in New York in 1894. His first turkey illustration, *Cousin Reginald Catches Thanksgiving Turkey,* appeared on the cover of *The Country Gentleman* in 1917. In it, a very large tom is in hot pursuit of "Cousin Reginald," who is running as fast as he can. *Freedom from Want,* Rockwell's most famous Thanksgiving dinner scene (and among the most famous images of the holiday), appeared on the *Saturday Evening Post*'s cover on the unseasonable date of March 6, 1943, as one of a series entitled the "Four Freedoms" to illustrate the values for which America was fighting. In *Freedom from Want* a grandmother brings an uncarved, steaming turkey to the table. Next to the grandfather's plate are carving knives, and children and grandchildren smile and chat around the table. The image has been frequently reproduced in prints and on tableware.[7]

Talking Turkey

For almost two hundred years the turkey has been a symbol of honesty in America. That symbol is reflected in a joke: A white man and an Indian go hunting together and end up with only a turkey and a buzzard. When it's time to divide the spoils, the white man says, "You may take the buzzard and I will take the turkey, or I will take the turkey and you may take the buzzard." The Indian replies, "You never once said turkey to me."[8]

The first known reference to this "heads I win; tails you lose" joke appeared in 1821, but it likely circulated for decades before becoming enshrined in print.

An 1837 newspaper article reported that it had been current in colonial times.[9] In the first published reference, the author comments that he hopes that none of the readers will accuse him "of *not talking Turkey* to them in this article."[10]

The joke was repeated for dozens of years, and variations developed. The "white man" became the Yankee, particularly in the South where Yankees were not always appreciated. The buzzard was sometimes replaced by the crow or bustard, and "said turkey to me" changed to "talk turkey." Since then, "talking turkey" has meant "to speak frankly."[11] The phrase has survived in the United States for almost two hundred years and is now common among other English-speakers as well.

A variant phrase, to "talk cold turkey," also meant to speak freely and give the cold, hard facts, even unpleasant ones. From talking cold turkey, the term evolved into "cold turkey," which meant quitting something addictive such as alcohol, smoking, or drugs by stopping suddenly and completely rather than tapering off. According to the *Oxford English Dictionary* it was first used in print in 1921 and referred to treatment applied to "the most pitiful figures" in a drug treatment program.[12] The phrase is also common in many English-speaking countries.

Wish Fulfillment

About the same time that Americans began to talk turkey the practice of pulling the bird's merrythought emerged as well, a tradition that likely was an English import and may have been a folk custom dating back millennia. It involves pulling apart the furcula, the forked bone between the neck and breast. Usually the bone was first dried, but at holiday time drying was dispensed with. Traditionally, the individual with the largest piece of the furcula would marry first. The *Oxford English Dictionary* traces the first use of the word *merrythought* to the sixteenth century; thereafter, numerous references to merrythoughts appear in English literature, but there is little mention of them in the United States until the nineteenth century.[13] Just before the Civil War the custom of pulling the furcula became very popular, and it broadened to include any wish. As a result, the name of the bone—and the practice—was changed to "wishing bone" and then "wishbone." In this modification the two people make silent wishes, and the person with the larger portion of the bone can expect to have the wish fulfilled. Of course, wishes made public will not be granted. Strategies were devised as to how to acquire the larger portion of the wishbone.[14] Any bird's furcula can be used, but in the United States it is usually the turkey's, which is larger than the chicken's; moreover, turkey is more commonly served than other large birds.

This custom was illustrated and enshrined in print beginning in the 1850s. Winslow Homer, for instance, drew a picture of two boys pulling at a wishbone, a work that was engraved and published in *Harper's Weekly*.[15] During the Civil War, Homer also drew Union soldiers breaking a wishbone, presumably wishing for an end to the war.[16] Many still practice the custom.

The Literary Turkey

The turkey was never a significant symbol in literary works, but it has frequently appeared in folk poetry and occasionally been mentioned in formal poetry and literature. In colonial America, European colonists appreciated the turkey as a source of sustenance but did not endow it with any particular symbolism although there are a few references in some early American literature and poetry. The Maryland lawyer and writer Ebenezer Cooke, for instance, referenced "turkies" in his epic poem *The Sot-weed Factor; or, A Voyage to Maryland* (1707). He added in a footnote: "Wild turkies are very good Meat, and prodigiously large in Maryland."[17] Timothy Dwight, an ordained minister who subsequently became president of Yale University, mentioned turkeys in his poem *The Triumph of Infidelity* (1788).[18] The popular ballad "American Taxation," purportedly written in 1765 as a protest song, tells us that the wealthy dined "on turkeys, fowls, and fishes." The ballad, sometimes with different lyrics, was popular throughout the mid-nineteenth century.[19]

The increased importance of the turkey in the United States in the nineteenth century is reflected in poetry, often published in newspapers and magazines. "A Merry Ode for Thanksgiving," which mentioned the turkey, was published in a Connecticut newspaper in 1801, and a poem in *Harper's Weekly* in 1864 identified it as the "king of birds."[20] Joseph Barber's "Turkey Poem" first appeared in the magazine *Round Table* in 1865 and was picked up by anthologies and reprinted elsewhere later in the nineteenth century; George Parsons Lathrop, whose wife was the daughter of Nathaniel Hawthorne, wrote the poem "Thanksgiving Turkey" in 1892; "The Turkey's Relief," also a poem, was published in the food magazine *Table Talk* in 1905. There were hundreds of such Thanksgiving verses, and many of them included references to the turkey.[21]

The turkey also appears occasionally in other literature. Henry Wadsworth

Longfellow included a reference in his epic *Song of Hiawatha,* first published in 1855.[22] In the twentieth century, D. H. Lawrence was fascinated by turkeys. His poem "The Turkey-Cock" (1922) presents the bird as a noble icon of pre-Columbian America, and in *The Plumed Serpent* (1926), Lawrence wrote, "No sound on the morning save a faint touching of water, and the occasional powerful yelping of the turkey-cock." In 1940 James Thurber wrote the fable "Two Turkeys."[23] As America urbanized and the poultry business became industrialized, the bird's power to evoke symbolic images declined, although turkey frequently appears in folk poetry, mainly as a food served on the Thanksgiving table, and in books written for children and juveniles.[24]

Charity and Gifts

The practice of giving turkeys at Thanksgiving became common in the late eighteenth century. One poor newspaper publisher in Cumberland, Maine, begged readers to send him "Turkies, Geese, Fowles, Butter and Eggs" for his Thanksgiving dinner in the 1780s, and in the 1790s the townspeople of Ridgefield, Connecticut, gave their parson a turkey for Thanksgiving.[25] This practice expanded during the nineteenth century. Businesses gave turkeys to employees, friends sent them to prominent persons, and kindly townspeople served the birds to incarcerated prisoners at the local jail.[26]

Charles Dickens's *A Christmas Carol* ends with Ebenezer Scrooge giving a "prize turkey" to his underpaid clerk, and a New York diarist, Philip Hone, credited Dickens's work with "a wonderful outpouring of Christmas good feeling" that led to "an awful slaughter of Christmas turkeys."[27] No doubt that provided extra impetus for employers to give turkeys to their staffs, and in 1852 a judge's son in Philadelphia sent the birds to local prisoners so they could have a proper dinner at Thanksgiving.[28] Frederick Douglass was given a turkey for Thanksgiving in 1853, a gift important enough for him to note in his newspaper, and in 1855 the Boston and Worcester Railroad Company provided each married employee with a Christmas bird. These practices continued until well after the Civil War.[29]

It is a logical step from giving turkeys to employees to using them as a sales promotion, a practice that began in the late nineteenth century and still continues. Many supermarkets, for instance, give turkeys to customers who purchase a specific amount of groceries or spend a specific amount at the store during the weeks preceding major holidays. To accommodate even more customers, some stores provide a vegetarian alternative such as frozen lasagna or a kosher turkey if requested.

By the late nineteenth century even the proprietors of bowling alleys were awarding turkeys as prizes for the best scores during the weeks before Thanksgiving and Christmas.[30] As time went on a "turkey" came to indicate three strikes in a row—all pins knocked down with the first ball three consecutive times—and lanes were made more difficult to make that task more challenging. Bowlers' skills and equipment have improved and bowling is a popular pastime; even though turkeys are no longer used as enticements the phrase remains a part of bowling jargon.[31]

Thanksgiving evolved into a day when religious and other groups sponsored turkey dinners for the poor. In 1850 the Ladies' home Missionary Society of the Methodist Episcopal Church opened a Five Points Mission in Manhattan, and on Thanksgiving Day they paraded poor children before benefactors while providing them with a turkey dinner. In one *Harper's Weekly* lithograph, hundreds of poor children stand in a large room, eating Thanksgiving dinner. The meal became an annual event held throughout much of the nineteenth century. In yet another issue of *Harper's Weekly,* a middle-class family shares leftovers from their dinner with a poor immigrant waif in a lithograph entitled *The First Thanksgiving Dinner.*[32] St. Barnabas's House in New York served 1,400 pounds of turkey to a thousand people, and the following year Mrs. Frederick W. Vanderbilt sponsored a "turkey dinner" with all the fixings for four hundred poor boys of Newport, Rhode Island.[33] Similar events for the homeless have been conducted in almost every city in America ever since.

Presidential Turkeys

It was during the run-up to the 1848 presidential election that the turkey moved into politics. James K. Polk had decided not to run for reelection, and the nominating conventions of three parties became free-for-alls. The Whigs nominated Zachary Taylor, a general who had participated in the American victory in the just-ended Mexican-American War, and the Democrats nominated Lewis Cass. To make matters more exciting, the former president Martin Van Buren was running on the Free-Soil Party ticket. The unnamed artist who drew the broadside entitled *Shooting the Christmas Turkey* has Taylor and Cass attacking each other while van Buren, disguised as a fox, makes off with the turkey.

The campaign's burning issue concerned the Wilmot Proviso, an amendment introduced into the House of Representatives by David Wilmot in 1846 that forbade slavery in territories acquired from Mexico as a result of the war. The Proviso split Whigs and Democrats along sectional lines and polarized Northerners against Southerners. Bills with the Proviso passed the House, which representatives from nonslave states controlled, but failed in the Senate, which was evenly split between slave and nonslave states. Taylor and Cass avoided taking a stand on the issue, which enraged antislavery forces, and Van Buren embraced the Proviso. Also in the broadside is Horace Greeley, editor of the *New York Tribune* and a strong supporter of the Proviso, who withheld support for Taylor until late in the campaign.[34] Taylor was elected but died in office. In 1850 the Wilmot Proviso was partly incorporated into the Compromise of 1850, which was hailed as the solution to the question of slavery in the territories. The matter reemerged, however, and eleven years later was a significant contributor to the Civil War.

The turkey again appeared in campaign literature during the 1852 presidential election, which pitted a Whig, Winfield Scott, against a Democrat, Franklin Pierce. A lithograph entitled *Ornithology* portrays Scott, associated with antislavery forces during the election, as a turkey and Pierce, whose main support was in the South, as a gamecock. They face each over the "Mason & Dixon's Line." Scott demands that Pierce get out of his way so he can head South, and Pierce taunts "Don't you wish you may get it! But you can't get over this line." Pierce won the election.

It may have been such references to the turkey that encouraged individuals to give the birds to presidents of the United States, a tradition that dates at least to the mid-nineteenth century. In February 1856, J. M. Mathews of Mathews, Hunt and Company of New York, bought a live, thirty-four-pound turkey from Ralph H. Avery of Wampsville in Madison County, New York. Mathews then presented the bird to James Buchanan at his inauguration. The turkey was evidently not eaten by the president, as it was subsequently observed roaming the White House gardens. Avery reported, tongue-in-cheek, that his turkey served "as a member of the 'kitchen cabinet,'" an allusion to the story that Andrew Jackson met with his unofficial cabinet in the White House kitchen.[35]

By the 1860s it had become customary for many "patriotic persons" to send choice turkeys to the president for Thanksgiving and Christmas dinners and inaugurations. Avery, for instance, sent a "Monster turkey" directly to President-elect Abraham Lincoln just in time for his inauguration in 1861, and Henry Vose of Westerly, Rhode Island, sent a turkey to Lincoln in 1863.[36]

It may have been Vose's first turkey that sparked a memorable incident. According to Noah Brooks, a newspaperman and a friend of Lincoln, the president was given a turkey in 1863 that his ten-year-old son Tad befriended and named Jack. When the time neared to prepare Jack for the Christmas meal, Tad burst into one of his father's cabinet meetings requesting that Jack be spared, which Lincoln did. On election day in 1864, Lincoln saw the turkey at the polling place at the White House and asked Tad, "What business has the turkey stalking about the polls in that way? Does he vote?" "No," Tad replied, "he's not of age." Lincoln loved Tad's quick-witted response and took pride in re-telling the story, which has been often repeated in various forms ever since.[37]

New York's Union League Club purchased an impressive forty-seven-pound turkey from a widow in Stamford, Connecticut, and gave it to Andrew Johnson as a New Year's gift in December 1865, a practice that continued throughout the nineteenth and twentieth centuries. Henry Vose, for instance, sent a turkey every Thanksgiving to every president for forty years, and many others did so as well.[38] In 1891 Jesse L. Moss of Chicago sent a turkey to William Henry Harrison, as did E. H. Miner of Westerly, Rhode Island. Theodore Roosevelt also received turkeys but didn't seem to need them; he hunted for wild turkeys and bagged his share while in the White House.[39]

In 1912 a Kentuckian sent President-elect Woodrow Wilson a forty-three-pound turkey that had been fed on sweet corn, celery, and pepper corns to improve its flavor. Wilson also received a turkey delivered by a Boy Scout who brought with it an invitation from the governor of Texas to attend the Turkey Trot festivities in Cuero. "Do you think I would make a good turkey?" the enigmatic Wilson asked the scout. History does not reveal what he may have meant, but he did not attend the Cuero, Texas, Turkey Trot.[40]

The turkey that the Harding Girls Club of Chicago sent Warren G. Harding via a Pullman railroad car in 1928 was photographed as its crate was being wheeled into the White House. Harding evidently liked turkeys and kept a pen of them at the White House. In 1936 the Norbest Turkey Company hit the publicity jackpot when it presented a large turkey to Franklin D. Roosevelt just before Thanksgiving.[41] Three years later Keys F. Carson, a student at the Agricultural and Mechanical College in Texas (now Texas A&M), hitchhiked to Washington with another live turkey for the president. The hotel in which he stayed permitted him to keep the bird in his bathroom, but a maid accidentally released it. The bird was recaptured, however, and given to the president. The wives of members of Congress plucked its feathers for souvenirs, and Carson received a gratifying amount of publicity. He later took another turkey to the president of Mexico, which generated even more visibility. In 1941 Roosevelt received at least five turkeys for Thanksgiving.[42]

Harry Truman was given several turkeys in 1948. He was going to eat the one from the Science Club of Ohio State University at Thanksgiving, he said, and the one from the National Turkey Federation for Christmas dinner. The federation subsequently gave turkeys to Dwight D. Eisenhower, but there is no evidence that he pardoned them. The federation's gift in December 1956 was to Vice-President Richard Nixon instead of President Eisenhower, who was busy at the time, but the turkey ended up on the Eisenhowers' Christmas table at their Gettysburg, Pennsylvania, farm.[43]

In 1963 Leo Pearlstein, president of the Los Angeles advertising firm Lee and Associates, had the California Turkey Advisory Board as a client. He convinced the National Turkey Federation to allow the board's chair, Bob McPherrin, to present John F. Kennedy with a turkey at the White House, and the photo-op occurred on November 18 in the Rose Garden. The legend "Good Eating, Mr. President!" appeared under the turkey. Kennedy reported that he didn't plan to eat the bird, and newspapers reported the following day that he had "pardoned" it. Photographs of the event were never sent out; four days later Kennedy was assassinated in Dallas, Texas.[44]

The tradition of pardoning, presuming Kennedy did so, was not continued by Lyndon Johnson although he received turkeys each year he was in the White House. In the 1970s President Nixon did not eat at least one of the birds he was given, but no mention was made of a pardon. Ronald Reagan may have pardoned his gift turkey in 1987, but if he did so he did not use the word *pardon.* George H. W. Bush, however, did officially pardon a turkey in 1989 and in each succeeding year of his presidency, a practice continued annually by each succeeding president.[45]

At the 1997 "pardoning" ceremony President Bill Clinton quipped, "We can all be grateful that there will be one less turkey in Washington." ("Do you know why President Clinton keeps a frozen turkey on Air Force One?" Republicans countered. "For spare parts.") In 2002 President George W. Bush pardoned a turkey named Katie, the first female bird to receive a reprieve. The president regarded the hen and said, "I see the turkey standing there, he looks a little nervous doesn't he? probably thinks he's going to have a press conference!"[46]

The pardoned turkeys were sent to a petting zoo at Frying Pan Park in Herndon, Virginia. Unfortunately, the birds did not live long there, and members of People for the Ethical Treatment of Animals complained about the way the pardoned turkeys were maintained at the park. In 2005 President Bush pardoned two Thanksgiving turkeys, Marshmallow and Yam, and announced that they were skeptical about being sent to a place called Frying Pan Park. He then sent them first-class on United Airlines to live out their lives at Disneyland in Anaheim, California.[47]

The turkeys that the National Turkey Federation selects for the president are broad-breasted strains bred for meat not longevity, and the pardoned birds die within a few years. But the event gives national visibility to turkey growers at very little cost to them. For the president, it is a holiday photo opportunity that casts the incumbent as a kindly sort who cannot eat a turkey he has seen alive (yet there seems to be no contradiction in the president eating an unpardoned turkey at Thanksgiving dinner).

Stupid Turkeys?

The turkey has appeared in songs and music since the late eighteenth century. "Turkey in the Straw" is a catchy number thought to have originated in the Midwest or Upper South during the early nineteenth century. Americans danced to the tune like they would to a Virginia reel, couples facing each other in two lines. The song is closely related to one named "Zip Coon." At the time, the word *coon* (for "raccoon") was not necessarily a derogatory reference to African Americans but meant "a rustic."[48] During 1830s and 1840s, "coon songs" were Whig political songs and had no derogatory connotations, but things changed just before the Civil War. The Ohioan fiddler Daniel Decatur Emmett is credited with popularizing "Zip Coon" at minstrel shows, which provided comedy, music, dance, and skits. The events frequently featured white performers in blackface, something considered humorous at the time. The turkey was connected with many minstrel shows; one, an "Ethiopian Whimsicality," was entitled *Turkeys in Season.*[49]

When the title "Zip Coon" was changed to "Turkey in the Straw," devoid of any negative connotations, the song became an American classic enshrined in school song textbooks and campfire song books and has remained a popular ballad that children still sing.[50] As the twentieth century rolled on, the song became the emblem of a ridiculous rustic hick. Pianists accompanying theatricals or silent movies played "Turkey in the Straw" to announce the entrance of a bumpkin or hillbilly, someone frequently stupid and slow. The song migrated into early vaudeville and then made its screen debut in Walt Disney's *Steam Boat Willie,* which was first released in 1928. In this, the first animated cartoon fully synchronized with sound, Mickey Mouse, in the role of a deckhand, plays "Turkey in the Straw" to entertain his girlfriend Minnie.

The idea of stupidity was also reinforced by what people thought they knew about turkeys. Domesticated birds are bred for certain characteristics, and intelligence is not one of them. What humans perceive as stupidity is a preferred trait in the large, ungainly birds. It's been said that turkeys are so stupid that they can drown in a rainstorm, and it's true, some do. A turkey's nostrils, tiny, oval-shaped openings alongside their beaks, are perfect funnels for falling rain. If a bird tilts its head skyward during a rainstorm it will indeed drown. The precise reason for such behavior is unknown, but observers have developed two explanations. First, turkey chicks usually spend their first several months in the wild with their mothers, who protect them and teach them how to survive. When it rains, hens cover their young with their wings. As they grow older, chicks consider rain to be part of their natural environment and do not react by looking up and hence do not drown. Today, domesticated turkeys are raised independently of their mothers, and when rain starts to fall they naturally look up to see what's hitting them. Their nostrils fill with water, and they can drown. A second explanation is offered by Tom Savage, a poultry scientist at Oregon State University, who reports that some turkeys have a genetic condition called "tetanic torticollar spasms" that predisposes them to cock their heads and look skyward for thirty seconds or more. If they do so during a rainstorm they may drown.[51]

With "Turkey in the Straw" a universally recognized tune, it's not surprising that the word *turkey* entered the lexicon of theatrical jargon. In 1927 the newspaper and gossip columnist Walter Winchell proclaimed that a "turkey" was "a third rate production."[52] By the 1950s the term was applied to people, according to the *Dictionary of American Slang,* and by the 1970s, someone acting stupid, foolish, or incompetent was being, in popular slang, a "turkey."

A turkey's stupidity has also been enshrined in the term *gobbledygook,* which refers to unintelligible jargon or bureaucratese. The word was coined by a member of Congress from Texas, Maury Maverick, who in March 1944 used it in a memo entitled "Lengthy Memoranda and Gobbledygook Language," his complaint against the unclear language used by congressional colleagues and Washington bureaucrats. Maverick's inspiration for the word came from an "old bearded gobbler back in Texas who was always gobbledygobbling and strutting with ridiculous pomposity. At the end of his gobble there was always a gook."[53] The word met a clear need in America and quickly became part of the English language.

Turkey Trotting

The phrase *turkey trot* refers in part to the speed at which wild turkeys move when startled and to their jerky, comically awkward gait. This strut inspired the turkey trot, an eponymous dance, in the early twentieth century. Dancers performing the turkey trot circle the floor in short, jerky steps while pumping their arms in imitation of a turkey's wings. The dance probably originated in Montana in the early 1900s, but it was popularized on the raucous Barbary Coast of San Francisco before 1910. By January 1911 the turkey trot was common in the dance halls of Coney Island. A few weeks later it became popular in Chicago, and by fall the craze had hit Newport and Philadelphia, where one young "society leader" proclaimed, "Everybody is doing it this season."[54]

The turkey trot became the "in" dance throughout America. Dance schools began to teach it, and variations on the theme emerged. There was, for instance, "The Turkey Gobbler's Ball" (1911), "Turkey Trot Glide" (1912), "The Yiddisha Turkey Trot" (1912), and "Oh You Turkey (A Rag Trot)" (1914). Books included instructions on how to do the turkey trot.[55] The dance even appealed to the renowned Russian ballerina Anna Pavlova, who tried it in San Francisco and declared it "artistically satisfying." She believed the turkey trot might be the basis of a new ballet and announced she planned to introduce it to Europe, and it did arrive there after spreading quickly across the United States.[56]

In Mansfield, Ohio, the turkey trot was called the dance of the "katy kids," who were the "wild" youth of their day.[57] The problem was that it varied from accepted dances such as the waltz. Indeed, it was considered so provocative that the San Francisco police commissioner banned it in that city, and many dance floors across the country did the same. The clergy also attacked the dance. Archbishop Henry Moeller in Cincinnati, for instance, condemned it, and Father Edward F. Hannigan, pastor of a Catholic church on Long Island, proclaimed that if he were a judge he "would sentence any woman who danced the turkey trot to a year in the penitentiary, and would send her partner to the county jail for three months." The dance was also "attacked as negroid and animal."[58]

Newspapers of the day reported that serious physical health problems resulted from dancing the turkey trot. The *Houston Chronicle,* for instance, referred to "Turkey Leg" as the latest disease. The cause, reported the *Chronicle,* was that turkey trotters favored one leg, and cramps resulted. The only cure, doctors maintained (perhaps tongue-in-cheek), was to shake the leg or have it pulled several times daily.[59]

Efforts to discourage the dance only made it more popular among the young. One *Puck* magazine writer observed in 1912, "Not in years have any forms of dancing enjoyed, or suffered, the publicity now accorded 'The Turkey Trot.'" The dance was not new but it was to "polite society."[60] In the end, what drove the turkey trot from dance floors was yet another rage, the fox trot, which was popularized by a vaudeville performer, Harry Fox, in 1914, and the tango, a European import. The fox trot and tango were condemned even more than the turkey trot—and became even more popular.

The Broadway Turkey

"Turkey" usually means bad news on Broadway, but the bird has also turned up in a couple of undeniable hits. From the musical *Promises, Promises,* written by Neil Simon with music by Burt Bacharach and lyrics by Hal David, came two turkey songs: "It's Turkey Lurkey Time" and the "Thanksgiving Song" (which has the memorable line "love to eat turkey").[61] More recently, in the off-Broadway *Dinner with Demons* a turkey was deep-fried onstage. Written and performed by Jonathan Reynolds, a *New York Times* food writer, the one-man show opened on December 16, 2003, and ran for more than a year. Reynolds offered a monologue as he prepared a turkey dinner for a group of guests, all of them old friends who had died. At the end of the show the dinner was brought to the table, ready for the guests. Unfortunately, reported Elyse Sommer, who reviewed the play for *Curtain Up,* the meal could not be sampled by the audience because of health laws.[62]

Turkey Racing

A different type of turkey trot developed in the Texas town of Cuero, which by the early twentieth century had become an important center for turkey raising. At the time, the area's roads turned to mud in the fall, making it difficult for farmers to transport birds to market at the time of highest demand. The solution was a revival of the old-fashioned turkey drive. Growers around Cuero drove their turkeys in flocks of five to ten thousand up to thirty miles, from their farms to turkey-processing plants in town. The birds ate grasshoppers and mast along the way and were fed corn at night. Drivers were paid only $2.50 per day but were eager for the jobs because most farm work had ended by November and at the end of the drive they could spend at least one night in Cuero. The need for turkey drives became obsolete by 1917 when roads improved and trucks became the main mode of transporting the birds.[63]

The Cuero turkey drives, however, were enough of a novelty that tourists in large number visited the town during the fall just to witness the spectacle. When the turkey trot became a popular dance, Cuero officials decided to create a turkey drive especially for tourists and call the event the Turkey Trot. While the first one was being planned in the summer of 1912 a New York newspaper carried a small story about it, and other publications picked up the account. That November, thirty thousand people showed up to watch eleven thousand turkeys being driven down Cuero's Main Street. Following the birds were the local high school football team, uniformed Boy Scouts and Girl Scouts, and floats, some decorated with turkey feathers and other turkey-connected displays. The Cuero Turkey Trot made national news.[64]

Turkey Trots were held sporadically in following years until Cuero designated itself the "turkey capital of the world." Then its citizens regularized and expanded the "Turkeyfest" with dinners, carnivals, entertainment, tours, dances, and an arts and crafts show. Inspired by the success of events in Cuero, other communities, such as McMinnville, Oregon, and Worthington, Minnesota, offered similar festivals. McMinnville was a major turkey-producing area in 1938 when its citizens launched Turkey Rama, which featured a turkey barbecue and turkey races. Even after turkey raising had moved from the area, residents kept Turkey Rama going and imported birds from elsewhere. Worthington citizens began King Turkey Day in 1946. Turkeys stopped trotting and began running in 1972 when the two towns began a competition—the Great Gobbler Gallop—to determine which had the fastest turkey.[65]

Turkey racing was discontinued in many communities due to pressure from animal rights activists, but turkey trot "fun runs" for human competitors often replaced it. Indeed, if turkeys could trot, why couldn't people do the same? Hundreds of communities now sponsor such events. Some feature "walks" for those who prefer a slower pace and allow skating and skate boards for the younger generation. Most events are held to benefit local charities, often (appropriately enough) food banks.

Turkey Drops

A far less common, and much less humane, preholiday event was undertaken by the Chamber of Commerce of Yellville, Arkansas, which has sponsored the Turkey Trot Festival since 1945. The two-day event features a turkey-calling contest, target shooting, and a Miss Drumsticks Pageant in which the contestant with the most shapely legs wins. The high point is the Turkey Drop, when live birds are thrown from a low-flying airplane in the general vicinity of the town square. People scramble for the birds, and whoever captures one gets to keep it.[66] In 1989 the *National Enquirer* published a photograph of the Turkey Drop that was seen across the nation, and since then animal rights activists have protested the event's cruelty to the turkey. Yellville is not the only community to sponsor a turkey drop, but most towns have canceled them due to public outrage. In Yellville, however, the event continues under "private sponsorship" without Chamber of Commerce backing.[67]

A fictional account of the turkey drop appeared in the classic "Turkeys Away" episode of the television series *WKRP in Cincinnati.* In the show, first aired October 30, 1978, Arthur Carlson, the radio station's manager, decides to develop a major promotion just before Thanksgiving. He'll have live turkeys dropped from an airplane and let the crowds below hustle for the live birds. The gruesome sight of the turkeys splattering on the ground (not shown on-air) is described by the station's newsman Les Nessman in a script patterned after Herb Morrison's famous radio broadcast of the crash of the *Von Hindenburg* zeppelin in Lakehurst, New Jersey, in 1937. After the mess, Carlson utters one of the show's best-remembered lines: "As God is my witness, I thought turkeys could fly." In honor of this episode, Illinois hot-air balloonists from Danville, Bismarck, Champaign, and Urbana have conducted a "Les Nessman Memorial Turkey Drop," and from their balloons dropped rubber turkeys into a bale of straw reminiscent of the song "Turkey in the Straw."[68]

Other meanings of the term *turkey drop* have evolved. The on-line Urban Dictionary describes a turkey drop as the situation when "a dating couple try the long-distance relationship thing when they go off to university or college in September. Typically, when Thanksgiving rolls around and everyone goes home for the holiday, someone gets dumped." A more positive connotation of the "turkey drop," again according to the Urban Dictionary, is the act of "dropping off" a frozen turkey to the Salvation Army, which then redistributes it to the poor.[69]

An Anti-Symbol

Perhaps due to the national significance of Thanksgiving, many Americans promote particular causes on that day. In 1835 William Alcott, a physician, wrote that he was opposed to the feast on moral grounds as well as for medical reasons. He called Thanksgiving a carnival "loaded with luxuries not only on the day of the general Thanksgiving, but for several days afterward." He was particularly concerned because New Englanders were also beginning to celebrate Christmas, and he claimed that the two feasts had already merged into one long period of overindulgence that caused serious health problems. William Alcott had other reasons to oppose the traditional Thanksgiving dinner: He had become a vegetarian in 1830 and was later one of the founders of the American Vegetarian Society.[70]

Few Americans paid attention to Alcott or other vegetarians at the time, but their concerns reemerged later in the century. John Harvey Kellogg, a Seventh-Day Adventist, managed a sanatorium in Battle Creek, Michigan. Kellogg was a dominant force in culinary Americana at the beginning of the twentieth century, and in 1894 his wife, Ella Kellogg, published a totally vegetarian menu for Thanksgiving. The problem was, however, that many vegetarians felt the lack of the pivotal holiday symbol until someone came up with "Mock Turkey." The first located recipe was published in 1899 by Almeda Lambert, wife of an employee of the Kellogg's sanatorium. Variations on Mock Turkey became a regular feature in vegetarian and other cookbooks.[71] Even if turkey itself does not appear on vegetarians' tables, simulated turkeys frequently do. Beginning in the 1980s, vegetarians could feast on tofu turkey or "Tofurkey," a soy-based product shaped like a turkey from Turtle Island Foods. Others prefer not to eat something shaped like a turkey or intended to taste like one.

Since the 1970s animal rights organizations such as PETA have gained visibility around Thanksgiving. For PETA members, Turkey Day is not a time to eat turkeys but to convince Americans to give up eating meat in general and turkeys in particular. PETA has sponsored petitions and published leaflets encouraging turkeyless Thanksgivings ("Give Turkeys Something to be Thankful For!"). To counteract the Butterball Turkey Talk-Line, intended to answer questions about proper cooking techniques, PETA has encouraged members to call the hot line with the message that there is no proper way to kill and cook turkeys.

The Farm Sanctuary, a nonprofit organization, launched the Adopt-a-Turkey Project in 1986 and has continued it annually ever since. This effort places turkeys that would otherwise be slaughtered into vegetarian households. At Farm Sanctuary shelters in Watkins Glen, New York, and Orland, California, turkeys are considered guests and at Thanksgiving are fed "squash, cranberries, pumpkin pie, and other vegetarian treats, and the turkeys have the pleasure of stuffing themselves." The Adopt-a-Turkey Project tries to attract media attention to encourage Americans to celebrate Thanksgiving without eating turkey and publishes "Thankful Turkey Recipes," which are "delicious Thanksgiving recipes that give the turkeys something to really be thankful for." The project also distributes a video, *The Making of a Turkey,* with "undercover footage obtained by Farm Sanctuary investigators of inhumane factory farming practices, transportation cruelties, and slaughterhouse abuses."[72]

Similarly, the nonprofit United Poultry Concerns "addresses the treatment of domestic fowl in food production, science, education, entertainment, and human companionship situations." It promotes respectful treatment of domestic fowl in laboratories and factory farms. It has developed a variety of programs related to turkeys and promoted works such as Karen Davis's *Instead of Chicken, Instead of Turkey: A Poultryless "Poultry" Potpourri* (1998).[73]

A Commercial Symbol

In the autumn, posters, banners, and decorations with images of male gobblers displaying their tail feathers appear in stores throughout America. These colorful items encourage shoppers to purchase seasonal products. Ironically, however, a gobbler displays his feathers only at mating time—in the spring. But it is the male display of its feathers that makes a turkey easily recognized, so the gobbler's display has become a symbol of fall.

Perhaps the most obvious use of the turkey as a commercial symbol is employed in the Macy's Thanksgiving Day Parade, which was started by Macy's employees on November 27, 1924. The parade stepped off on 145th Street in Harlem and ended in front of the Macy's store on Herald Square. Balloons, introduced in the late 1920s, have become signature attractions, and millions of television viewers watch them being paraded down the route. One traditional float and balloon, the turkey, has changed over the years. In 1955 the *Daily News* headlined "Turkey Is Stuffed with Helium," and the following year,

"Gobbler the Turkey" was carved up by the wind. Traditionally, the last float of the parade carries Santa Claus, who officially kicks off the Christmas shopping season.[74] The day following the parade, "black Friday," is supposed to be the first day of the year that retail stores get out of the red and into the black due to extensive sales. Many people feel that the parade and the materialistic mania it ushers in have made the Thanksgiving turkey a symbol of crass commercialism.[75] But businesses love it.

The turkey's image has also been used to sell specific products. Perhaps the best-known example is Wild Turkey Bourbon, which is produced by the Austin, Nichols Distilling Company of Lawrenceburg, Kentucky, which started as a wholesale grocer specializing in teas and other specialty items but in 1939 decided to focus on alcoholic beverages. As the story goes, Wild Turkey Bourbon was named after a company executive, Thomas McCarthy, who went hunting for the birds in South Carolina in 1940. He brought along some bourbon to keep the hunters warm in the blind, and his friends were so impressed that they asked for more of the same the following year. McCarthy decided to sell the bourbon and named it in honor of the bird being hunted. Austin, Nichols contracted with several distilleries, and in May 1942 Wild Turkey whiskey had its debut.[76] McCarthy was a successful promoter, and the association of wild turkey hunters and bourbon was a powerful advertising gimmick. The name *Wild Turkey* was prominently lettered on the label along with a picture of the bird itself—an autumnal, masculine image with commercial appeal. Unlike the standard American turkey symbol—a broad-breasted male turkey with tail feathers displayed—the wild bird is shown with its tail modestly folded. Some bottles shaped like turkeys are now collectors' items.

Wild Turkey Bourbon and the National Wild Turkey Federation now sponsor the annual National Turkey Calling Championships. To reach the finals, which are witnessed by thirty thousand enthusiasts, contestants must make their way through local and state contests.[77]

The Wild Turkey Bourbon logo is one of the few uses of the wild turkey image. Many Americans have never seen a wild turkey, and those who do have a difficult time recognizing it because a wild bird differs so much from the more familiar broad-breasted commercial strains. Without the brand name on the bottle many Americans would not recognize the image as one of a turkey because it violates the standard American turkey symbol. As another reflection of economic globalization, this American symbol of a wild turkey has been exported. Since 1991 a French multinational, Pernod Ricard Group, has owned Austin, Nichols, and Wild Turkey Bourbon is now sold extensively abroad.

Although each of these social and symbolic images of the turkey is significant in its own right, it is the diversity of symbols that makes the bird one of America's most important national icons.

10 THE AMERICAN TURKEY; OR, HOW THE TURKEY CAME HOME TO ROOST

When wild turkeys were fast disappearing from the American landscape many states passed laws restricting hunting seasons and regulating the number of birds a hunter could kill.[1] These laws, however, were generally unenforced or ineffective. As many species became threatened, Congress enacted legislation intended to protect America's remaining wildlife. The Lacey Act of 1905 blocked the sale of frozen wild turkeys between states and thus gave a small measure of protection to the surviving wild birds.

Some attempts were made to transplant birds to environments that were more protected. In 1876, for instance, J. D. Caton transported wild turkeys to the uninhabited Santa Clara Island off the coast of Santa Barbara, California.[2] During the early twentieth century wild turkeys were reintroduced into areas from which they had disappeared years before, but those efforts were generally unsuccessful. Wild turkeys raised in captivity did not adapt well to wild conditions.

During the depression many farms were abandoned, and some land gradually reverted to forest, creating an ideal habitat for wild turkeys. The Federal Aid in Wildlife Restoration (the Pittman-Robertson Act) of 1937 imposed an excise tax on sporting goods ammunition to pay for the restoration of wildlife, and by 1940 projects began using those funds to try and reestablish wild turkey populations in eighteen states.[3]

The main problem in doing so was how to capture enough birds without harming them in the process. The cannon net provided a solution. The device, propelled by black-powder cannons detonated by an operator stationed in a nearby blind, could fling a concealed net over a flock. The first wild turkeys known to have been captured this way were taken in South Carolina in 1951, and after that "trap and transplant" programs accelerated. In the 1960s other methods were employed; sleep-inducing drugs, for instance, placed in food helped capture live birds, and once the birds were transplanted to their new environments, efforts weref made to track them with solar-powered transmitters and motion sensors.[4]

The results of these restoration efforts were astounding. From the verge of extinction in the late 1930s, wild turkey populations had increased to an estimated five hundred thousand birds in 1959 when the first National Wild Turkey Symposium was held to enhance communication among the wildlife specialists working on improving the birds' chances to thrive in America. When the National Wild Turkey Federation was formed in 1973, an estimated 1.5 million wild turkeys were spread throughout most of their ancestral regions and a few new areas. Since then the federation has supported scientific wildlife management on public, private, and corporate lands and has restored wild turkey hunting as a traditional North American sport. By 2005 an estimated seven million wild turkeys roamed America nationwide.[5] They range though more square miles than any other game bird in North America and inhabit every state except Alaska, several provinces in Canada, and several countries in Europe.

The revival of the wild turkey has indeed meant the return of turkey hunting, which is one of the fastest-growing gun sports in the United States. There are an estimated 2.4 million turkey hunters in America, and outfitting them has become big business. Turkey-calling devices are but one component of a much larger commercial interest in the birds. Other paraphernalia—decoys, special "turkey" socks to wear, patterning targets, pocket knives, mosquito repellant, outdoor seats, scent dispensers, gun racks, and so forth—are also big business. In 1989 turkey hunters spent an estimated $567 million in pursuit of their sport, and by 2003 the direct retail sales were estimated to be $1.79 billion.[6]

The Turkey Industry

During the last century the turkey industry grew exponentially, greatly increasing supply, and now retail prices of turkey are lower than those of any other meat. In the United States, per-capita turkey consumption increased from 8.1 pounds in 1970 to more than 17.4 pounds in 2004. Moreover, Americans now enjoy turkey throughout the year. Turkey products have diversified so the industry is no longer totally dependent upon sales of whole birds during the fall holidays. During 2004 the turkeys raised in the United States weighed an estimated 7.16 billion pounds and were valued at $2.68 billion. North Carolina is the top turkey-producing state followed by Minnesota, Arkansas, Missouri, Virginia, California, Indiana, and Pennsylvania.[7]

Turkey has been promoted as a health food since World War II. Beginning in the 1970s, diets that stress high-protein foods and limited carbohydrates provided a substantial boost to the turkey industry and hit a high point in the early twenty-first century. Turkey breast, nutritious yet rich in protein and low in fat and calories, is the ideal meat for nearly any diet.

The Revival of Heritage Turkeys?

Virtually all of the estimated 240 million turkeys now consumed by Americans each year are strains of the Broad-breasted White. The rise of that strain's popularity largely meant the demise of historical turkey breeds that had emerged during the nineteenth and early twentieth centuries. According to a 1938 nationwide survey by *Turkey World,* 63.9 percent of the turkey crop consisted of Bronze turkeys, 13.5 percent were White Holland, 9.7 percent were Narragansett, 9.1 percent were Bourbon Red, and 3.8 percent were Black.[8]

The case for conserving genetic diversity has been put forth by Roy D. Crawford: "The need for conservation of genetic variability is perhaps more critical in the turkey than it is even for domestic chickens and is far more urgent than for most domesticated mammalian species."[9] Beginning in 1995, the American Livestock Breeds Conservancy, a nonprofit membership organization that serves as a clearinghouse for information on livestock and genetic diversity, conducted a census of nonindustrial turkey breeds and encouraged their conservation. Twenty-five seasonal hatcheries that sell turkeys were surveyed to determine the status of each traditional breed. From its study the Conservancy concluded that any breed with fewer than five hundred breeding birds is endangered because disease or predators can easily destroy a single flock. It placed seven turkey breeds into the "critical" category.[10] By 2000 the Conservancy concluded that its call for action had spurred farmers to double their heritage breeding stock.

In 1998 and again in 1999, the Society for the Preservation of Poultry Antiquities conducted its own surveys to find out precisely how many "historical farm" turkeys were still being bred in America. The survey, conducted by Paula Johnson, focused on hatcheries as well as individual flock owners. The

1999 study found a total of 3,388 breeding "historical turkeys," 2,662 females and 726 males. The most numerous variety was the Bourbon Red, with 834 breeding females and 158 toms in four primary flocks; the Royal Palm followed, with 624 females in two primary flocks. The historical Bronze turkey, defined as a Bronze turkey that could reproduce without artificial insemination, had 312 breeding females in a single primary flock. For Blacks (Spanish or Norfolk) there were 192 hens and 53 males. Only one small flock of Black turkeys is kept for research purposes at North Carolina State University, and another can be viewed at Colonial Williamsburg in Virginia. The Slates had 122 breeding females. There were only sixty-six hens and twenty-eight toms of the Narragansett breed among thirteen breeders and only nineteen hens and nine toms of the White Holland breed. Of the Buffs, the survey located only sixty-eight hens and twenty-two toms, and they found only two flocks of the Beltsville Small Whites—one of which has been isolated for research purposes by the U.S. Department of Agriculture since 1961.[11]

Table 1. Number of Breeding Populations

	ALBC 1995–57[1]	SPPA 1998[2]	SPPA 1999[3]	ALBC 2003[4]
Beltsville Small-breasted White	NA	NA	NA	44
Bourbon Red	664	782	834	1,519
Bronze Broad-breasted	7,049	NA	NA	930
Bronze Standard	NA	281	312	441
Black	62	164	192	478
Buffs	NA	NA	68	NA
Jersey Buff	NA	NA	NA	42
Large White	4,600	NA	NA	NA
Narragansett	3	70	66	368
Royal Palm	381	589	624	818
Silver Auburn	NA	NA	NA	16
Slate	60	108	122	437
White Holland	4	22	19	61
White Midget	NA	NA	NA	106

ALBC: American Livestock Breeds Conservancy
SPPA: Society for the Preservation of Poultry Antiquities
Sources: 1. Carolyn J. Christman and Robert O. Hawes, *Birds of a Feather: Saving Turkeys from Extinction* (Pittsboro, N.C.: American Livestock Breeds Conservancy, 1999), 28.
2. Christman and Hawes, *Birds of a Feather,* 29.
3. For a summary of the survey, see www.feathersite.com/Poultry/SPPA/TurkCensusRept99.html.
4. Marjorie E. F. Bender, *Heritage Turkeys in America: The American Livestock Breeds Conservancy 2003 Heritage Turkey Census* (Pittsboro, N.C.: American Livestock Breeds Conservancy, 2003), 3.

Little breeding of historical turkey varieties was underway in the United States in 1999, and it appeared that some breeds would soon disappear. In 2002, however, another census of heritage turkeys by the American Livestock Breeds Conservancy found that populations of standard varieties continued to increase although the number of hatcheries that actually bred standard birds had decreased.[12]

Many groups were formed to preserve turkey breeds, particularly those that originated in the United States. In 1996 Slow Food launched its Ark of Taste Project, which aimed "to rediscover, catalog, describe and publicize forgotten flavors." But helping animals and plants survive was not enough. Slow Food then launched the Presidia Project, which was intended to find ways to make endangered species economically viable. In 2001 Slow Food USA identified the turkey as the "all-American farm animal" and nominated it for its "Ark of Taste," an honor roll of foods worthy of preservation. The following year Slow Food USA began its Heritage Turkey Project, which sought to preserve genetic diversity by creating a market for noncommercial breeds. The year after the Turkey Heritage Project was launched, more than five thousand of the birds were raised on twenty-two family farms. These were sold through local Slow Food chapters and through restaurants, although they are smaller and much more expensive than broad-breasted turkeys sold in supermarkets.

The Turkey Heritage Project encouraged Patrick Martins, founder and former director of Slow Food USA, and Todd Wickstrom, managing partner of Zingerman's Deli in Ann Arbor, Michigan, to launch Heritage Foods USA, the for-profit arm of Slow Food USA, which raises, buys, and sells endangered plants and animals such as heritage turkeys. Animals are raised outdoors, and seasonal Web-cams permit Internet users to view the conditions under which they are raised. Turkeys are numbered, and the consumer can select a specific bird for purchase. Also on the Web site are seasonal evaluations of the turkeys' medical and feed histories.

The food press was rhapsodic over this development. *Food and Wine* noted that it was ironic that Americans had to "eat turkeys in order to save them," but commercialization meant that farmers raised twice as many Bourbon Red turkeys in 2004 than they had in the previous year. Thanks to Heritage Foods USA and other groups, Narragansett, Bronze, and Bourbon Red turkeys are now being raised commercially. According to an article in *Bon Appétit,* "Heritage turkeys bring more flavor to the table and buying one could help preserve small farms and endangered breeds." It continues, "Genetic diversity is being preserved and Americans who have never tasted heirloom turkeys have the ability to do so. Heritage turkey meat is denser and more flavorful and complex; in comparison, regular turkey is one-note and almost spongy."[13]

Other companies sell organic turkey meat and still others promote sustainable agriculture.[14] There were an estimated twenty thousand heritage turkeys in 2003, a figure that greatly increased during 2004. But the effort to save heritage turkeys faces some obstacles. At present few hatcheries are willing to invest the time and money to produce the birds, which need to be processed before they are shipped. Perhaps if demand continues to increase such challenges will be met.

It is still too early to proclaim success in the preservation of heritage turkey breeds, but there is room for hope. According to Marjorie Bender, research and technical program manager of the American Livestock Breeds Conservancy, "With many of us working together and with luck we will succeed and these wonderful standard varieties will once again claim their place as useful market birds."[15]

Concerns about health issues as well as objections to factory farming methods and the modern turkey's lack of flavor have opened the market to alternatives to large producers. Some small companies stress varieties that flourished before the Broad-breasted turkey became the standard. The movement toward organic and free-range turkeys is a related development. Turkeys can be labeled "organic" if they comply with labeling laws relating to feed certification, genetic engineering, and the use of ionizing radiation. Partisans may disagree, but organic turkeys are not necessarily tastier, juicier, or more tender.

Likewise, the term *free range* has different meanings. To comply with labeling restrictions, a turkey grower wishing to acquire the free-range label would have only to open pens to a common outside area for a short time every day. Commercial turkeys are given a bland (if nutritionally balanced) feed, whereas range-raised birds in an open environment eat virtually anything available. Free-range turkeys suffer less stress because they have not been caged, debeaked, de-toed, or subjected to severe crowding, factors that some consumers feel produce a more tender bird.

Turkey Cookery

The return of the wild turkey has occasioned an increase in recipes for preparing the bird for the table. Game cookbooks now include wild turkey recipes, and two, one by Rick Black and the other by A. D. Livingston, are both entitled the *Wild Turkey Cookbook.*[16]

Commercial turkey cookery has also experienced a revival. Turkey producers, or companies that made products related to turkey cookery, have long issued small cookbooks that feature the company's products and are usually given free to consumers.[17] Beginning in the 1970s, cookbooks specifically related to turkeys began to be published. The first was by S. I. Reese, *The Complete Turkey Cookbook: The Good Cook's Guide to Unusual Turkey Dishes and Exciting Accompaniments* (1971), and dozens have since been published.[18]

Deep-frying is a popular means of cooking turkeys, a southern tradition that has gained national attention. The deep-frying process produces ultra-crisp skin while the interior remains very juicy. Deep-frying is generally done commercially, but it is possible to purchase forty- to sixty-quart kettles to be filled with cooking oil and fired outdoors. The heat is so intense that an average turkey can be cooked in less than an hour. The risks of this kind of cookery have more to do with fire safety than with food safety. The year 2003 saw the first cookbook devoted solely to preparing turkeys through deep-frying.[19]

The Turkey Today

No other American bird has received the lavish amount of attention bestowed upon the turkey. It is not hard to understand this fascination. The wild turkey is not America's biggest bird—the swan and crane are larger—but turkeys do not migrate and are abundant throughout the eastern United States. Wild turkeys are much larger than domesticated poultry such as chickens. They are also handsome birds that command the attention of anyone who sees them. A wild turkey's habits are unusual, its behavior extraordinary, and its vocalizations quite singular in the avian world. Then again, the wild turkey also played an important role in American history. Without deer and the wild turkey, early European settlements would have been even more tenuous than they were, and westward expansion from the East Coast would have been long delayed. The turkey remains a potent American symbol, and it will likely remain so. It is not just another answer to the question, What's for dinner? It is a powerful social symbol, closely enmeshed with the nation's history and culture.

PART 2
Historical Recipes

Thousands of turkey recipes were published in the United States and the United Kingdom, whether in cookbooks, agricultural and horticultural journals, newspapers, popular magazines, turkey processors' promotional pamphlets, or a host of other sources. The recipes that follow form a representative sample of historical recipes; some were selected because they are typical, others because they are unusual. As a collection, they reflect the diversity of turkey recipes. The spelling, grammar, and style of the recipes have been left in their original form.

Before the twentieth century, most cookbook authors took for granted a certain level of knowledge, understanding, and experience among readers—as well a good supply of common sense. Instructions in old cookbooks often seem confusing and vague to modern readers accustomed to step-by-step directions accompanied by color photographs. The quintessential example is the phrase "cook until done." At what heat? a modern reader may wonder. In what shape and size of pan, for how long, and how do you *tell* when it's done?

These recipes are valuable from a historical standpoint—for what they tell us about the history of the turkey and, more broadly, culinary history. Many, however, can be brought successfully to the table if a cook is willing to allow for some trial and error in the cooking process and for changes wrought in ingredients and kitchen technology by the passage of time. Don't hesitate to experiment and take up the challenges and joys of turkey cookery. Enjoy!

Turkey Cookery and Safety

Food safety is a serious consideration when cooking turkey. Like all poultry, turkey can be a breeding ground for salmonella bacteria, but proper handling will minimize that risk. Above all, avoid contact between raw turkey and other foods, raw or cooked. Wash your hands before handling any food, and after handling raw turkey, wash your knives, cutting boards, countertops, and sink—whatever the turkey or its juices have touched—with a mild bleach solution.

Uncooked poultry should be kept separate from produce and cooked and ready-to-eat food in the refrigerator. Frozen turkeys should not be thawed on the kitchen countertop or in the sink; the temperature of the bird can easily rise above the 40°F considered safe. It's best to thaw it in the refrigerator on a platter or pan big enough to prevent dripping juices from contaminating other foods. Unfortunately, a big turkey takes up considerable space in the refrigerator, and most people don't want to wait several days for the bird to thaw. You can speed the process by placing the turkey in a basin of cold water, but the bird should be wrapped in leakproof plastic and the water changed every thirty minutes.

When you're ready to cook the turkey, wash it under cold running water and pat it dry with paper towels. Don't stuff the bird until you are ready to cook it. For maximum safety, cook the stuffing outside the bird, in a separate pan.

Because oven thermostats are frequently inaccurate, most sources recommend inserting a meat thermometer in the outside of the thigh, not touching the bone. When the turkey is done its juices should run clear and there should be no trace of pinkness in the meat. Traditional advice has been to roast the bird at 325° or 350°F; its internal temperature and that of the stuffing needs to reach 165°F. White meat cooks faster than dark, and stuffing cooked in the turkey adds about twenty-five minutes to the cooking time, which dries out the white meat even more.

Various methods have been devised to balance the cooking times of different parts of the turkey, such as tenting the bird with foil or shrouding it with cloth. Others cook the bird breast-down and then turn it to a higher oven temperature—450°F—for a shorter cooking time. Still others recommend brining, which through the process of osmosis absorbs marinades such as salt, herbs, and other flavorings. Critics claim that brining puts water (and weight) into the bird but does not add flavor. What does make a turkey more flavorful is to smoke it, and several smokers are on the market for indoor or outdoor use. Frequently, turkeys are brined, smoked, and then heated in a conventional oven.

When serving a roast turkey, scoop out all its stuffing at once and don't leave it or the bird at room temperature for longer than two hours. The danger zone for bacteria growth is above 40°F and below 140°F, so refrigerate leftovers as soon as possible in shallow containers so they cool quickly. The stuffing, meat, and gravy should be stored separately. Unfrozen leftovers should be reheated to 165°F and are good within two days.

À la Daube

TO DRESS A TURKEY IN THE FRENCH MODE, OR TO EAT COLD, CALLE[D] A LA DOODE

Take a turkey and bone it, or not bone it, but boning is the best way, and lard it with good big lard as big as your little finger and season it with pepper, cloves, and mace, nutmegs, and put a piece of interlarded bacon in the belly with some rosemary and bayes, whole pepper, cloves and mace, and sew it up in a clean cloth, and lay it in steep all night in white-wine, next morning close it up with a sheet of course paste in a pan or pipkin, and bake it with the same liquor it was steept in; it will ask four hours baking, or you may boil the liquor; then being baked and cols, serve it on a pie-plate, and stick it with rosemary and bays, and serve it up with mustard and sugar in saucers, and lay the fowl on a napkin folded square, and the turkey laid corner-ways.

Thus are large fowl or other meat, as a leg of mutton, and the like.

Source: Robert May, *The Accomplished Cook* (London: Obadiah Blegrave, 1685), 216–17.

GEESE, TURKEYS AND CAPONS, A LA DOBE

First lard your Fowl with gross Lard season'd with Pepper, Salt, Cloves and Mace, Thyme and Parsly minc'd; pass them off brown in a Stew-pas in Butter, or brown them off very quick on a Broach at a good Fire, which is the best Way; put them in a Stew-pan, or Boat-pan; cover them over with good Gravy and Broth; put some Red-wine, and season them very well, and stove them over a gentile Fire; put in a Faggot of sweet Herbs and Parsly, some Onions, and a Piece of Bacon stuck with Cloves, and a few Bay-leaves, and a Carrot cut in Pieces; stove it till very tender, then have some Forc'd meat roll'd up in Cauls of Veal, or sheets of Landere wash'd over with Eggs, and bake them; then make a ragoust of good Gravy thicken'd; put in Sweetbreads dic'd, Cocks-combs, Chestnuts blanch'd; Mushrooms, Morelles and Trouffles; stove it, and toss it up pretty thick: Dish your Fowl; lay round some Forc'd-meat, and put over your Ragoust, and then garnish with Petit-patties and sliced Lemon.

Source: Charles Carter, *The Complete Practical Cook: or, A New System of the Whole Art and Mystery of Cookery* (London: W. Meadows, 1730), 55.

Boiled

BOILED CHICKENS AND TURKIES, THE DUTCH WAY.

Boil them, season them with salt, pepper, and cloves; then to every quart of broth, put a quarter of a pound of rice or vermicelli: it is eat with sugar and cinnamon. The two last may be left out.

Source: Hannah Glasse, *The Art of Cookery Made Plain and Easy* (Alexandria: Cotton and Stewart, 1805), 278.

BOILED TURKEY AND FOWL

Select a fat, young fowl; prepare the dressing of cracker or bread crumbs, made fine; chop bits of raw salt pork very fine; sift in sage, savory, thyme, or any other sweet herbs you prefer; add to this pepper, salt, and considerable butter; mix with hot water. An egg is sometimes added. After the turkey is stuffed, wrap closely in cloth. Put in cold water to boil, having all parts covered. Boil slowly, removing the scum as it rises. A small turkey will boil in less than two hours. If you use oysters for the dressing, it is better to steam the turkey instead of boiling. When tender, take it up, strain the gravy found in the pan, thicken with flour; stew the oysters intended for the sauce, mix this liquor with the gravy, add butter, salt and pepper to suit the taste; a trifle of cream improves the color.

Source: Jonathan Periam, *The Home and Farm Manual: A Pictorial Encyclopedia of Farm, Garden, Household, Architectural, Legal Medical and Social Information* (New York: N. D. Thompson, 1884), 825.

Boned

BONED TURKEY

With a sharp-pointed knife slit the skin the entire length of the back. Cut the flesh from the bones, disjoint the wings and legs, cut off the last joint of the wing and be careful of the skin of the second joint. When the flesh is all loosened from the bones, remove the skeleton and entrails, saving the giblets. Make a filling of bread crumbs and butter mixed with the giblets, minced fine, and the flesh of the fowl. Keep the entire skin intact if possible, and prepare filling enough to replace the bones that have been taken out. Shape nicely sew the slit in the back, tie the wings and legs close to the body and bake until done, using salt and water and butter to baste with. Of course the proper seasoning must be used to make it palatable. Use sage or savory in the filling, and the juice of a lemon is an improvement. Carve in slices across the breast.

Source: Ladies' Aid Society of the Church of Our Father (Universalist), *Helps to Housekeeping* (Chicago: Commercial Printing, 1888), 51–52.

Braised

BRAISED TURKEY

Take two carrots, one onion, and one turnip, cut them in thin slices, with a little celery and parsley; lay three sheets of paper on the table, on these spread your vegetables, and pour over them two or three table-spoonsful of oil. Your turkey must be trussed cover the breast with thin slices of bacon and lay the back of the bird on the vegetables; a few slices of lemon on the breast to keep it white; tie the paper round with string, then put some paper over the breast and legs also, to keep them from burning. Roast it three hours, at a pretty good distance from the fire.

Source: Mrs. A. M. Collins, *The Great Western Cook Book; or, Table Receipts adapted to Western Housewifery* (New York: A. S. Barnes, 1857), 89.

Croquettes

TURKEY OR CHICKEN CROQUETTES, MRS. S. GERHART

Mince turkey or chicken as fine as possible; season with pepper, salt, a little nutmeg, and a very little onion. Take a large tablespoonful of butter, two of flour, one-half glass of cream; mix, boil, and stir the meat in. When cold, take a spoonful of the mixture and dip into the yolk of an egg; then in bread-crumbs; roll lightly in your hand into the proper shape, and fry in boiling lard deep enough to cover them.

Source: Ladies of the First Presbyterian Church, *Presbyterian Cook Book* (Dayton: John H. Thomas, 1875).

Cutlets

TURKEY CUTLETS

Kill a large gobbler; hang him up several days before using; then, with a sharp knife, take as many cutlets from the thighs and breasts as may be needed, and fry or fricassee them. Continue to cut them until all that will answer the purpose is used, then put the carcass, dissected, into the soup-kettle, with a slice or two of ham or fresh meat; it will aid in making good soup. Serve without gravy, and pour over melted butter. Season upon the plate with French mustard or any kind of catsup preferred. Should the common gravy be preferred, make it as for brown fricassee.

Source: Mrs. A. P. Hill, *Mrs. Hill's New Cook Book* (New York: Carleton Publishers, 1872), 126.

Deviled

DEVILED TURKEY'S LEGS, WITH CHOW CHOW

Use the legs from a broiled or roasted turkey. Season with salt and pepper, spread some French mustard all over the surface, roll in bread crumbs, and broil; or fry in pan with a piece of butter. When nice and brown dish up on platter, and garnish with large leaves of lettuce filled with chow chow.

Source: Victor Hirtzler, *The Hotel St. Francis Cook Book* (Chicago: Hotel Monthly Press, 1919), 19.

Eggs

TURKEY'S EGGS SAUCE

Turkey's eggs are superior to others for sauce. Boil three eggs gently in plenty of water twenty minutes. Break the shells by rolling them on the table; separate the whites from the yolks, divide all the yolks into quarter inch dice pieces, mince one and a half of the whites rather small, mix them lightly and stir them into a pint of white sauce, and serve hot. The eggs of common fowl may be prepared for sauce according to these directions, using four yolks and two whites, and boiling four or five minutes less. The eggs of guinea fowl also make a good sauce after ten minutes.

Source: Mrs. J. C. Croly, *Jennie June's American Cookery Book* (New York: American News Company, 1866), 100.

TURKEY, GEESE, AND DUCK EGGS

Put the eggs into a bowl filled with boiling water for five minutes, keeping the bowl covered tight and in a hot place; then pour off the first water, replace it with more boiling water, and let them stand for five minutes longer; serve them like ordinary boiled eggs; or, actually boil the eggs for five minutes: either of these methods will cook the eggs medium hard. From ten to fifteen minutes boiling will cook the eggs hard, according to size. Duck eggs will cook in less time than turkey or goose eggs.

Source: Juliet Corson, *Miss Corson's Practical American Cookery and Household Management* (New York: Dodd, Mead, 1886), 253.

Escalloped

ESCALLOPED TURKEY

Cut the remnants of cold roast turkey in small pieces; there should be one and one-half cupfuls. Melt two table-spoonfuls of butter, add two table-spoonfuls of flour, mixed with one fourth of a tea spoonful of salt and a few grains of pepper, and stir until well blended. Then pour on gradually, while stirring constantly, one cupful of turkey stock (obtained by cooking bones and skin of a roast turkey in water) and bring to the boiling point. Sprinkle the bottom of a buttered baking dish with three fourths of a cupful of buttered cracker crumbs, add turkey, pour over sauce, and cover with three fourths of a cupful of buttered cracker crumbs. Bake in a hot oven until crumbs are brown.

Source: Fannie Merritt Farmer, "An Old Fashioned Thanksgiving Dinner," *Woman's Home Companion* 41 (Nov. 1914): 48.

Galatine

GALATINE OF TURKEY

Bone the turkey, and push the wings and legs inside of the body. Make three pints of ham force-meat. Cut a cold boiled tongue in thin slices. Season the turkey with salt and pepper, and spread on a board, inside up. Spread a layer of the force-meat on this, and then a layer of tongue. Continue this until all the tongue and force-meat are used up. Roll the bird into a round form, and sew up with mending cotton. Wrap tightly in a strong piece of cotton cloth, which must be either pinned or sewed to keep it in position. Put in a porcelain kettle the bones of the turkey, two calf's feet, four pounds of the knuckle of veal, an onion, two slices of turnip, two of carrot, twenty pepper-corns, four cloves, two stalks of celery, one table-spoonful of salt and three quarts of water. When this comes to a boil, skim, and put the turkey in. Set back where it will just simmer for three hours. Take up and remove the wrapping, put on a clean piece of cloth that has been wet in cold water, and place in a dish. Put three bricks in the flat baking pan, and place on a dish, the smooth side up. Melt four table-spoonfuls of glaze, and brush the turkey with it. Garnish with the jelly, and serve. Or, the galatine can be cut in slices and arranged on a number of dishes, if for a large party. In that case, place a little jelly in the centre of each slice, and garnish the border of the dish with jelly and parsley. The time and materials given are for a turkey weighing about nine pounds. Any kind of fowl or bird can be prepared in the same manner.

To make the jelly: Draw forward the kettle in which the turkey was cooked, and boil the contents rapidly for one hour. Strain, and put away to harden. In the morning scrape off all the fat and sediment. Put the jelly in a clean sauce-pan with the whites and shells of two eggs that have been beaten with four table-spoonfuls of cold water. Let this come to a boil, and set back where it will just simmer for twenty minutes. Strain through a napkin, and set away to harden.

Source: Maria Parloa, *Miss Parloa's New Cook Book: A Guide to Marketing and Cooking* (Boston: Estes and Lauriat, 1880), 177–78.

Giblets

TURKY GIBLETS

Blanch them in fresh water, and seeth them with good broath, when they are almost sod, pass them in the pan with lard, and good seasoning. Let the sauce be short, and serve.

Source: [François Pierre] de la Varenne, *The French Cook,* 2d ed. (London: Printed for Charles Adams, 1654), 51.

TURKEY GIBLETS À LA BOURGEOISE

The giblets of turkey consist of the pinions, feet, neck and gizzard. After hav-ing scalded pick them well and put in a saucepan with a piece of butter, some parsley, green onions, clove of garlic, sprig of thyme, bay-leaf, a spoonful of flour moistened with stock, salt and pepper. Brown to a good color.

Source: Rufus Estes, *Good Things to Eat as Suggested by Rufus* (Chicago: Published by the Author, 1911), 39.

Gravy

TURKEY GRAVY

Heart, liver, gizzard and neck slashed and dredged thickly with flour. Put in a sauce pan with a little salt, a few peppercorns and allspice and a little mace, outside skin of three onions, lump of butter the size of a walnut. When well browned, add boiling water till of proper thinness: let it cook slowly on the back part of the stove all the morning. After removing the turkey from the dripping-pan and pouring off any grease, put the prepared gravy into the dripping-pan, and proceed to make gravy same as any.

Source: Par Excellence, *Manual of Cookery* (Chicago: Published by the St. Agnes Guild of the Church of the Epiphany, 1888), 36.

Gumbo

NEW ORLEANS GUMBO

Take a turkey fowl, cut it up, with a piece of fresh beef; put them in a pot, with a little lard, an onion, and water sufficient to cook the meat. After they have become soft, add a hundred oysters, with their liquor. Season to your taste; and just before taking up the soup, stir in until it becomes mucilaginous two spoonsful of pulverized sassafras-leaves.

Source: [Sarah Rutledge], *The Carolina Housewife* (Charleston: W. R. Babcock, 1847), 43.

Hashed

TURKIE WITH RASPIS

When it is dressed, take up the brisket, and take out the flesh, which you shall mince with suet and some little of Veal-flesh, which you shall mix together with yolkes of Eggs and young Pigeons, & all being well seasoned, you shall fill your Turkie with it, and shall season it with Salt, Pepper, beaten Cloves and Capers, then you shall spit it, and turne it very softly; When it is almost rosted, take it up, and put it into an earthen pan with good Broath, Mushrums, and a bundle, which you shall make with Parsley, Thime, and Chibols tyed together; for to thicken the sauce, take a little sliced Lard, passe it in the pan, and when it is melted, take it out, and mix a little flower with it, which you shall make very brown, and shall allay it with a little Broath and some Vinegar; then put it into your Earthen pan with some Lemon juice, and serve.

If it be in the Raspis season, you shall put a handfull of them over it, if not, some Pomegranate.

Source: [François Pierre] de la Varenne, *The French Cook,* 2d ed. (London: Printed for Charles Adams, 1654), 30–31.

TURKEY, HASHED

Cut the remnants of turkey from a previous dinner into pieces of equal size. Boil the bones in a quart of water, until the quart is reduced to a pint; then take out the bones, and to the liquor in which they were boiled add turkey gravy, if you have any, or white stock, or a small piece of butter with salt and pepper; let the liquor thus prepared boil up once; then put in the pieces of turkey, dredge in a little flour, give it one boil-up, and serve in a hot dish.

Source: Mrs. Bliss, *The Practical Cook Book* (Philadelphia: David McKay, 1885), 79.

Jelly

TURKEY, &C. IN JELLY

Boil a turkey, or fowl, as white as you can let it stand till cold, and have ready a jelly made thus: take a fowl, skin it, take off all the fat, do not cut it in to pieces, nor break the bones; take four pounds of a leg of veal, without any fat or skin, put it into a well-tinned sauce-pan, put to it full three quarts of water, set it on a very clear fire till it begins to simmer; be sure to skim it well. but take great care it does not boil. When it is well skimmed, set it so as it will but just seem to simmer; put two large blades of mace, half a nutmeg, and twenty corns of white-pepper, a little bit of lemon-peel as big as a six-pence. This will take six or seven hours doing. When you think it is a stiff jelly, which you will know by taking a little out to cool, be sure to skim off all the fat, if any, and be sure not to stir the meat in the sauce-pan, A quarter of an hour before it is done, throw in a large tea-spoonful of salt, squeeze in the juice of half a fine Seville orange or lemon; when you think it is enough, strain it off through a clean sieve, but do not pour it off quite to the bottom, for fear of settling. Lay the turkey or fowl in the dish you intend to send it to the table in, beat up the whites of six eggs to a froth, and put the liquor to it, then boil it five or six minutes, and run it through a jelly-bag till it is very clear, then pour the liquor over it, let it stand till quite cold; colour some of the jelly in different colours, and when it is near old, with a spoon sprinkle it over in what form or fancy you please, and send it to the table. A few nastertium flowers stuck here and there look pretty, if you can get them; but lemon, and all those things are entirely fancy. This is a very pretty dish for a cold collation, or a supper.

All sorts of birds or fowl may be done this way.

Source: Hannah Glasse, *The Art of Cookery Made Plain and Easy* (Alexandria: Cotton and Stewart, 1805), 232–33.

MEAT JELLIES

Put in a saucepan two ounces of gelatine with three eggs and shells, a table-spoonful of salt, the rind of half a lemon, a liquor-glass of rum or brandy, or a wine-glass of wherry, port, or madeira wine; mix well the whole. Add one quart of broth, twelve pepper-corns; beat the whole well with an egg-beater and set on a good fire; stir gently till it comes to a boil; then move it on a rather slow fire; boil slowly for about eight minutes and turn into the jelly-bag. Have two bowls at hand to be used alternately; have one under the bag before turning the jelly into it; and when it has passed through the bag once, turn it into the bag again, putting the other bowl under; repeat this three or four times, and it will be perfectly clear. Just before turning into the bag the first time, a few drops of burnt sugar are added to give the jelly an amber color. Use the jelly immediately if wanted in liquid form, as to fill a meat-pie, etc., or put it on ice to congeal.

Boned-turkey Jelly.—As soon as the water in which you have boiled a boned turkey is cold, skim off the fat and strain it. Then proceed exactly as for meat jelly, except that you take one quart of the above instead of one quart of beef broth.

Source: Pierre Blot, *Hand-Book of Practical Cookery* (New York: D. Appleton, 1869), 53–54.

Leftovers

FRICASSEED TURKEY (COLD MEAT COOKERY)

The remains of cold roast or boiled turkey, a strip of lemon peel, a bunch of savory herbs, one onion; pepper and salt to taste. 1 pint of water, 4 tablespoons of cream, the yolk of an egg. Cut some nice slices from the remains of cold turkey and put bones and trimmings into a stewpan with the lemon peel, herbs, onion, pepper and salt and the water; stew for an hour, strain the gravy and lay in the pieces of turkey. When warm through add the cream and the yolk of an egg; stir, and when getting thick take out the pieces of turkey. When warm through add the cream and the yolk of an egg; stir, and when getting thick take out the pieces, lay them on a hot dish and pour the sauce over. Garnish with snippets of toast. Celery or cucumbers cut into small pieces may be put into the sauce; if the former, it must be boiled first. Time one hour to make the gravy.

Source: *The Portland Woman's Exchange Cook Book* (Portland, Ore.: Wells, Aug. 1913), 97.

Miscellaneous

BALLOONS FROM TURKEY'S CROPS

Free the crop from the thick coat of fat; turn the inside out, and wash the food away; soak it in water for a day or two, then lay it on a cloth, and with a bone or knife scrape off the internal coat of the stomach; wash it well and dry it with a clean cloth; then turn the crop and make an incision through the external coats, taking particular care not to cut through the membrane; draw the coats at once over the neck, which must be cut long for greater convenience in using the balloon when finished. Proceed with the other neck in the same way; tie it firm with silk, and cut it close to the body of the balloon; it must be then distended with wind and hung to dry, it may then be painted and varnished, but will not be made large enough to contain a gallon of gas, and so light as to weigh only thirty grains.

Source: Mrs. Elizabeth Fries Ellet, *The Practical Housekeeper: An Cyclopedia of Domestic Economy* (New York: Stringer and Townsend, 1857), 577.

CHICKENS OR SMALL TURKEYS, WITH JERUSALEM ARTICHOKES

Wash the chickens clean, and rub them all over with salt; also rub them inside with salt, pepper, a little marjoram or sweet basil, and parsley chopped up fine;

and stuff them with bread-crumbs, a good lump of butter, pepper, salt, a little parsley chopped fine, and plenty of celery cut up. Turkeys and chickens are improved in flavor by being rubbed inside and stuffed some days before they are used, if the weather will admit. Have some slices of middling, or lard boiling hot, in a dutch oven, and brown the chickens in it. When sufficiently so on one side, turn the other. After they are browned all over, pour off the grease from the oven. Have ready a kettle of boiling water, and pour in enough to cover the chickens about an inch (it will take about a quart.) Put in now, with the chickens and gravy you are cooking, an atom of onion, celery tops or celery tied in a bunch. Put on the chickens an hour and a half before dinner, having previously prepared them. Stew slowly until about to serve, occasionally ladling the gravy over them. Put in the pinions, &c., to make the gravy.

When about half done, put in a quart of Jerusalem artichokes carefully peeled, and let them stew until dinner time, in the gravy, occasionally turning them and ladling the gravy over them to brown.

Source: Mrs. B. C. Howard, *Fifty Years in a Maryland Kitchen* (Baltimore: Turnbull Brothers, 1873), 59.

TURKEY IN A HURRY

Truss a turkey with the legs inward, and flatten it as much as you can: then put it into a stew-pan, with melted lard, chopped parsley, shallots, mushrooms, and a little garlic; give it a few turns on the fire, and add the juice of half a lemon to keep it white. Then put it into another stew-pan, with slices of veal, one slice of ham, and melted lard, and every thing as used before; adding whole pepper and salt; cover it over with slices of lard, and set it about half an hour over a slow fire then add a glass of white wine and a little broth, and finish brazing; skim and sift the sauce, add a little cullis to make it rich, reduce it to a good consistence, put the turkey into your dish, and pour the sauce over it. Garnish with lemon.

Source: Mrs. Jane Astor, *The New York Cook-Book* (New York: G. W. Carleton, 1880), 149–50.

TURKEY SOUSED IN IMITATION OF STURGEON

Dress a fine large turkey, dry and bone it, then tie it up as you do a sturgeon, and put it into the pot, with a quart of white wine, a quart of water, the same quantity of good vinegar, and a large handful of salt; but remember that the wine, water, and vinegar, must boil before you put in the turkey, and that the pot must be well skimmed before it boils. When it is enough, take it out, and tie it tighter; but let the liquor boil a little longer. If you think the pickle wants more vinegar or salt, add them when it is cold, and pour it upon the turkey. If you keep it covered close from the air, and in a cool dry place, it will be equally good for some months. Some admire it more than sturgeon, and it is generally eaten with oil, vinegar, and sugar, for sauce.

Source: Mrs. Jane Astor, *The New York Cook-Book* (New York: G. W. Carleton, 1880), 307–8.

TURKEY EN PAIN

Take a fine turkey, bone it, and put into the carcase a ragout composed of large livers, mushrooms, and streaked bacon, all cut in small dice, and mingled with salt, fine spices, and shred parsley and onions. Sew the turkey up, but take care to shape it nicely; then put a thin slice of bacon upon the breast, and wrap it in a cloth. Stew it in a pot, but not too large a one, with good broth, a glass of white wine, and a bunch of sweet herbs; when it is done, strain the liquor the turkey was done in into a stew-pan, after having taken off the fat; reduce it to a sauce, adding a spoonful of cullis; then unwrap your turkey, take off the bacon, dry away the grease, and serve it up with the sauce.

Source: Mrs. Jane Astor, *The New York Cook-Book* (New York: G. W. Carleton, 1880), 90.

TURKEY WITH CÈPES (DINDE AUX CÈPES)

Pick out four dozen good unopened cèpes, weighing about four pounds, having them fresh, sound, and of equal size; cut off and peel the stalks, chop them up and cook in butter with a little chopped onion. Prepare a fine hash with one pound of veal, and one pound of fresh fat pork, seasoning it highly, add the chopped cèpes and a handful of soaked and pressed out bread-crumbs. Crack the breastbone of a fat turkey, remove the bone and fill in the empty space with the prepared dressing, sew the skin underneath and truss for entrée. Lay the bird in a buttered stewpan covering the bottom with small squares of bacon; surround it with the peeled and seasoned cèpes heads, and a bunch of parsley; season and moisten with a quart of stock (No. 194a); baste the turkey with butter, salt well, and place it in the oven to leave until the moistening is entirely reduced, then moisten again to half its height with more stock; boil, close the pan, and keep it cooking in the oven for three hours, pouring in a little broth at times while basting it occasionally. At the last moment drain off the turkey to untruss and dress on a dish surrounding it with the cèpes and bacon. Strain the stock, skim it free of fat, then thicken and reduce with some good béchamel, and a few spoonfuls of half-glaze. Pour a part of this over the turkey and the surplus in a sauce boat.

Source: Charles Ranhofer, *The Epicurean* (New York: R. Ranhofer, 1894), 631–32.

TURKEY-GRENADES À LA JULES VERNE (GRENADES DE DINDE À LA JULES VERNE)

Raise and pare the fillets from one to two turkeys weighing eight pounds each; shape them into half hearts rounded on one side and pointed on the other; remove the skin and lard the tops with small lardons of larding pork, and then braise in mirepoix stock being careful to baste occasionally and to glaze toward the end so that they assume a fine color. Dress them on a rice socle placed in the center of a dish, pour over the strained and reduced stock, lay on top croustades made of thin foundation paste, having them one inch and three quarters in diameter and filled with a fresh mushroom salpicon cut in quarter inch squares and fried in butter; then moisten with a little Maderia and let fall to a glaze; garnish around with truffles. Serve in a sauce-boat a velouté sauce reduced with cream and butter just at the last moment.

Source: Charles Ranhofer, *The Epicurean* (New York: R. Ranhofer, 1894), 633.

TURKEYS' LIVERS EN BROCHETTE

Take three turkey livers and cut each in four slices. Broil three slices of bacon, and cut in four pieces also. Now stick a piece of liver on a skewer, then a piece of bacon, then another piece of liver, then another piece of bacon, and so continue until the skewer is full. Season with salt and pepper, roll in fresh bread crumbs, sprinkle with olive oil, and broil. When done on all sides place on a piece of toast, put some maitre d'hotel sauce over it, and garnish with quarters of lemon and water-cress.

Source: Victor Hirtzler, *The Hotel St. Francis Cook Book* (Chicago: Hotel Monthly Press, 1919), 66.

BLANQUETTE OF TURKEY

Heat one tablespoonful of best butter in the blazer of the chafing-dish; stir in one dessert-spoonful of flour, and cook for two minutes; then add one-half cupful of highly seasoned white stock, one-half cupful of thick cream, a dash of lemon juice, salt, Paprika and grated nutmeg to taste, and a few drops of onion juice. Reduce the flame and simmer three minutes; then add one pint of breast of cold turkey, cut in small pieces, and cook five minutes more. Stir in the well-beaten yolks of two eggs, and serve at once.

Source: L. L. McLaren, comp., *High Living: Recipes from Southern Climes* (San Francisco: Paul Elder, 1904), 26.

BOUDINS OF COLD CHICKEN OR TURKEY

1 pt. chopped meat, 1–2 cup water or stock, 2 tbs. white bread crumbs, 1 tb. butter, 3 eggs, 1 tsp. salt, 1–4 tsp. pepper. Heat stock add the crumbs, boil a moment. Take from fire and add butter and eggs slightly beaten, add meat and seasoning; mix thoroughly put into greased custard cups, stand in baking pan, half filled with boiling water. Bake in moderate oven 20 min. While cooking prepare thin white sauce. Take from the fire and add yolk of 1 egg, 1–2 tsp. salt and dash of pepper. Strain this into serving dish and turn into it the boudins. Garnish dish with parsley or celery.

Source: Dallas Free Kindergarten and Training School, *Lone Star Cook Book* (Dallas: Ladies of the Dallas Free Kindergarten and Training School, 1901), 42.

MOCK TURKEY

1 pint bread-crumbs
1 pint mixed nuts
1 pint boiled rice
6 hard-boiled eggs
3 raw eggs
1 tablespoonful grated onions
1 tablespoonful salt
1 saltspoonful pepper

Put the bread-crumbs in a saucepan with a pint of water; cook for a few minutes; add the hard-boiled eggs, chopped; take saucepan from the fire and add the nuts (a mixture of peanuts and pine nuts is best), and the rice. When this is well mixed, add the raw eggs, slightly beaten. Form this into the shape of a turkey, reserving a portion for the legs and wings. Take a tablespoonful of the mixture in your hand and press it into the shape of a leg; put a piece of dry macaroni into it for the bone and fasten it to the turkey. Do the other side the same. Form the remaining portion into small pieces looking like wings tucked under; press them to the side of the turkey. Brush the turkey with butter and bake for one hour. Serve with cranberry sauce.

Source: Sarah Tyson Rorer, *Mrs. Rorer's Vegetable Cookery and Meat Substitutes* (Philadelphia: Arnold, 1909), 45.

VEGETABLE TURKEY

2 cups each of mixed nuts, chopped or ground, and coarse whole wheat bread crumbs, add 1 cup cream, 2 eggs salt, paprika and powdered sage. Mix well, shape into a loaf somewhat resembling a dressed turkey. Place in a baking pan, surround with pared and quartered potatoes, and roast about thirty minutes until the potatoes are tender and the loaf nicely browned. Baste with equal parts hot water and melted butter. Transfer carefully to a heated platter, garnish with parsley and sections of lemon. Serve in a border of the roasted potatoes, with brown gravy and cranberry sauce.

Source: Anna Lindlahr and Henry Lindlahr, *The Lindlahr Vegetarian Cook Book and A B C of Natural Dietics,* 15th ed. (Chicago: Lindlahr Publishing, 1922), 3:254–55.

Pies

GOOSE, TURKEY OR BUSTARD PIE

First bone your Fowl, and season it with Pepper, Salt, Cloves and Mace; then raise a Coffin according to the Pattern as is set down hereafter: You may put a Goose and a Turkey together, that is, you may put the Turkey, when bon'd, within the Goose, and lay the Turkey in the Bottom: You may likewise put a couple of Rabbets cut in Quarters, season'd well, and laid round to fill up the vacant Places; let all be well season'd; cover it with Butter, and close it, and bake it, and give it good Soaking.

Source: Charles Carter, *The Complete Practical Cook; or, A New System of the Whole Art and Mystery of Cookery* (London: W. Meadows, 1730), 157–58.

YORKSHIRE CHRISTMAS-PYE.

First make a good standing Crust, let the Wall and Bottom be very thick, bone a Turkey, a Goose, a Fowl, a Partridge, and a Pigeon, season them all very well, take half an Ounce of Mace, half an Ounce of Nutmegs, a quarter of an Ounce of Cloves, half an Ounce of black Pepper. all beat fine together, two large Spoonfuls of Salt, mix them together. Open the Fowls all down the Back, and bone them; first the pigeon, then the Partridge, cover them; then the Fowl, then the Goose, and then the Turkey, which must be large; season them all well first, and lay them in the Crust, so as it will look only like a whole Turkey; then have a Hare ready cased, and wiped with a clean Cloth. Cut it to Pieces, that is jointed; season it, and lay it as close as you can on one side; on the other Side Woodcock, more Game, and what Sort of Wild fowl you can get. Season them all well, and lay them close; put at least four Pounds of Butter into the Pye. then lay on your Lid, which must be a very thick one, and let it be well baked. It must have a very hot Oven, and will take at least four Hours.

This Pye will take a Bushel of Flour. in this Chapter, you will see how to make it. These Pies are often sent to *London* in a Box as Presents; therefore the Walls must be well built.

Source: Hannah Glasse, *The Art of Cookery Made Plain and Easy* (London: Published by the Author in London, 1747), 73.

Potted

POTTED TURKEY

Hash roughly the stock . . . and cook slowly in a kettle with melted lard and a little water; it must not cook dry, the water will help to soften the meat so it can absorb the lard, flavor with mixed spices, can hot in tins or glass, seal airtightly and process 30 minutes at 222 degrees. Shake several times the cans or jars while they are cooling off in order to keep the fat well mixed with the meat.

Source: Jean Pacrette, *The Art of Canning and Preserving as an Industry,* deluxe ed. (New York: Henry I. Cain and Son, 1901), 190–91.

Ragoût

RAGOÛT OF TURKEY

This is also a cheap, yet nice dish. Cut the cold turkey from the bones and into bits an inch long with a knife and fork, tearing as little as possible. Put into a skillet or saucepan the gravy left from the roast, with hot water to dilute it should the quantity be small. Add a lump of butter the size of an egg, a teaspoonful of pungent sauce, a half-teaspoonful of cloves, a large pinch of nutmeg, with a little salt. Let it boil, and put in the meat. Stew very slowly for ten minutes—not more—and stir in a tablespoonful of cranberry or currant jelly, another of browned flour which has been wet with cold water; lastly, a glass of brown sherry or Madeira. Boil up once, and serve in a covered dish for breakfast. Leave out the stuffing entirely; it is no improvement to the flavour, and disfigures the appearance of the ragoût.

Source: Marion Harlan, *Common Sense in the Household: A Manual of Practical Housewifery* (New York: Charles Scribner's Sons, 1871), 86–87.

Roast

TO ROAST A TURKEY

The best way to roast a turkey is to loosen the skin on the breast of the turkey, and fill it with force-meat, made thus[:] take a quarter of a pound of beef-suet, as many crumbs of bread, a little lemon peel, an anchovy, some nutmeg, pepper, parsley, and a little thyme. Chop and beat them all together, mix them with the yolk of an egg, and stuff up the breast; when you have no suet, butter will do: or you may make your force-meat thus: spread bread and butter thin, and grate some nutmeg over it; when you have enough roll it up, and stuff the breast of the turkey; then roast it of a fine brown, but be sure to pin some white paper on the breast till it is near enough. You must have good gravy in the dish, and bread-sauce, made thus: take a good piece of crumb, put it into a pint of water, with a blade or two of mace, two or three cloves and some whole pepper. Boil it up five or six times, then with a spoon take out the spice you had before put in, and then you must pour off the water, (you may boil an onion in it, if you please); then beat up the bread with a good piece of butter and a little salt. Or onion-sauce made thus: take some onions, peel them and cut them into thin slices, and boil them half an hour in milk and water; then drain the water from, and beat them up with a good piece of butter; shake a little flour in, and stir it all together with a little cream, if you have it (or milk will do); put the sauce into boats, and garnish with lemon.

Another way to make sauce: take half a pint of oysters, strain the liquor, and put the oysters with liquor into a sauce-pan, with a blade or two of mace, let them just lump, then pour in a glass of white-wine, let it boil once, and thicken it with a piece of butter rolled in flour. Serve this up in a basin by itself, with good gravy in the dish for every body does not love oyster-sauce. This makes a pretty side-dish for supper, or a corner-dish of a table for dinner. If you chafe it in a dish, add half a pint of gravy to it, and boil it up together. This sauce is good either with boiled or roasted turkies or fowls; but you may leave the gravy out, adding as much butter as will do for sauce, and garnishing with lemon.

Another bread-sauce. Take some crumbs of bread, rubbed through a fine cullender, put to it a pint of milk, a little butter, and some salt, a few corns of white pepper, and an onion; boil them for fifteen minutes, take out the onion and beat it up well, then toss it up, and put it in your sauce-boats.

Source: Hannah Glasse, *The Art of Cookery Made Plain and Easy* (Alexandria: Cotton and Stewart, 1805), 77–78.

Salads

FLESH SALLET OF A CAPON OR TURKEY

Take of either, slice it very thin, as for a Hash, put that which is white of the breast and wings by itself, and that which is black of the legs, or other part of the Fowl, by itself; put the rump and sides of the rump in the dish, and the other bones of the legs and wings about sides of the dish like sippets; then season your meat with a few Sives [chives], a little Tarragon, Speermint and Parslee, with the Cabbage or two of Lettice; mince these exceedingly small, add a little small Pepper Salt, and sliced Nutmeg, with a little Horse Raddish, scraped and minced, mingle your seasoning together, and strow it on your Sallet, pour on Oyl and Vinegar, so toss it up together; let your blackest flesh be laid, all over the bottom of your dish and bones, and your whitest on the top of all; strow on a Lemmon cut in Dice, and garnish it at your pleasure.

Source: William Rabisha, *The Whole Body of Cookery Dissected* (London: George Calvert and Ralph Simpson, 1682), 114–15.

CHICKEN [AND TURKEY] SALAD

Cut up the white parts of a cold chicken, season it with oil, or drawn butter, mustard, pepper, salt, and celery, chopped very fine, and a little vinegar. Turkey salad is made in the same manner as above.

Source: Elizabeth Ellicott Lea, *The Domestic Cookery*, 5th ed. (Baltimore: Cushings and Bailey, 1853), 30.

TURKEY SALAD

Remove the bones from some cold cooked Turkey, trim off all the skin and thick fat, and cut the meat into long stripes and then across, making the smallest possible squares. If celery be in season, procure about two-thirds as much celery as there is Turkey, and cut it in the same way. Lettuce or white cabbage, or a mixture of both, can be used in place of the celery, adding celery salt or extract of celery vinegar. Mix the meat and vegetables together, and season them with pepper and salt. Mix _ teaspoonful of vinegar and _ teacupful of salad-oil together, then stir in with the salad. Cover the bottom of a salad-bowl with a highly seasoned mayonnaise, spread the salad on the top of it, and serve.

Source: Theodore Francis Garrett, ed., *The Encyclopædia of Practical Cookery: A Complete Dictionary of All Pertaining to the Art of Cookery and Table Service* (London: L. Upcott Gill, Bazaar Buildings, W.C., [1890]), 7:657.

Salmagundi

TO MAKE A COLD HASH, OR SALAD-MAGUNDY

Take a cold Turkey, two cold Chickens, or, if you have neither, a piece of fine white Veal will do; cut the Breasts of these Fowls into fair slices, and mince all the rest; to the Quantity of two Chickens you must take eight or ten large Anchovies, wash and bone them, eight large Pickled Oisters, the Anchovies, the Cucumbers, and one whole Lemon small; mix them with the shred Meat, lay it in the middle of the Dish, lay the Slices of the white Part round the Dish, with halv'd Anchovies, whole Pickled Oisters, quater'd Cucumbers, sliced Lemon, whole Pickled Mushrooms, Capers or any Pickle you like; cut also some fine Lettuce and lay round among the Garnish; but put not Oil and Vinegar to the minced Meat, 'till it comes to Table.

Source: Mary Kettilby, *A Collection of above Three Hundred Receipts in Cookery, Physick and Surgery*, 4th ed. (London: Printed for Mary Kettilby, 1728), 204–5.

Sandwiches

TURKEY SANDWICH

Finely chop the dark meat of a cold roast Turkey, put it into a saucepan with about 2 tablespoonfuls of finely-chopped celery, season it with salt and pepper, and stir over the fire till hot; then add a soft-boiled egg, and leave it till cool, Cut some slices of bread about _ in. in thickness, toast them inside. Spread a layer of the Turkey mixture on one of them, lay the other side over, and press them gently with the blade of a knife. Cut the sandwiches into halves or quarters, put them on a folded napkin or a fancy dish-paper that has been placed on a dish, and serve them.

Source: Theodore Francis Garrett, ed., *The Encyclopædia of Practical Cookery: A Complete Dictionary of All Pertaining to the Art of Cookery and Table Service* (London: L. Upcott Gill, Bazaar Buildings, W.C., [1890]), 7:657.

CLUB-HOUSE SANDWICHES

Club-House sandwiches may be made in a number of different ways, but are served warm as a rule on bread carefully toasted at the last moment. Put on top of a square of toasted bread a thin layer of broiled ham or bacon; on top of this a thin slice of Holland pickle, on top of that a thin slice of cold roasted chicken or turkey, then a leaf of lettuce in the center of which you put a teaspoonful of mayonnaise dressing; cover this with another slice of buttered toast. Press the two together, and cut from one corner to another, making two large triangles, and send at once to the table.

People not using ham may make a palatable sandwich by putting down first a layer of cold boiled tongue, then a layer of Holland cucumber, a layer of turkey or chicken, another layer of cucumber and the slice of toast. Garnish with little pieces of water cress before putting on the last slice.

Source: S[arah] T[yson] Rorer, *Sandwiches* (Philadelphia: Arnold, 1894), 68–69.

Sauces

OYSTER SAUCE FOR A BOILED TURKEY

Take one Pint of oysters draw out the Liquor which you will set apart, put them in cold water, wash and clean them well, put them in an earthen dish with the Liquor, in which you will put a shred of Nutmeg, with a little butter strewed with flour and a quarter of a Lemon; boil them, then, put in a half Pint of Cream and boil slowly, all together; this done take out the Lemon, the Nutmeg, squeeze the Juice of a Lemon in the Sauce, then serve it in a Sauceboat.

Source: Benjamin Franklin, *On the Art of Eating* (Princeton: Princeton University Press for the American Philosophical Society, 1958), 49, 63–64.

TO MAKE A CELERY-SAUCE, EITHER FOR ROASTED OR BOILED FOWL, TURKIES, PARTRIDGES, OR ANY OTHER GAME

Take a large bunch of celery, wash and pare it very clean, cut it into little thin bits, and boil it softly in a little water till it is tender; then add a little beaten mace, some nutmeg, pepper, and salt, thickened with a good piece of butter rolled in flour; then boil it up, and pour it into your dish.

You may make it with cream thus: boil your celery as above, and add some mace, nutmeg, a piece of butter as big as a walnut rolled in flour, and a half pint of cream; boil them altogether.

Source: Hannah Glasse, *The Art of Cookery Made Plain and Easy* (Alexandria: Cotton and Stewart, 1805), 78–79.

Sausage

TURKEY SAUSAGE

Draw a Turkey, cut the skin down the back and round the joints, then pull it off as nearly whole as possible. Separate the meat from the bones, remove all the gristle, chop the meat, then put it in a mortar and pound it. Chop and pound half the quantity of fat bacon, and mix it with the pounded Turkey. Season the mixture with pepper, salt, and sage, roll it in the skin of the Turkey, and then in a cloth, fastening this securely at the ends. Put the rolled Turkey into a saucepan with the bones and trimmings, cover it with lightly-seasoned broth, and boil it gently for a hour. When cooked, put the Turkey on a dish, leaving it in the cloth, place another dish on top, with a weight on the top of that, and leave it till cold. Remove the cloth from the sausage, cut it into slices, arrange them on a dish, ornament it with chopped aspic jelly and small sprays of parsley, and serve.

Source: Theodore Francis Garrett, ed., *The Encyclopædia of Practical Cookery: A Complete Dictionary of All Pertaining to the Art of Cookery and Table Service* (London: L. Upcott Gill, Bazaar Buildings, W.C., [1890]), 7:657.

Scallop

TURKEY SCALLOP

Cut the meat from the bones of a cold boiled or roasted turkey left from yesterday's dinner. Remove the bits of skin and gristle, and chop up the rest very fine. Put in the bottom of a buttered dish a layer of cracker or breadcrumbs; moisten slightly with milk, that they may not absorb all the gravy to be poured in afterward; then spread a layer of the minced turkey, with bits of the stuffing, pepper, salt, and small pieces of butter. Another layer of cracker, wet with milk, and so on until the dish is nearly full. Before putting on the topmost layer, pour in the gravy left from the turkey, diluted—should there not be enough—with hot water, and seasoned with Worcester shire sauce, catsup, and butter. Have ready a crust of cracker-crumbs soaked in warm milk, seasoned with salt and beaten up light with two eggs. It should be just thick enough to spread smoothly over the top of the scallop. Stick bits of butter plentifully upon it. And bake. Turn a deep plate over the dish until the contents begin to bubble at the sides, showing that the whole is thoroughly cooked; then remove the cover, and brown. A large pudding-dish full of the mixture will be cooked in three-quarters of an hour.

This, like many other economical dishes, will prove as savory as to claim a frequent appearance upon any table.

Cold chicken may be prepared in the same way;

Or,

The minced turkey, dressing, and cracker-crumbs may be wet with gravy, two eggs beaten into it, and the forcemeat thus made rolled into oblong shapes, dipped in egg and pounded cracker, and fried like croquettes, for a side dish, to "make out" a dinner of ham or cold meat.

Source: Marion Harlan, *Common Sense in the Household: A Manual of Practical Housewifery* (New York: Charles Scribner's Sons, 1871), 86–87.

Soups

TURKEY SOUP

1 turkey carcass, cover with water,
1 small onion,
1 stock of celery,
_ teaspoon of extract of beef,
2 tablespons of rice,
Seasoning to taste.

Break the carcass in pieces and remove all dressing, cover with water and let simmer for 2 hours with celery and onion, then remove the bones and strain. Add the extract of beef, then the rice, which should have been previously cooked, let the soup reach the boiling point, season and serve with croutons.

Source: Senior Amona Class, *Echoes from the Kitchen: A Careful Compilation of Tried and Approved Recipes by the Ladies of the Church and Congregation of the Bales Avenue Baptist Church* (Kansas City, Mo.: Tingle Titus Printing, 1916), 148.

TURKEY BONE SOUP

Turkey bones, water to cover bones, 1 onion, 1 stalk celery, 2 carrots, 1 tablespoon barley, 1 teaspoon rice, 1 sprig parsley, pepper and salt. Put turkey bones in kettle and cover with water; boil slowly for 3 hours; add the other ingredients, chopping the onion, parsley and celery, and cutting the carrot and 1 potato into small dice. Boil until the vegetables are tender, season to taste and serve.

Source: Women's Guild, *Grace Church Cook Book,* 2d ed. (Astoria, Ore.: J. S. Dellinger, 1922), 17.

Steamed

STEAMED TURKEY

Cleanse the fowl thoroughly: then rub pepper and salt well mixed into the inside of it. Fill up the body with oysters mixed with a small cupful of breadcrumbs. Sew up all the apertures; lay the turkey into a large steamer and place over a kettle of boiling water; cover closely, and steam thoroughly for two hours and a half. Now take it up; set the platter in a warm place, and turn whatever gravy there is in the steamer, straining it first into the oyster sauce which you have prepared, in the following manner: Take a pint of oysters, turn a pint of boiling water over them in the colander. Put the liquor on to boil, skim off whatever rises on the top. Thicken it with a tablespoonful of flour rubbed into two tablespoonfuls of butter; season it well with pepper and salt. Add two or three tablespoonfuls of cream or milk to whiten it; and pour it over the turkey and plate; serve boiling hot. This sauce must be made while the turkey is still in the steamer, so that it can be poured over the turkey as soon as it is taken up.

Source: Jonathan Periam, *The Home and Farm Manual: A Pictorial Encyclopedia of Farm, Garden, Household, Architectural, Legal Medical and Social Information* (New York: N. D. Thompson, 1884), 825.

Stewed

TO STEW A TURKEY OR FOWL

First let your pot be very clean, lay four clean skewers at the bottom, and your turkey or fowl upon them, put in a quart of gravy; take a bunch of celery, cut it small, and wash it very clean, put it into your pot, with two or three blades of mace, let it stew softly till there is just enough for sauce, then add a good piece of butter rolled in flour, two spoonful of red-wine, two of catchup, and just as much pepper and salt as will season it; lay your fowl or turkey in the dish, pour the sauce over it, and send it to the table. If the fowl or turkey is enough before the sauce, take it up, and keep it up till the sauce is boiled enough, then put it in, let it boil a minute or two, and dish it up.

Source: Hannah Glasse, *The Art of Cookery Made Plain and Easy* (Alexandria: Cotton and Stewart, 1805), 67–68.

STEWED TURKEY—A FRENCH RECEIPT

Keep a large fat turkey several days after being killed. When ripe for cooking, stuff it; upon the bottom of a large stew-pan that will hold the fowl without cramping it, put a trivet to elevate it a few inches. Rub over the turkey a coat of flour, shake off all that does not stick; lay it upon the trivet; cover over the breast with slices of pickled pork or bacon. Cut up two or three calf's feet, lay these around it. Season highly with pepper, chopped onions, mace or nutmeg, a few cloves, or a stick of cinnamon broken up. Mix together a pint of cold water, the same of Sherry wine; pour to the turkey; cover well with a well-fitting cover; keep a wet towel or cloth over and around the edges of the cover;

wet it as often as is required to keep it from becoming dry. Stew slowly five hours; turn the turkey when half done. For sauce, strain the gravy; send it to the table in a sauce-boat.

Source: Mrs. A. P. Hill, *Mrs. Hill's New Cook Book* (New York: Carleton Publishers, 1872), 75.

Stuffing/Dressing

A FOWL OR TURKEY ROASTED WITH CHESTNUTS

Roast a quarter of a hundred of chestnuts, and peel them; save out eight or ten, the rest bruise in a mortar, with a liver of a fowl, a quarter of a pound of ham well pounded, and sweet herbs and parsley chopped fine: Season with mace, nutmeg, pepper, and salt: mix all these together, and put them into the belly of your fowl: Spit it, and tie the neck and vent close. For sauce, take the rest of the chestnuts, cut them in pieces, and put them into a strong gravy, with a glass of white wine: thicken with a piece of butter rolled in flour. Pour the sauce in the dish, and garnish with orange and water-cresses.

Source: Susannah Carter, *The Frugal Housewife; or, Complete Woman Cook; Wherein the Art of Dressing All Sorts of Viands Is Explained in Upwards of Five Hundred Approved Receipts* (New York: Printed and Sold by G. and R. Waite, No. 64, Maidenlane, 1803), 33.

A TURKEY STUFFED AFTER THE HAMBURGH WAY

Take one pound of beef, three quarters of a pound of suet, mince it very small, season it with salt, pepper, cloves, mace, and sweet marjoram; then mix two or three eggs with it, loosen the skin all round the turkey, and stuff it. It must be roasted.

Source: Hannah Glasse, *The Art of Cookery Made Plain and Easy* (Alexandria: Cotton and Stewart, 1805), 277.

LIVER AND TRUFFLE STUFFING FOR A PIG OR TURKEY

Pare and cut into small pieces a pound of truffles, put them into a stewpan with a large spoonful of butter, one-half pound of fat bacon, chopped very fine; add a spoonful of black pepper, a clove of garlic, a little salt, a bunch of sweet basil and thyme, dried and powdered; add also half a pound of nice veal liver, boiled and grated. Set this all on the fire, let it cook until the truffles are soft, then mash with a wooden spoon; take it off to cool it, and stuff the pig with the forcemeat. Baste the pig with sweet oil [olive oil], which is better than butter. It is supposed the pig comes from the butchers all ready for stuffing and baking. If the stuffing is desired for a turkey, add a quarter of a pound of bread crumbs and two beaten eggs, and baste the turkey with butter, instead of oil.

Source: [Lafcadio Hearn], *La Cuisine Creole: A Collection of Culinary Recipes from Leading Chefs and Noted Creole Housewives, Who Have Made New Orleans Famous for Its Cuisine,* 2d ed. (New Orleans, F. F. Hansell and Bro., 1885), 37.

STUFFINGS FOR TURKEYS AND DUCKS

Wild turkeys should be stuffed with corn bread, pecan nuts and truffles. Take a piece of corn bread left over from breakfast, moisten with a teaspoonful of sauce. Add about a dozen peeled pecan nuts, three or four cut truffles, mix well. Cook in saucepan. Stuff your turkey the day before. Always let your fowls hang by the legs. A wild turkey should cook an hour, perhaps a little more or less. Be careful it does not dry. as the flesh is rather dry. Carve it as you would a wild duck, to prevent its drying. Tame turkeys can be cooked and stuffed in the same way. Sausages well fried, with mashed potatoes, salt, and red pepper, make delicious stuffing for fowls.

Source: Celestine Eustis, *Cooking in Old Creole Days* (New York: R. H. Russell, 1904), 28–29.

PICKLED PORK STUFFING FOR TURKEYS

Chop up very fine a quarter of a pound of fat and lean salted pork, break quite fine a quarter of breakfast cupfuls of bread and put them in a frying pan over the fire with two heaping tablespoonfuls of butter, fry to a brown and season with salt, pepper and any sweet herbs except sage.

Source: Rufus Estes, *Good Things to Eat as Suggested by Rufus* (Chicago: Published by the Author, 1911), 41.

CHESTNUT STUFFING FOR TURKEY

Shell 1 pint of large chestnuts; pour on boiling water and remove the inner skin. Boil in salted water, or stock until soft. Mash fine and mix with them 1 cup of fine rolled crackers. Season with 1 teaspoon of salt, 1 saltspoon of pepper and 1 teaspoon of chopped parsley. Moisten with 1–3 cup of melted butter. This stuffing is especially nice for quail. *Mrs. H. E. Blossom.*

Source: *The Portland Woman's Exchange Cook Book* (Portland, Ore.: Wells, Aug. 1913), 98.

Wild Turkey

AU CHASSEUR (HUNTER'S OR SPORTSMAN'S SOUP)

A potage *au chasseur* is always made with game, such as rabbit, prairie-hen, grouse, venison, wild turkey, wild pigeon, etc., but never with aquatic birds. It might be made with quail, but that bird is really too delicate to make soup with. A whole bird or animal is never used, but the bones and trimmings only. After having cut off the fleshy parts, the bones are cracked and used to make the potage.

Take the bones of two prairie-hens after having cut off the flesh on both sides of the breast-bone, also the legs; cut the bones in pieces about half an inch long and set them on the fire with half an ounce of butter, stir for two or three minutes, cover with broth, or game broth, and boil gently till well cooked, or about two hours.

Put in another pan, and set it on the fire at the same time as above, half a head of cabbage, one carrot, one turnip, and one onion, all cut fine; about half a pound of lean salt pork; cover with cold water, and boil gently for about two hours also.

In case the water or broth should boil away, add a little more.

After having boiled both vegetables and bones about two hours, take off the salt pork from the pan in which the vegetables are, and turn what you have in the other pan over the vegetables, through a strainer; add some broth if it is too thick; boil ten minutes, and serve.

Proceed as above with the bones and trimmings of other birds.

Source: Pierre Blot, *Hand-Book of Practical Cookery* (New York: D. Appleton, 1869), 86–87.

WILD TURKEY

This stately bird stalker of Southern forests and Western prairies is eagerly sought after by the lovers of good eating in those regions. The dark meat and game flavor proclaim his birthright of lordly freedom as truly after he is slain and cooked, as did his lithe grace of figure, lofty carriage, and bright eye where he trod his native wilds. I have heard sportsmen declare that when they have inveigled him up to a blind by imitating the call of his harem or younglings, they have stood in covert, gun at shoulder and finger on the trigger, spell-bound by pitying admiration of his beauty. But I have never seen that sensibility curbed appetite while they told the story at the table adorned by the royal bird, have noted, indeed, that their mouths watered rather than their eyes, as he crumbled, like a dissolving view, under the blade of the carver.

Draw and wash the inside carefully, as with all game. Domestic fowls are, or should be, kept up without eating for at least twelve hours before they are killed; but we must shoot wild when we can get the chance, and of course it often happens that their crops are distended by a recent hearty meal of rank or green food. Wipe the cavity with a dry soft cloth before you stuff. Have a rich forcemeat, bread-crumbs, some bits of fat pork, chopped fine, pepper, and salt. Moisten with milk, and beat in an egg and a couple of tablespoonfuls of melted butter. Baste with butter and water for the first hour, then three or four times with the gravy; lastly, five or six times with melted butter. A generous and able housekeeper told me once that she always allowed a pound of butter for basting a large wild turkey. This was an extravagant quantity, but the meat is drier than that of the domestic fowl, and not nearly so fat. Dredge with flour at the last, froth with butter, and when he is of a tempting brown, serve. Skim the gravy, add a little hot water, pepper, thicken with the giblets chopped fine and browned flour, boil up, and pour into a tureen. At the South the giblets are not put in the gravy, but laid whole, one under each wing, when the turkey is dished. Garnish with small fried sausages, not larger than a dollar, crisped parsley between them.

Send around currant and cranberry sauce with it.

Source: Marion Harlan, *Common Sense in the Household: A Manual of Practical Housewifery* (New York: Charles Scribner's Sons, 1871), 179–80.

WILD TURKEY À LA DELAGRANGE-STUFFED (DINDE SAUVAGE FARCIE À LA DELAGRANGE)

Singe and draw a young wild turkey, then truss for an entrée. Prepare a dressing composed of bread-crumbs soaked in warm water and the liquid entirely extracted, season with salt, fine spices, sage, chopped onions fried in butter, and finely chopped beef marrow; add some roasted chestnuts, and broiled sausages free of skin, and cut into slices. When all the ingredients are thoroughly mixed, fill the turkey with it and braise in a saucepan garnished with bards of pork, and moistened with a white wine mirepoix stock; when nearly done, glaze with bénchamel sauce reduced with the mirepoix stock, thickening with raw egg-yolks and cream; when ready to serve incorporate a little chicken glaze, and a piece of fine butter. Pour part of this sauce over the turkey serving the rest in a sauce-boat.

Source: Charles Ranhofer, *The Epicurean* (New York: R. Ranhofer, 1894), 630.

Notes

Chapter 1: The Prehistoric Turkey

1. R. A. Donkin, *The Muscovy Duck,* Carina moschata domestica, *Origin, Dispersal, and Associated Aspects of the Geography of Domestication* (Rotterdam: A. A. Balkema, 1989); R. D. Crawford, "Introduction to Europe and Diffusion of Domesticated Turkeys from America," *Archivos de Zootecnia* 41 (1992): 314.

2. Richard Howard and Alick More, *The Howard and More Complete Checklist of Birds of the World,* 3d ed., edited by Edward C. Dickinson (London: Christopher Helm, 2003), 44; *Check-list of North American Birds: The Species of Birds of North America from the Arctic through Panama, including the West Indies and Hawaiian Islands, Prepared by the Committee on Classification and Nomenclature of the American Ornithologists' Union,* 7th ed. (Washington: The Union, 1998), 122.

3. Janet Vorwald Dohner, *The Encyclopedia of Endangered Livestock and Poultry Breeds* (New Haven: Yale University Press, 2001), 443.

4. Alfred M. Tozzer and Glover M. Allen, *Animal Figures in the Maya Codices* (Cambridge, Mass.: The Museum, 1910), 326–29, plate 16.

5. "California's Tar Pit Turkeys Closely Related to Modern Wild Turkeys," press release at the National Wild Turkey Federation Web site: www.nwtf.org/nwtf_newsroom/press_releases.php?id=10220; Zbigniew Bochenski and Kenneth E. Campbell, *The Extinct California Turkey,* Melegris californica (Los Angeles: Natural History Museum of Los Angeles County, [2004]), 1 (interim report).

6. James Earl Kennamer, Mary Kennamer, and Ron Brenneman, "History," in *The Wild Turkey: Biology and Management,* edited by James G. Dickson (Mechanicsburg, Pa.: Stackpole Books, 1992), 39.

7. John James Audubon, *The Birds of America* (New York: J. J. Audubon; Philadelphia: J. B. Chevalier, 1840–44), 5:49; W. Clift, "The Narragansett Turkey," *Poultry World* 1 (Dec. 1872): 151; George Enty, "The Wild Turkey," in *Turkeys and How to Grow Them,* edited by Herbert Myrick (New York: Orange Judd, 1897), 9; Sylvester D. Judd, *The Grouse and Wild Turkeys of the United States, and Their Economic Value* (Washington: U.S. Department of Agriculture, Biological Survey, 1905), 49–50; Florence Merriam Bailey, *Birds of New Mexico* (Sante Fe: New Mexico Department of Game and Fish in Cooperation with the State Game Protective Association and the Bureau of Biological Survey, 1928), 233.

8. Dohner, *The Encyclopedia of Endangered Livestock and Poultry Breeds,* 444.

9. The term *tom* is an Americanism that originated in the mid-nineteenth century. For the first located use in print, see George W. Henry, *Tell Tale Rag, and Popular Sins of the Day* (Oneida: Published for the author, 1861), 110, 182. Thanks to Barry Popik for locating this reference.

10. M. W. Olsen, "The Sex of Parthenogenetic Turkey Embryos," *Journal of Heredity* 48 (1957): 217–18; M. W. Olsen, "Performance Record of a Parthenogenetic Turkey Male," *Science* 132 (Dec. 1960): 1661; M. W. Olsen,

"Twelve Year Summary of Selection for Parthenogenesis in Beltsville Small White Turkeys," *British Poultry Science* 6 (1965): 1–6; T. F. Savage, G. L. Bradley, and J. Hayat, "The Incidence of Parthenogenesis in Medium White Turkey Hens When Fed a Breeder Diet Containing Yeast Cultures of Saccharomyces Cerevisiae," *Poultry Science,* supp. 1, 72 (1993): 80; Thomas F. Savage and Elzbieta I. Zakrzewska, "A Guide to the Recognition of Parthenogenesis in Incubated Turkey Eggs," at www.oregonstate.edu/Dept/animal-sciences/poultry/index.html.

11. *Check-list of North American Birds,* 122; Carolyn J. Christman and Robert O. Hawes, *Birds of a Feather: Saving Turkeys from Extinction* (Pittsboro, N.C.: American Livestock Breeds Conservancy, 1999), 3–5; Howard and More, *The Howard and More Complete Checklist of Birds of the World,* 44.

12. Sophie D. Coe, *America's First Cuisines* (Austin: University of Texas Press, 1994), 141.

13. Stanley J. Olsen, "Turkeys," in *The Cambridge World History of Food,* edited by Kenneth F. Kiple and Kriemhid Conee Ornelas (New York: Cambridge University Press, 2000), 2:579.

14. Richard S. MacNeish, "Ancient Mesoamerican Civilization," *Science* 143 (Feb. 1964): 537.

15. Crawford, "Introduction to Europe and Diffusion of Domesticated Turkeys from America," 309.

16. A. Starker Leopold, "The Wild Turkey of Mexico," in *Transactions of the Thirteenth North American Wildlife Conference,* edited by Ethel M. Quee (Washington: Wildlife Management Institute, 1948), 393–400; Board on Science and Technology for International Development, National Research Council, *Microlivestock: Little-known Small Animals with a Promising Economic Future* (Washington: National Academy Press, 1991), 162.

17. Crawford, "Introduction to Europe and Diffusion of Domesticated Turkeys from America," 310.

18. Bernardino de Sahagún, *General History of the Things of New Spain* (*Florentine Codex*), Book 11: *Earthly Things,* translated by Charles Dibble and Arthur J. O. Anderson (Santa Fe: School of American Research and University of Utah, 1963), 52.

19. Bernardino de Sahagún, *Florentine Codex,* Book 9: *The Merchants,* pt. 10, no. 14, translated by Arthur Anderson and Charles E. Dibble (Santa Fe: School of American Research and University of Utah, 1959), 48.

20. James Cooper Clark, trans. and ed., *Codex Mendoza: The Manuscript Known as the "Collection of Mendoza" and Preserved in the Bodleian Library, Oxford* (London: Waterlow and Sons, 1938), 1:92n4; Frances F. Berdan, and Patricia Rieff Anawalt, eds., *The Essential Codex Mendoza* (Berkeley: University of California Press, 1997), 169.

21. W[illiam] Bullock, *Six Months' Residence and Travels in Mexico* (London: John Murray, 1824), 311.

22. Berdan and Anawalt, eds., *The Essential Codex Mendoza,* 169.

23. de Sahagún, *General History of the Things of New Spain* (*Florentine Codex*), Book 11: *Earthly Things,* 53–54.

24. Codex Borbonicus in the Bibliotèque de l'Assemblée Nationale, Paris, 17; *Tezcatl-Ipoca* (electronic journal) at www.thing.net/~grist/ld/bot/ky-ab4.htm or www.thing.net/~grist/ld/bot/ky-abt.htm.

25. Codex Huejotzingo, 1531, 6, Library of Congress, Washington; Berdan and Anawalt, eds., *The Essential Codex Mendoza,* 169, 218.

26. A. W. Schorger, *The Wild Turkey: Its History and Domestication* (Norman: University of Oklahoma Press, 1966), 467; John W. Aldrich, "Historical Background," in *The Wild Turkey and its Management,* edited by Oliver H. Hewett (Washington: Wildlife Society, 1967), 9.

27. F. d'Alva Ixlilxochitl, *Historia des Chichimègues: Ternaux-compan voyages* (Paris, 1840): 12–13:211, as cited in Schorger, *The Wild Turkey,* 490.

28. Board on Science and Technology for International Development, National Research Council, *Microlivestock,* 158–59; Dohner, *The Encyclopedia of Endangered Livestock and Poultry Breeds,* 446.

29. Bernardino de Sahagún, *Códice florentino Historia general de las cosas de Nueva España* [Mexico City: Secretaría de Gobernación, 1979], folio 57.

30. Giovanni da Udine, *Turkey* (Villa Madama, Sala de Giulio Romano) and *Turkey-cock* and *Turkey-hen* (attributed to Hans Verhagen, Biblioteca Universitaria, ms. 514, folio 147), all in Sabine Eiche, *Presenting the Turkey: The Fabulous Story of a Flamboyant and Flavourful Bird* (Florence: Centro Di, 2004), 14, 23–24, 74.

31. Emanuel Breitburg, "The Evolution of Turkey Domestication in the Greater Southwest and Mesoamerica," in *Culture and Contact: Charles C. Di Peso's Gran Chichimeca,* edited by Anne I. Woosley and John C. Ravesloot (Albuquerque: University of New Mexico Press, 1993), 156.

32. Stephen Jett, *House of Three Turkeys* (Santa Barbara: Capra Press, 1977).

33. Jean M. Pinkley, "The Pueblos and the Turkey: Who Domesticated Whom?" *American Antiquity* 31 (1965): 70–72.

34. Breitburg, "The Evolution of Turkey Domestication," 160.

35. Charmion R. McKusick, "Three Groups of Turkeys from Southwestern Archaeological Sites," *Contributions in Science Natural History Museum, Los Angeles County* (Los Angeles: The Museum, 1980), 225–35; Crawford, "Introduction to Europe and Diffusion of Domesticated Turkeys from America," 307–14.

36. "Casteñeda's History of the Expedition," in *Narratives of the Coronado Expedition, 1540–1542,* edited and translated by George P. Hammond and Agapito Rey (Albuquerque: University of New Mexico Press, 1940), 255.

37. Breitburg, "The Evolution of Turkey Domestication," 168.

38. F. M. Buckelew, *Life of F. M. Buckelew: The Indian Captive as Related by Himself; Written by T. S. Dennis and Mrs. T. S. Dennis* (Bandera, Tex.: Hunter's Printing House, 1925), 90.

39. Willard W. Hill, *The Agricultural and Hunting Methods of the Navaho Indians* (New Haven: Published for the Department of Anthropology by the Yale University Press, 1938), 174.

40. William Byrd, *Histories of the Dividing Line betwixt Virginia and North Carolina* (Raleigh: North Carolina Historical Commission, 1929), 194.

41. Edward Franklin Castetter, *Pima and Papago Indian Agriculture* (Albuquerque: University of New Mexico Press, 1942), 69.

42. Henry C. Keeling, "The Indians: My Experience with the Cheyenne Indians," Kansas State Historical Society *Collections for 1909–1910* 11 (1910): 308.

43. Don C. Talayesva, *Sun Chief: The Autobiography of a Hopi Indian,* edited by Leo W. Simmons (New Haven: Published for the Institute of Human Relations by Yale University Press; London, H. Milford, Oxford University Press, 1942), 55; George Henry Loskiel, *History of the Mission of the United Brethren among the Indians in North America* (London: Brethren's Society for the Furtherance of the Gospel, 1794), 91.

44. Hill, *The Agricultural and Hunting Methods of the Navaho,* 174.

45. Thomas Morton, *New English Canaan* [Washington: P. Force, 1838], 2:22; William Strachey, *Historie of the Travaile into Virginia Britania* (London: Printed for the Hakluyt Society, 1849), 65 (quotation); John Ettwein, "Some Remarks and Annotations upon the Traditions, Customs, Languages of the Indians of North America," *Bulletin of the Historical Society of Pennsylvania* 1 (1845–47): 32; "Heckewelder's Indian History, Manners and Customs," *North American Review* 9 (June 1819): 176; Charles Colcock Jones Jr., *Antiquities of the Southern Indians, Particularly of the Georgia Tribes* (New York: D. Appleton, 1873), 77, 87; John Josselyn, *An Account of Two Voyages to New-England* (London: G. Widdows, 1674), 99; Roger Williams, *A Key into the Language of America* (London: Printed by G. Dexter, 1643), 65; "Journal of New Netherland," in E. B. O'Callaghan, *The Documentary History of the State of New-York* (Albany: Weed, Parsons, 1851), 4:3–4; Alexander Scott Withers, *Chronicles of Border Warfare* (Clarksburg, Va.: J. Israel, 1831), 37; Thomas Nuttall, "Travels into the Arkansas Territory, 1819," in *Early Western Travels,* edited by Reuben Gold Thwaites (Cleveland: A. H. Clark, 1905), 13:258–59; Loskiel, *History of the Mission of the United Brethren,* 48.

46. Jens Knudsen Jensen, "Notes on the Nesting Birds of Northern Santa Fe, New Mexico," *The Auk* 40 (July–Sept. 1923): 455; Hill, *The Agricultural and Hunting Methods of the Navaho,* 174; Pinkley, "The Pueblos and the Turkey," 70–72.

47. Castetter, *Pima and Papago Indian Agriculture,* 228; Edward F. Castetter and Ruth M. Underhill, *The Ethnobiology of the Papago Indians* (New York: AMS Press, 1978), 41, 71.

48. Le Page du Pratz, *The History of Louisiana* (London: T. Becket and P. A. De Hondt, 1763), 2:85.

49. Samuel de Champlain, *Voyages of Samuel de Champlain,* edited by Edmund F. Slafter (Boston: Published by the Prince Society, 1878), 88; Andrew White, "A Briefe Relation of the Voyage into Maryland," in *Narratives of Early Maryland 1633–1684* (New York: Charles Scribner's Sons, 1910), 34, 43–44, 10, 75, 80, 98; Robert Beverly, *History and Present State of Virginia* (London: Printed for R. Parker, 1705), 60; William Byrd, *The Westover Manuscripts: Containing the History of the Dividing Line Betwixt Virginia and North Carolina* (Petersburg [Va.]: Printed by E. and J. C. Ruffin, 1841), 39; Thomas C. Battey, *The Life and Adventure of a Quaker among the Indians* (Boston: Lee and Shepard; New York: Lee, Shepard and Dillingham, 1875), 323.

50. James Mooney, *The Ghost-Dance Religion and the Sioux Outbreak of 1890* (Washington: Government Printing Office, 1896), 1024.

51. Castetter, *Pima and Papago Indian Agriculture,* 228, 227; Castetter and Underhill, *The Ethnobiology of the Papago,* 41, 71; Jens Knudsen Jensen, "Notes on the Nesting Birds of Northern Santa Fe, New Mexico," *The Auk* 40 (July-Sept. 1923): 455; Hill, *The Agricultural and Hunting Methods of the Navaho,* 174; Jean M. Pinkley, "The Pueblos and the Turkey: Who Domesticated Whom?" *American Antiquity* 31 (1965): 70–72; Don C.

Talayesva, *Sun Chief; the Autobiography of a Hopi Indian,* edited by Leo W. Simmons (New Haven: Published for the Institute of Human Relations by Yale University Press; London: H. Milford, Oxford University Press, 1942), 55.

52. Thomas F. O'Donnell, ed., *A Description of the New Netherlands by Adriaen van der Donck* (Syracuse: Syracuse University Press, 1968), 50; Kennamer, Kennamer, and Brenneman, "History," 12.

53. W. P. Baldwin, "Trapping Wild Turkeys in South Carolina," *Journal of Wildlife Management* 11 (1947): 24–36.

54. John D. Hunter, *Memoirs of a Captivity among the Indians of North America* (London: Longmans, Hurst, Rees, Orme, and Brown, 1823), 382–83.

55. Samuel Kercheval, *A History of the Valley of Virginia* (Winchester: Samuel H. Davis, 1833), 372–73.

56. Morris E. Opler, *An Apache Life-way: The Economic, Social, and Religious Institutions of the Chiricahua Indians* (Chicago: University of Chicago Press, 1941), 328.

57. Thomas Loraine McKenney, *Memoirs, Official and Personal; with Sketches of Travels among the Northern and Southern Indians* (New York: Paine and Burgess, 1846), 1:163; Henry Timberlake, *The Memoirs of Lieut. Henry Timberlake* (London: Printed for the author, 1765), 45–46; Hunter, *Memoirs of a Captivity,* 283.

58. McKenney, *Memoirs, Official and Personal,* 1:163.

59. Timberlake, *The Memoirs of Lieut. Henry Timberlake,* 45–46.

Chapter 2: The Globe-trotting Turkey

1. A. W. Schorger, *The Wild Turkey: Its History and Domestication* (Norman: University of Oklahoma Press, 1966), 4.

2. Pietro Martire d' Anghiera, *The Decades of the Newe Worlde or West India,* translated by Richard Eden (London: Guilhelmi Powell, 1555), 79.

3. Schorger, *The Wild Turkey,* 4.

4. Ibid., 9.

5. Gonzalo Fernández de Oviedo y Valdés, *Historia general y natural de las Indias* (Madrid: Impr. de la Real Academia de la Historia, 1851), 1:507; Bernal Díaz del Castillo, *Verdadera y notable Relación del Descubrimiento y Conquesta de la Nueva España y Guatemala* (Guatemala: [Tipografíía Nacional], 1933), 1:26, as cited in Schorger, *The Wild Turkey,* 6.

6. William Hickling Prescott, *History of the Conquest of Mexico, with a Preliminary View of the Ancient Mexican Civilization, and the Life of the Conqueror Hernando Cortez* (Philadelphia: J. P. Lippincott, 1867), 1:440.

7. Alessandro Geraldini, *Itinerarium ad regiones sub aequinoctiali plaga constitutas* (Rome: Typis G. Facciotti, 1631), 253; Sabine Eiche, *Presenting the Turkey: The Fabulous Story of a Flamboyant and Flavourful Bird* (Florence: Centro Di, 2004), 22.

8. Fernández de Oviedo y Valdés, *Historia general y natural de las Indias,* in Eiche, *Presenting the Turkey,* 13.

9. As of 2005, this manuscript was owned by the William Reese Company, New Haven, Connecticut. The estimate of the dates 1530–40 for the manuscript is also supported by Christopher de Hamel, formerly the expert in charge of illuminated manuscripts at Christie's and now librarian at Corpus Christi College at Cambridge.

10. Diego Granado, *Libro del arte de cocina* (Madrid: 1599), 321.

11. Joop Witteveen, "The Great Birds: Part 4, Peacocks in History," *Petits Propos Culinaires* 32 (1989): 23–24.

12. Ken Albala, *Eating Right in the Renaissance* (Berkeley: University of California Press, 2002), 205–6.

13. Giovanmaria della Porta to the Duke of Urbino, dated Sept. 1531, in Eiche, *Presenting the Turkey,* 21–22.

14. Antonio Zannon, *Letters sull' agricoltura, le arti e el commercio* (Venice: 1763), 1:32, as cited in Schorger, *The Wild Turkey,* 465; Agostino Gallo, *Le vinti giornate dell'agricultura et de' piaceri della villa* (1565), in Eiche, *Presenting the Turkey,* 50–51.

15. Nicola Zingarelli, *Vocabolario della lingua italiana,* 12th ed. (Bologne: Zanichelli, 1993), 4:708.

16. Bartolomeo Scappi, *Opera Dell'Arte del Cucinare; Presentazione di Giancarlo Roversi* (1570, repr. Bologne: Arnaldo Forni Editore, 1981); Roy Strong, *Feast: A History of Grand Eating* (New York: Harcourt, 2002), 144.

17. Scappi, *Opera Dell'Arte del Cucinare,* bk. 1, ch. 39, pp. 10 (back)–11; bk. 1, ch. 40, p. 11 (back); bk. 2, ch. 115, p. 50 (back); bk. 2, ch. 127, p. 54; and bk. 2, ch. 141, p. 61.

18. Conrad Heresbach, *Rei rvsticae libri qvatvor* (Cologne: Apud Ioannem Birckmannum, 1570), 172.

19. Marx Rumpolt, *Ein New Kochbuch* (Frankfurt am Main: Feyerabends, 1581), sec. 66.

20. Rumpolt, *Ein New Kochbuch,* 35.

21. Eiche, *Presenting the Turkey,* 74.

22. Jean Baptiste Bruyerin, *De re cibaria libri XXII, omnium ciborum genera, omnium gentium moribus & usu probata complectentes* (Lyon: Apud Sebast. Honoratum, 1560), 831.

23. Barbara Ketcham Wheaton, *Savoring the Past: The French Kitchen and Table from 1300 to 1789* (Philadelphia: University of Pennsylvania Press, 1983), 81.

24. R. de. Maulde, "De l'origine des dindons," translated by Carolin Young in *Bibliothèque de l'école des chartes: Revue d'érudition consacré spécialement à l'étude du moyen-age* 40 (1879): 332–34.

25. Jean-Louis Flandrin, "Introduction: The Early Modern Period," in *Food: A Culinary History from Antiquity to the Present,* edited by Jean-Louis Flandrin, Massimo Montanari, and Albert Sonnenfeld (New York: Columbia University Press, 1999), 359.

26. Pierre J. B. D'Aussy, *Histoire de la vie privée des Français* (Paris: P. D. Pierres, 1782), 1:290.

27. Adam Anderson, *Historical and Chronological Deduction of the Origin of Commerce* (London: A. Millar et al., 1764), 2:177.

28. Charles Estienne, *Maison rustique; or, The Coventrie Farme,* translated by Richard Svrflet (London: Edm. Bollifant, 1600), 117.

29. François Pierre de la Varenne, *Le cuisinier françois* (Paris: Chez Pierre David, 1652), 132, 135, 141, 144, 106, 152, 203.

30. Cardinal Jacques Davey du Perron, *Perroniana et thuana* (Cologne: 1691), 71, as quoted in Schorger, *The Wild Turkey,* 466.

31. Marc Antoine René de Voyer Argenson, *Précis d'une histoire générale de la vie*

privée des français dans tous les temps et dans toutes les provinces de la monarchie (Paris: Chez Moutard, imprimeur-libraire de la reine, de Madame, et de Madame la comtesse d'Artois, 1779), 23.

32. John Cook Bennett, *The Poultry Book* (Boston: Phillips, Sampson, 1850), 18.

33. Brillat-Savarin as quoted in *Cassell's Dictionary of Cookery* (London: Cassell, Petter, and Galpin, ca. 1870), n.p.

34. Giovanni da Udine, *Turkey* (Villa Madama, Sala de Giulio Romano), in Eiche, *Presenting the Turkey,* 14, 71.

35. Eiche, *Presenting the Turkey,* 77.

36. F. Rabelais, *Le quart livre des faicts et dictc heroques du bon Pantagruel,* as cited in Schorger, *The Wild Turkey,* 465.

37. Pieter Brueghel, *Seven Deadly Sins: Envy* (Metropolitan Museum of Art, New York).

38. Jan Brueghel, *Birds of Paradise* (Herzog Anton Ulrich-Museum, Lower Saxony), in Eiche, *Presenting the Turkey,* 76.

39. Jacopo Bassano, *Animals Entering the Ark* (The Prado Museum, Madrid).

40. Vincenzo Campi, *The Poulterer* (Pinacoteca di Brera, Milan), in Eiche, *Presenting the Turkey,* 84, 90.

41. Gillian Riley, *Renaissance Recipes* (San Francisco: Pomegranate Artbooks, 1993), 87.

42. Eiche, *Presenting the Turkey,* 72.

43. Charles Avery, *Giambologna: The Complete Sculpture* (Oxford: Phaidon, Christie's Limited, 1987), 154; www.liripipe.com/travel/index.cgi#.

44. da Udine, *Turkey,* Angelo Bronzino, *Abundance* (Pitti Palace, Florence), Willem Pannemaker, *Tapestry with Garden* (Kunsthistorisches Museum, Vienna), and Francisco Mingucci, *Barchetto,* (Vatican Biblioteca), all in Eiche, *Presenting the Turkey,* 14, 71, 16, 72, 19, 21, 23.

45. Ibid., 68.

46. Roy Strong, *Feast: A History of Grand Eating* (New York: Harcourt, 2002), 146.

47. Vincenzo Cervio, *Il Trinciante* (1593, repr. Bologne: Arnaldo Forni Editore, 1980), 25–28.

48. Jacques Vonlett, *La vraye mettode de bien trencher tant à la l'Itaeinne qu' à la main* (1647), as cited in Ken Albala, "The Banquet: A Culinary History of Europe, 1520–1660" (forthcoming).

49. P. Gyllius, *Ex Aeluani historia per P. Gyllium* (Lyon: Seb. Gryphius, 1533), 456.

50. Pierre Belon du Mans, *L'histoire de la nature des oyseaux* (Paris: G. Cauellat, 1555), 248–49; Conrad Gesneri, *Historiæ animalium* (Zurich: Apud Christoph. Froschouerum, 1555), 464.

51. Ulysse Aldrovandi, *Ornithologiae hoc est, de avibus historiae,* pt. 2 (Bononiae: Apud Io: Francisain de Franciscis Senensem, 1599–1603), 2: 41.

52. P. von Möller, *Strödda utkast rörande svenska jordbtukets historia* (Stockholm: 1881), as cited in Schorger, *The Wild Turkey,* 112; R. D. Crawford, "Introduction to Europe and Diffusion of Domesticated Turkeys from America," *Archivos de Zootecnia* 41 (1992): 311.

53. Reay Tannahill, *Food in History,* rev. ed. (New York: Crown, 1988), 212.

54. John Bell, *Travels from St. Petersburg, in Russia, to Diverse Parts of Asia* (Glasgow: Printed for the author by R. and A. Foulis, 1763), 1:124; Schorger, *The Wild Turkey*, 743.

55. Tannahill, *Food in History*, 212.

56. John Bardot, "A Description of the Coast of North and South Guinea," in *A Collection of Voyages and Travels*, edited by Awmsham Churchill (London: J. Walthoe et al., 1732), 5:217.

57. John Beckmann, *A History of Inventions and Discoveries*, 3d ed., translated by William Johnston (London: Printed for Longman, 1817), 2:367.

58. T. Webster, and Mrs. Parkes, *An Encyclopedia of Domestic Economy* (New York: Harper and Brothers, 1848), 418.

59. Alfred W. Crosby Jr., *The Columbian Exchange: Biological and Cultural Consequences of 1492* (Westport: Greenwood Press, 1973); Immanuel Wallerstein, *The Modern World-System I: Capitalist Agriculture and the Origins of the European World-Economy in the Sixteenth Century* (New York: Academic Press, 1974), 41–44.

Chapter 3: The English Turkey

1. Alfred Newton, *A Dictionary of Birds* (London: A. and C. Black, 1896), 994; Edward Avery McIlhenny, *The Wild Turkey and Its Hunting* (New York: Doubleday-Page, 1914), 44; Morley A. Jull, "Fowls of Forest and Stream Tamed by Man," *National Geographic Magazine* 57 (Mar. 1930): 366; A. W. Schorger, *The Wild Turkey: Its History and Domestication* (Norman: University of Oklahoma Press, 1966), 16.

2. Jull, "Fowls of Forest and Stream," 366.

3. E. Henderson, "The Turkey," in *Turkeys and How to Grow Them*, edited by Herbert Myrick (New York: Orange Judd, 1897), 3, 4.

4. James C. Clark, ed. and trans., *Codex Mendoza: The Mexican Manuscript Known as the Collection of Mendoza and Preserved in the Bodleian Library, Oxford* (London: Waterlow and Sons, Limited, 1938), 1:58; Reay Tannahill, *Food in History*, rev. ed. (New York: Crown, 1988), 211.

5. John Cook Bennett, *The Poultry Book* (Boston: Phillips, Sampson, 1850), 106.

6. John Leland, *Joannis Lelandi antiquarii de rebvs britannicis collectanea* (London: Gvl. & J. Richardson, 1770), 38.

7. Joan Thirsk, ed., *The Agrarian History of England and Wales*, vol. 4: *1500–1640*. (Cambridge: Cambridge University Press, 1967), 44.

8. Hugh Platt, *The Jewell House of Art and Nature* (London: Printed by P. Short, 1594), 1:13.

9. P. E. Jones, *The Worshipful Company of Poulters of the City of London: A Short History*, 2d ed. (London: Oxford University Press, 1965), 82 (quotation), 116, 139–43.

10. Thomas Tusser, *Five Hundred Pointes of Good Husbandrie*, edited by W. Payne and Sidney J. Herrtage (London: Published for the English Dialect Society by Trübner, 1878), 70.

11. A.W., *A Booke of Cookrye* (London: Ednard Allde, 1584), 20.

12. Thomas Dawson, *The Good Huswives Iewell* (London: Iohn Wolfe, 1587), 13.

13. Henry Wadsworth Longfellow, *Hyperion, a Romance* (New York: S. Colman, 1839), vii.

14. Gervase Markham, *Cheape and Good Husbandry* (London: Roger Jackson, 1614),

126 (quotation); J[ohn] Mortimer, *The Whole Art of Husbandry* (London: Printed by J. H. for H. Mortlock, 1708), 197; John Laurence, *A New System of Agriculture, Being a Complete Body of Husbandry and Gardening* (London: T. Woodward, 1726), 152; Charles Millington, *The Housekeeper's Domestic Library; or, New Universal Family Instructor* (London: F. Flint, 1810), 361.

15. Gervase Markham, *The English Hus-wife,* in *The English Housewife,* edited by Michael R. Best (1615, repr. Kingston: McGill-Queen's University Press, 1986), 123.

16. William Rabisha, *The Whole Body of Cookery Dissected* (London: George Calvert and Ralph Simpson, 1682), 94; T. Hall, *The Queen's Royal Cookery,* 2d ed. (London: Printed for C. Bates et al., 1713), 121–22.

17. E. S. Dallas, *Kettner's Book of the Table: A Manual of Cookery, Practical, Theoretical, Historical* (London: Dulau, 1877), 101.

18. Markham, *The English Hus-wife,* 79 (boiled), 88 (roasted), 89 (sauce), 92 (sauces), 96 (carbonated and pastry).

19. Pieter Claesz, *Laid Table with a Turkey Pie* (Rijksmuseum, Amsterdam), in Sabine Eiche, *Presenting the Turkey: The Fabulous Story of a Flamboyant and Flavourful Bird* (Florence: Centro Di, 2004), 45.

20. François Pierre de la Varenne, *Le cuisinier françois* (Paris: Chez Pierre David, 1652), 132, 135, 141, 144, 106, 152, 203; [François Pierre] de la Varenne, *The French Cook,* 2d ed. (London: Printed for Charles Adams, 1654), 26, 30–31, 34, 38, 42, 51, 63, 65–66, 38; Karen Hess, "Historical Notes and Commentary," in Mary Randolph, *The Virginia House-wife,* facsimile (Columbia: University of South Carolina Press, 1984), 257.

21. La Varenne, *The French Cook,* 9, 20.

22. W. M.'s *The Queen's Closet Opened* was a trilogy. These two recipes appear in the first volume entitled *The Compleat Cook* (London: E. B. for *Nath. Brook,* at the Angel in *Cornhill,* 1656), 64, 106.

23. Kenelme Digbie, *The Closet of the Eminently Learned Sir Kenelme Digby* (London: E.C., 1660), 253.

24. John Evelyn, *Acetaria: A Discourse of Sallets* (London: B. Tooke, 1699), 27–28.

25. William Salmon, *The Family-Dictionary; or, Household Companion* (London: H. Rhodes, 1705), 330–32.

26. T. Hall, *The Queen's Royal Cookery,* 2d ed. (London: Printed for C. Bates, etc., 1713), 121–22.

27. Robert May, *The Accomplished Cook* (London: Obadiah Blegrave, 1685), 217–18.

28. May, *The Accomplished Cook,* 214–16.

29. Charles Carter, *The Complete Practical Cook; or, A New System of the Whole Art and Mystery of Cookery* (London: W. Meadows, 1730), 55–56; Susannah Carter, *The Frugal Housewife; or, Complete Woman Cook; Wherein the Art of Dressing All Sorts of Viands Is Explained in Upwards of Five Hundred Approved Receipts* (New York: Printed and sold by G. and R. Waite, no. 64, Maidenlane, 1803), n.p.; [Lafcadio Hearn], *La Cuisine Creole: A Collection of Culinary Recipes from Leading Chefs and Noted Creole Housewives, Who Have Made New Orleans Famous for Its Cuisine,* 2d ed. (New Orleans, F. F. Hansell and Bro., 1885), 74.

30. William Rabisha, *The Whole Body of Cookery Dissected* (London: George Calvert and Ralph Simpson, 1682), n.p.

31. Rabisha, *The Whole Body of Cookery Dissected,* 94, 223–24.

32. Ibid., 114–15.

33. "The Forme of Cury," in Richard Warner, *Antiquitates Culinaræ; or, Curious Tracts Relating to the Culinary Affairs of the Old English* (London: R. Blamine, 1791), 16.

34. The first reference to a "turkey drive" in England is indirect. A contemporary observer, Bulstrode Whitlocke, reported that after the battle of Dunbar in 1650 Cromwell ended up with 5,100 Scottish prisoners who were driven "like turkies" down the road. Of those prisoners, 1,600 died. John Lingard, *The History of England from the First Invasion of the Romans to the Accession of William and Mary in 1688* (London: J. Mawman, 1819–30), 316; William Ellis, *The Country Housewife's Family Companion,* introduction by Malcolm Thick (1750, repr. Devon, U.K.: Prospect Books, 2000), 218–19; B.E., *A New Dictionary of the Terms Ancient and Modern of the Canting Crew* (London: W. Hawes, P. Gilbourne and W. Davis, 1690?).

35. Daniel Defoe, *A Tour through England and Wales* (London: Everyman Edition, 1928), 1:59–60.

36. Judy Urquhart, *Animals on the Farm: Their History from the Earliest* (London: MacDonald, 1983), 162–63.

37. Isabella Beeton, *Book of Household Management* (London: S. O. Beeton, 1861), 497.

38. Mary Kettilby, *A Collection of above Three Hundred Receipts in Cookery, Physick and Surgery,* 2d ed. (London: Printed for Mary Kettilby, 1719), 205.

39. Hess, "Historical Notes and Commentary," 292.

40. Thomas Blount, *Glossographia,* 4th ed. ([London]: Printed by T. Newcomb, sold by R. Boulter, 1674), n.p.

41. *The Family Receipt-Book; or, Universal Repository* (London: Printed for the Editors, n.d. [ca. 1810]), 6–7.

42. Mary Kettilby, *A Collection of above Three Hundred Receipts in Cookery, Physick and Surgery,* 4th ed. (London: Printed for Mary Kettilby, 1728), 205.

43. Charles Carter, *The Complete Practical Cook: or, A New System of the Whole Art and Mystery of Cookery* (London: W. Meadows, 1730), 55–59, 85, 92, 116, 157.

44. E. Smith, *The Compleat Housewife; or, Accomplished Gentlewoman's Companion,* 15th ed. (London: R. Ware, etc., 1753), 6, 22, 25, 40, 83.

45. Hannah Glasse, *The Art of Cookery Made Plain and Easy* (London: Published by the Author, 1747), 5, 7, 18, 34, 35, 36, 62, 129, 37.

46. Bartolomeo Scappi, *Opera Dell' Arte del Cucinare; Presentazione di Giancarlo Roversi* (1570, repr. Bologne: Arnaldo Forni Editore, 1981), ch. 115, 50 (back). Thanks to Ken Albala for pointing out this recipe.

47. Robert May, *The Accomplished Cook* (London: Obadiah Blegrave, 1685), 214.

48. Vincent LaChapelle, *The Modern Cook* (London: Nicolas Prevost, 1733), 138.

49. Dallas, *Kettner's Book of the Table,* 464.

50. Richard Bradley, *The Country Housewife and Lady's Director,* 6th ed. (London: D. Browne, 1736), 179.

51. Carter, *The Frugal Housewife,* 33.

52. Glasse, *Art of Cookery Made Plain and Easy,* 73.

53. Elizabeth Raffald, *The Experienced English Housewife* (Manchester: Printed by J. Harrop, for the Author, 1769), 129–30.

54. John Madden, "Turkduckens and Touchdowns," Thanksgiving Classics, Nov. 20, 2001; Dan Sewell, "A Holiday Hybrid of Birds When Plain Turkey Just Isn't Enough," *Augusta* (Ga.) *Chronicle,* Nov. 17, 1997, n.p.

55. Launcelot Sturgeon, *Essays, Moral, Philosophical, and Stomachical of the Important Science of Good-Living,* 2d ed. (London: G. and B. Whittaker, 1823), 39–40.

56. Beeton, *Book of Household Management,* 506 (quotation), 954–55; Margaret Visser, *The Rituals of Dinner: The Origins, Evolution, Eccentricities and Meaning of Table Manners* (New York: Penguin Books, 1991), 240–41.

57. Alexis Soyer, *The Modern Housewife or Méagère* (New York: D. Appleton, 1850), 147; Anne Cobbett, *The English Housekeeper,* 6th ed. (London: A. Cobbett, 1851), 168; Mrs. A. M. Collins, *The Great Western Cook Book; or, Table Receipts Aaapted to Western Housewifery* (New York: A. S. Barnes, 1857), 89; Mrs. Elizabeth Ellet, *The Practical Housekeeper: An Cyclopedia of Domestic Economy* (New York: Stringer and Townsend, 1857), 357; Theodore Francis Garrett, ed., *The Encyclopædia of Practical Cookery: A Complete Dictionary of All Pertaining to the Art of Cookery and Table Service* (London: L. Upcott Gill, Bazaar Buildings, W. C., [1890]), 7:448–49; *Cassell's New Universal Cookery Book* (London: Cassell, 1906), 945.

58. Sturgeon, *Essays, Moral, Philosophical,* 149–56.

59. Thomas Tusser, *Five Hundred Pointes of Good Husbandrie,* edited by W. Payne and Sidney J. Herrtage (London: Published for the English Dialect Society by Trübner, 1878), 70.

60. John Gay, *Fables* (London: J. F. and C. Rivington, 1792), pt. 1: 39.

61. Jones, *The Worshipful Company of Poulters of the City of London,* 47–48.

62. Susan M. Rossi-Wilcox, *Dinner for Dickens: The Culinary History of Mrs. Charles Dickens's Menu Books* (Devon, U.K.: Prospect Books, 2005); Charles Dickens, *A Christmas Carol* (Glasgow: George Routledge and Sons, 1843), 244.

63. "Lady Maria Clutterbuck" [Catherine Thomson Dickens], *What Shall We Have for Dinner? Satisfactorily Answered by Numerous Bills of Fare for from Two to Eighteen Persons* (London: Bradbury and Evans, 1851); Rossi-Wilcox, *Dinner for Dickens,* 262.

64. Beeton, *Book of Household Management,* 506; Marianne Mays and Sam Mays, *The Twelve Days of Christmas Turkey* (Glenageary, Ire.: Sugar Loaf, 1973).

Chapter 4: The Call of the Wild Turkey

1. Theodor De Bry, *Americae* (Frankfort: Gedruckt durch M. Becker, 1599), pt. 2, plate 5.

2. "Sir George Peckham's True Report of the Late Discoueries," pt. 2, in *The Principal Navigations, Voyages, Traffiques and Discoveries of the English Nation,* edited by Richard Hakluyt (Edinburgh: E. and G. Goldsmid, 1889), 13:271.

3. Thomas Wentworth Higginson, *Life of Francis Higginson, First Minister in the Massachusetts Bay Colony, and Author of "New England's Plantation"* (1630, repr. New York: Dodd, Mead, 1891), 101.

4. Charles Francis Adams Jr., "The Maypole of Merrymount," *Atlantic Monthly* 39 (May 1877): 566.

5. Adriaen van der Donck, *A Description of the New Netherlands,* edited by Thomas F. O'Donnell (Syracuse: Syracuse University Press, 1968), 50.

6. William Byrd, *William Byrd's Natural History of Virginia; or, The Newly Discovered Eden,* translated and edited by Richmond Croom Beatty and William J. Mulloy (Richmond, Va.: Dirtz Press, 1940), 71.

7. John Lawson, *The History of Carolina; Containing an Exact Description of the Inlets, Havens, Corn, Fruits, and Other Vegetables of That Country* (London: Printed for W. Taylor and J. Baker, 1714), 27; John Brickell, *The Natural History of North-Carolina* (1737, repr. New York: Johnson, 1969), 181–82.

8. Adams, "The Maypole of Merrymount," 566; Richard Blome, *The Present State of His Majesties Isles and Territories in America* (London: H. Clark, for D. Newman, 1687), 187.

9. "Narrative of a Voyage to Maryland, 1705–1706," *American Historical Review* 12 (Jan. 1906): 330–31.

10. John Clayton, "Mr. John Clayton, Rector of Crofton at Wake-Field, His Letter to the Royal Society," *Philosophical Transactions* 17 (1693): 992.

11. John Josselyn, *New-England Rarities Discovered* (1672, repr. Boston: Massachusetts Historical Society, 1972), 8–9.

12. "Narrative of a Voyage to Maryland," 330–31.

13. Christian Schultz, *Travels on an Inland Voyage through the States of New York, Pennsylvania, Virginia, Ohio, Kentucky and Tennessee, and through the Territories of Indiana, Louisiana, Mississippi, and New-Orleans; Performed in the Years 1807 and 1808* (New York: Printed by Isaac Riley, 1810), 122–23.

14. James Adair, *Adair's History of the American Indians,* edited by Samuel Cole Williams (New York: Promontory Press, 1986), 387.

15. William Wood, *New Englands Prospect; a True, Lively and Experimentall Description of That Part of America Commonly Called Nevv England* (London: Printed by T. Cotes for I. Bellamie, 1634), 28–29.

16. John Bakeless, *America as Seen by Its First Explorers: The Eyes of Discovery* (New York: Dover Publications, 1989), 267.

17. Van der Donck, *A Description of the New Netherlands,* 50.

18. Pierre Esprit Radisson, *Voyages of Peter Esprit Radisson, Being an Account of His Travels and Experiences among the North American Indians, from 1652 to 1684* (New York: B. Franklin [1967]), 152.

19. John F. D. Smyth, *A Tour in the United States of America* (London: For G. Robinson et al., 1784), 1:337.

20. C.C., "The Prairie," *Southern Literary Messenger; Devoted to Every Department of Literature and the Fine Arts* 2 (May 1836): 354.

21. Father Sébastien Rasles to his Brother, dated Oct. 12, 1723, in *The Jesuit Relations and Allied Documents: Travels and Explorations of the Jesuit Missionaries in New France, 1610–1791: The Original French, Latin, and Italian Texts, with English Translations and Notes,* edited by Reuben Gold Thwaites (Cleveland: Burrows Brothers, 1900), 67: 169.

22. Henri Joutel, *A Journal of the Last Voyage Perform'd by Monsr. De La Sale* (London: A. Bell, 1714), 82.

23. Georges-Henri-Victor Collot, *A Journey in North America, Containing a Survey of the Countries Watered by the Mississippi, Ohio, Missouri, and Other Affluing Rivers*, 2 vols. (Paris: Printed for Arthus Bertrand, 1826), 1:128.

24. "Narrative of a Voyage to Maryland," 330–31.

25. Robert Beverly, *History and Present State of Virginia* (London: Printed for R. Parker, 1705), 59.

26. H. H. Lane, "Oklahoma," in *Naturalist's Guide to the America*, edited by Victor E. Shelford (Baltimore: Williams and Wilkins, 1926), 496.

27. Robert M. Wright, *Dodge City, the Cowboy Capitol and the Great Southwest* (Wichita: Wichita Eagle Press, [1913]), 71.

28. "The Rancho," *New Orleans Picayune*, Nov. 19, 1859, 1.

29. H. L. Bingham, "A Thousand Wild Turkeys," *Forest and Stream* 11 (1878): 410–11.

30. J. Elgin, "Christmas Dinner on the Upper Brazos in 1872," West Texas Historical Association *Year Book* 14 (1938): 86.

31. A. W. Schorger, *The Wild Turkey; Its History and Domestication* (Norman: University of Oklahoma Press, 1966), 61.

32. Thomas Hariot, *A Briefe and True Report of the New Found Land of Virginia* (Frankfurt am Main: De Bry, 1590), 20.

33. William Strachey, *Historie of the Travaile into Virginia Britania* (London: Printed for the Hakluyt Society, 1849), 125.

34. Byrd, *William Byrd's Natural History of Virginia*, 71.

35. S. P. Hildreth, "Biographical Sketch of Isaac Williams," *American Pioneer* 1 (1842): 345.

36. John Heckewelder, "Notes of Travel . . . to Gnadenhuetten, 1797," *Pennsylvania Magazine of History and Biography* 10 (1886): 146.

37. Joseph Doddridge, *Notes on the Settlement and Indian Wars of the Western Parts of Virginia and Pennsylvania from 1763 to 1783, Inclusive* (Wellsburgh, Va.: Printed at the Office of the Gazette, for the Author, 1824), 101.

38. John H. Jenkins, *Recollections of Early Texas: The Memories of John Holland Jenkins*, 3d ed. (Austin: University of Texas Press, 1958), 8.

39. W. A. Covington, *History of Colquitt County* (Spartanburg, S.C.: Reprint Co., 1980), 63.

40. Jean Anthelme Brillat-Savarin, *The Physiology of Taste; or, Meditations on Transcendental Gastronomy*, translated by M. K. F. Fisher (Washington: Counterpoint, 1986), 71, 77–78.

41. Brillat-Savarin, *The Physiology of Taste*, 350.

42. John James Audubon, *The Birds of America* (New York: J. J. Audubon; Philadelphia: J. B. Chevalier, 1840–44), 5:42.

43. Todd S. Goodholme, ed., *Goodholme's Domestic Cyclopedia of Practical Information*, 2d ed. (New York: Charles Scribner's Sons, 1889), 541.

44. Auguste Levasseur, *Lafayette in America in 1824 and 1825*, translated by J. D. Godman (Philadelphia: Carey and Lea, 1829), 2:10, 2:120; C. N. Bement, *The American Poul-*

terer's Companion (New York: Saxton and Miles, 1845), 215; *American Farmer,* May 6, 1825, 55; "The Herdbook of John Hartwell Cocke," July 20, 1825, Papers of the Cocke Family, box 1 (1777–1866), Alderman Library, University of Virginia, as cited in Richard E. Powell, *Turkey Husbandry in Virginia and the Chesapeake Region, 1750–1830,* Colonial Williamsburg Research Report 327 (1992), 17.

45. City Hotel Menu, Feb. 18, 1842, in honor of Charles Dickens, in Lately Thomas, *Delmonico's: A Century of Splendor* (Boston: Houghton, Mifflin, 1967), 110.

46. Charles Ranhofer, *The Epicurean* (New York: R. Ranhofer, 1894), 629.

47. Lia Rand, *The Philosophy of Cooking Comprising Forty-One Explanatory Letters and Three Hundred and Ten Foreign Recipes; French, German and Italian, Adapted for the American Home Table* ([Brooklyn]: Published for the Author, 1894), 101.

48. G. Fay, "The Wild Turkey," *Harper's Weekly* 28 (1884): 848.

49. John. R. Cook, *The Border and the Buffalo: An Untold Story of the Southwest Plains; the Bloody Border of Missouri and Kansas, the Story of the Slaughter of the Buffalo* (Topeka: Crane, 1907), 114.

50. Philadelphia Museum of Art. See www.pafa.org/paintingsPreview.jsp?id=975.

51. Alexander Wilson, *American Ornithology; or, The Natural History of Birds of the United States* (Philadelphia: Bradford and Inskeep, 1808–14).

52. Richard Rhodes, *John James Audubon: The Making of an American* (New York: Alfred A. Knopf, 2004), 4–6, 11–12.

53. Rhodes, *John James Audubon;* Audubon, *The Birds of America,* 5:42.

54. John James Audubon, *The Birds of America; from Original Drawings* (London: Published by the Author, 1827–38); John James Audubon, *Ornithological Biography; or, An Account of the Habits of the Birds of the United States of America; Accompanied by Descriptions of the Objects Represented in the Work Entitled the Birds of America, and Interspersed with Delineations of American Scenery and Manners* (Edinburgh: A. Black, 1831–49); Audubon, *The Birds of America.*

55. Audubon, *The Birds of America,* 5:55.

56. Ibid., 5:42–43.

57. Ibid., 5:45.

58. Ibid., 5:44–45.

59. Ibid., 5:47–48.

60. Ibid., 5:47–48.

61. Ibid., 5:48–49.

62. Eliza Leslie, *The Lady's Receipt-book: A Useful Companion for Large or Small Families* (Philadelphia: Carey and Hart, 1847), 100–103.

63. Pierre Blot, *Hand-Book of Practical Cookery* (New York: D. Appleton, 1869), 86–87.

64. Marion Harlan, *Common Sense in the Household: A Manual of Practical Housewifery* (New York: Charles Scribner's Sons, 1871), 179–80.

65. Marion Cabell Tyree, ed., *Housekeeping in Old Virginia* (New York: G. W. Carleton, 1877), 92.

66. [Lafcadio Hearn], *La Cuisine Creole: A Collection of Culinary Recipes from Leading Chefs and Noted Creole Housewives, Who Have Made New Orleans Famous for its Cuisine,* 2d ed. (New Orleans: F. F. Hansell & Bro., 1885), 72.

67. *Aunt Babette's Cook Book: Foreign and Domestic Receipts for the Household: A Valuable Collection of Receipts and Hints for the Housewife, Many of Which Are Not to Be Found Elsewhere* (Cincinnati: Bloch Pub. and Print, 1889), 82–83; François Tanty, *La Cuisine Francaise: French Cooking for Every Home, Adapted to American Requirements* (Chicago: Baldwin, Ross, 1893), 126; Commissary General of Subsistence, *Manual for Army Cooks* (Washington: Government Printing Office, 1896), 114.

68. Isabella Kruse Schaffner, *Turkeys in Texas: A History of the Turkey Industry in Texas* (San Antonio: Naylor, 1954), 5.

69. William T. Hornaday, *Our Vanishing Wild Life, Its Extermination and Preservation* (New York: C. Scribner's Sons, 1913), 4.

70. Van der Donck, *A Description of the New Netherlands,* 50.

71. Wood, *Nevv Englands Prospect,* 29.

72. Robert Beverly, *The History of Virginia, in Four Parts* (Richmond: J. W. Randolph, 1855), 256.

73. John Oldmixon, *The British Empire in America* (London: J. Nicholson, B. Tooke, R. Parker, and R. Smith, 1708), 312.

74. Schorger, *The Wild Turkey,* 53.

75. Audubon, *The Birds of America,* 5:52–53.

76. Ibid., 5:52.

77. Josselyn, *New-England Rarities Discovered,* 8–9.

78. Doddridge, *Notes on the Settlement and Indian Wars,* 69.

79. Audubon, *The Birds of America,* 5:42.

80. Bradford Torrey, "The Bird of Thanksgiving," *Youth's Companion,* Nov. 29, 1888, 605.

81. Thomas F. De Voe, *The Market Assistant* (New York: Hurd and Houghton, 1867), 58–59.

82. Robert Jennings, *Sheep, Swine, and Poultry* (Philadelphia: J. E. Potter, 1864), 66.

83. Women's Centennial Committees of the International Exhibition, *National Cookery Book* (Philadelphia: Women's Centennial Executive Committee, 1876), 85.

84. City Hotel Menu, Feb. 18, 1842, in honor of Charles Dickens.

85. Gaston Fay, "The Wild Turkey," *Harper's Weekly,* Dec. 20, 1884, 848.

86. George Enty, "The Wild Turkey," in *Turkeys and How to Grow Them,* edited by Herbert Myrick (New York: Orange Judd, 1897), 5.

87. "Big Parade of the Turkey; Thanksgiving Bird Is Becoming Scarce," *New York Times,* Nov. 21, 1926, 6.

88. Henry S. Mosby and Charles O. Handley, *The Wild Turkey in Virginia: Its Status, Life History and Management* (Richmond: Pittman-Robertson Projects, Division of Game Commission of Game and Inland Fisheries, 1943), 15; Schorger, *The Wild Turkey,* 12; John W. Aldrich, "Historical Background," in *The Wild Turkey and its Management,* edited by Oliver H. Hewett (Washington: The Wildlife Society, 1967), 12; James Earl Kennamer, Mary Kennamer, and Ron Brenneman, "History," in *The Wild Turkey: Biology and Management,* edited by James G. Dickson (Mechanicsburg, Pa.: Stackpole Books, 1992), 11.

89. Henry S. Mosby, "The Status of the Wild Turkey in 1974," *Proceedings of the National Wild Turkey Symposium* 3 (1975): 22–26.

90. Harold L. Blakley, "Status and Management of the Eastern Wild Turkey," *American Wildlife* 30 (1941): 139–40.

91. Janet Vorwald Dohner, *The Encyclopedia of Endangered Livestock and Poultry Breeds* (New Haven: Yale University Press, 2001), 443.

92. Telephone interview with James G. Dickson, Jan. 10, 2005.

Chapter 5: The Well-dressed Turkey

1. Ralph Hamor, *A True Discourse of the Present Estate of Virginia* (London: Iohn Beale for W. Welby, 1615), 23; Francis Wyatt, "Proclamation against Stealing of Beasts and Birds of Domesticall and Tame Nature," Sept. 21, 1623, in *Records of the Virginia Company* (Washington: Government Printing Office, 1935), 4:283–84.

2. "Extract of a Letter of Captain Thomas Yong to Sir Toby Matthew, 1634," in *Narratives of Early Maryland, 1633–1684,* edited by Clayton Coleman Hall (New York: Charles Scribner's Sons, 1910), 60.

3. "Records of the Governor and Company of the Massachusetts Bay in New-England," in Alexander Young, *Chronicles of the First Planters of the Colony of Massachusetts Bay* (1629, repr. Boston: Charles C. Little and James Brown, 1846), 42–43.

4. Robert Pringle to Gedney Clarke, Dec. 20, 1744, in *The Letterbook of Robert Pringle,* edited by Walter B. Edgar (Columbia: Published for the South Carolina Historical Society and the South Carolina Tricentennial Commission by the University of South Carolina Press, 1972), 2:787–89; John Mair, *Book-keeping Modernized,* 1784, in Richard E. Powell, *Turkey Husbandry in Virginia and the Chesapeake Region, 1750–1830,* Colonial Williamsburg Research Report 327 (1992), 6.

5. John Cook Bennett, *The Poultry Book* (Boston: Phillips, Sampson, 1850), 18.

6. Le Page du Pratz, *The History of Louisiana* (London: Printed for T. Becket, 1774), 276–77; Bonington Moubray [John Lawrence], *A Practical Treatise on Breeding, Rearing and Fattening All Kinds of Domestic Poultry, Pheasants, Pigeons, and Rabbits,* 5th ed. (London: Sherwood, Jones, 1824), 27; Charles Egbert Craddock, "The Prophet of the Great Smoky Mountains," *Atlantic Monthly* 55 (Jan. 1885): 8.

7. Edwin Valentine Mitchell, *It's an Old New England Custom* (New York: Vanguard Press, [1946]), 26.

8. Fanny Field, *Practical Turkey Raising: Turkeys for Market and Turkeys for Profit* (Chicago: R. B. Mitchell, 1887), 22; Herbert Myrick, ed., *Turkeys and How to Grow Them* (New York: Orange Judd, 1897), 82–84.

9. S. W. Hamilton, *Profitable Turkey Management,* 8th ed. (Cayuga: Beacon Milling, 1951), 90.

10. William Tatham, *Essay on the Culture and Commerce of Tobacco* (London: Vernor and Hood, 1800), as cited in Powell, *Turkey Husbandry in Virginia and the Chesapeake Region,* 6.

11. John F. D. Smyth, *A Tour in the United States of America* (London: Printed for G. Robinson, 1784), 2:132.

12. "On the Worm," *American Farmer,* Feb. 23, 1821, 383.

13. James Fenimore Cooper, *The Spy: A Tale of the Neutral Ground* (New York: Wiley and Halsted, 1821), 2:92–93.

14. J. S. Skinner, "Use of Turkies at the South," *The Sun,* Feb. 1, 1844, 4; *Debow's Review* 12 (June 1852): 656; *Gardener's Monthly* 19 (June 1877): 175.

15. W. A. Browning, *A Complete System of Raising Turkeys, Hens, Geese &c* (Norwich, [Conn.]: Gordon Wilcox, 1873), 2.

16. "Raising Turkeys," *Christian Recorder*, July 25, 1863, n.p.

17. S. W. Fletcher Jr., *Pennsylvania Agriculture and Country Life, 1640–1840* (Harrisburg: Pennsylvania Historical and Museum Commission, 1950–55), 1:409–10; Julius Friedrich Sachse, *The Wayside Inns on the Lancaster Roadside between Philadelphia and Lancaster* (Lancaster: [Press of the New Era Printing Company], 1912), 200.

18. Edgar Gilbert, *History of Salem, N.H.* (Concord: Rumford Printing, 1907), 325.

19. Andrew W. Cain, *History of Lumpkin County* (Atlanta: Stein Printing, 1932), 54.

20. Wilma Dykeman, *The French Broad* (New York: Rinehart, 1955), 139–40; I. F. King, "The Coming and Going of Ohio Droving," *Ohio Archaeological and Historical Society Publication* 17 (1908): 248.

21. George A. Bruffey, *Eighty-one Years in the West* (Butte: Butte Miner Printers, 1925), 27.

22. Helen Walker Linsenmeyer, *From Fingers to Finger Bowls: A Sprightly History of California Cooking* (San Diego: Union-Tribune Publishing, 1972), 44.

23. J. F. Flagg, "A Philadelphia Forty-Niner," *Pennsylvania Magazine of History and Biography* 70 (1946): 417.

24. Frank C. Lockwood, *Arizona Characters* (Los Angeles: Times-Mirror Press, 1928), 142.

25. Stephen Powers, "The California Ranch," *Atlantic Monthly* 35 (June 1875): 693.

26. Morely A. Jull, "Fowls of the Forest and Stream Tamed by Man," *National Geographic* (Mar. 1930): 348.

27. "Manuscript Cookbook of D. Petre" (1705), 7, University of Pennsylvania Library, Rare Book and Ms Library Manuscripts Call Number Ms. Codex 624. Thanks to Mark Zanger for locating this source: http://dewey.library.upenn.edu/sceti/codex/public/PageLevel/index.cfm?WorkID=43&Page=88.

28. Gail Weesner, ed., *Mrs. Gardiner's Receipts from 1763* (Boston: Rowan Tree Press, 1984), 10–11, 13. It is likely that most of this manuscript was written after 1763. The published versions contain several errors, and the original manuscript has not been located.

29. Amelia Simmons, *American Cookery: A Facsimile of the First Edition with an Essay by Mary Tolford Wilson* (New York: Oxford University Press, 1958), 18.

30. Karen Hess, "Historical Glossary," in Mary Randolph, *The Virginia House-wife*, facsimile (Columbia: University of South Carolina Press, 1984), 81–83, 188–89, 257–58.

31. [N. K. M. Lee], *The Cook's Own Book and Housekeeper's Register* (Boston: Munroe and Francis, 1832), 64, 184, 192, 216–17, 227–28.

32. Eliza Leslie, *Domestic French Cookery, Chiefly Translated from Sulpice Barué* (Philadelphia: Carey and Hart, 1832), 48, 51.

33. Eliza Leslie, *Directions for Cookery; Being a System of the Art in Its Various Branches* (Philadelphia: E. L. Carey and A. Hart, 1837), 54.

34. James R. Mellow, *Nathaniel Hawthorne in His Times* (Boston: Houghton, Mifflin, 1980), 216.

35. Thomas Hamilton, *Men and Manners in America* (Edinburgh: W. Blackwood; London, T. Cadell, 1833), 242.

36. Adam Hodgson, *Remarks during a Journey through North America in the Years 1819, 1820, and 1821* (New York: Samuel Whiting, 1823), 106–7.

37. "Hodgson's Remarks on America," *North American Review* 18 (April 1824): 226.

38. George Henry Loskiel, *History of the Mission of the United Brethren among the Indians in North America* (London: Brethren's Society for the Furtherance of the Gospel, 1794), 91.

39. Charles Estienne, *Maison Rustique; or, The Coventrie Farme,* translated by Richard Surflet (London: Edm. Bollifant, 1600), 117.

40. Gervase Markham, *Cheape and Good Husbandry* (London: Roger Jackson, 1614), 127.

41. J[ohn] Mortimer, *The Whole Art of Husbandry* (London: Printed by J. H. for H. Mortlock, 1708), 197 (quotation); John Laurence, *A New System of Agriculture* (London: T. Woodward, 1726), 152.

42. Alexis Soyer, *The Pantropheon; or, History of Food, and Its Preparation, from the Earliest Ages of the World* (London: Simpkin, Marshall, 1853), 166.

43. *The History of Montgomery County, Ohio* (Chicago: W. H. Beers, 1882), 293; James Nourse, "Journey to Kentucky in 1775," *Journal of American History* 19 (1925): 127.

44. Israel Donalson, "Captivity of Israel Donalson," *American Pioneer* 1 (Dec. 1842): 430.

45. John Heckewelder, "Notes of Travel . . . to Gnadenhuetten, 1797," *Pennsylvania Magazine of History and Biography* 10 (1886): 146.

46. Sarah Brewer-Bonebright, *Reminiscences of Newcastle, Iowa, 1848* (Des Moines: Historical Department of Iowa, 1921), 76.

47. Charles Ranhofer, *The Epicurean* (New York: R. Ranhofer, 1894), 629.

48. Theodore Adolphu Babb, *In the Bosom of the Comanches* (Dallas: Press of John F. Worley Printing, 1912), 78; Brewer-Bonebright, *Reminiscences of New Castle, Iowa,* 77.

49. Thomas F. De Voe, *The Market Assistant* (New York: Hurd and Houghton, 1867), 406.

50. Carolyn J. Christman and Robert O. Hawes, *Birds of a Feather: Saving Turkeys from Extinction* (Pittsboro, N.C.: American Livestock Breeds Conservancy, 1999), 7.

51. Alexis Soyer, *The Modern Housewife or Méagère* (New York: D. Appleton, 1850), 147.

52. Mrs. A. M. Collins, *The Great Western Cook Book; or, Table Receipts Adapted to Western Housewifery* (New York: A. S. Barnes, 1857), 89; Elizabeth Fries Ellet, *The Practical Housekeeper: An Cyclopedia of Domestic Economy* (New York: Stringer and Townsend, 1857), 358.

53. "Turkey Braised," *Living Age,* Dec. 13, 1862, 505.

54. Ranhofer, *The Epicurean,* 180, 263, 354, 369, 379, 387, 629–35, 706, 744–45, 758–59, 800–801.

55. Elizabeth Ellicott Lea, *The Domestic Cookery,* 5th ed. (Baltimore: Cushings and Bailey, 1853), 30.

56. Pierre Blot, *Hand-Book of Practical Cookery* (New York: D. Appleton, 1869), 264.

57. [Alex Rivington], *Reminiscences of America in 1869* (London: S. Low, Son, and Marston, 1870), 66.

58. Marion Cabell Tyree, ed., *Housekeeping in Old Virginia* (New York: G. W. Carleton, 1877), 167.

59. Theodore Francis Garrett, ed., *The Encyclopædia of Practical Cookery: A Complete*

Dictionary of All Pertaining to the Art of Cookery and Table Service (London: L. Upcott Gill, Bazaar Buildings, W.C., [1890]), 7:657.

60. [Mrs. Alexander Orr Bradley], *Beverages and Sandwiches for Your Husband's Friends by One Who Knows* (New York: Brentano's, 1893).

61. Advertising card for "Huckins' Soups [and] Sandwich Meats," Boston, J. H. W. Huckins, 1893.

62. "Huckins' Soups Sandwich Meats"; Artemas Ward, *The Grocer's Encyclopedia* (New York: James Kempster, 1911), 503–4.

63. S[arah] T[yson] Rorer, *Sandwiches* (Philadelphia: Arnold, 1894), 14, 68–69.

64. Joseph Vachon, *Vachon's Book of Economical Soups and Entrees* (Chicago: Hotel Monthly Press, 1903), 54.

65. Mary L. Booth, *History of the City of New York, from Its Earliest Settlement to the Present Time* (New York: W. R. C. Clark, 1860), 192.

66. David Sturges Copeland, *History of Clarendon from 1810 to 1888* (Buffalo: Courier, 1889), 362.

67. Samuel H. Hammond and L. W. Mansfield, *Country Margins and Rambles of a Journalist* (New York: J. C. Derby, 1855), 64–65.

68. Sylvester Judd, *Margaret: A Tale of the Real and the Ideal, Blight and Bloom* (Boston: Jordan and Wiley, 1845), 84.

69. James Fenimore Cooper, *The Pioneers; or, The Sources of the Susquehanna, a Descriptive Tale* (New York: Charles Wiley, 1823), 237.

70. Cooper, *The Pioneers,* 238.

71. Charles Deas, *Turkey Shoot* (Virginia Museum of Fine Arts, Richmond); *Godey's Magazine and Lady's Book* 33 (Dec. 1846): 250.

72. William Walcutt, *The Turkey Shoot* (Smithsonian American Art Museum); Tompkins H. Matteson, *The Turkey Shoot* (New York State Historical Association, Cooperstown); John Whetten Ehninger, *Turkey Shoot* (Museum of Fine Arts, Boston).

73. Other artists who have depicted a turkey shoot include Julian Scot (1846–1901) and William Robinson Leigh (1866–1955).

74. George C. McWhorter, "The Holidays," *Harper's New Monthly Magazine* 32 (Jan. 1866): 168.

75. "Turkeys and Turkey Raising," *Poultry World* 8 (Nov. 1879): 343.

76. Karen Davis, *More Than a Meal: The Turkey in History, Myth, Ritual and Reality* (New York: Lantern Books, 2001), 108–9. The term *turkey shoot* has remained alive in the American language and evolved to mean a one-sided victory, particularly in war, that is easily accomplished. Historically, the term emerged during World War II. While protecting Americans landing in the Marianas Islands on June 19, 1944, fifty-eight American aircraft easily shot down an estimated three hundred Japanese planes in what was called the "Great Marianas Turkey Shoot." The term came up again during the Iraqi war in 1991, when coalition air forces lead by the United States destroyed an Iraqi column retreating from Kuwait City.

77. Lockwood Lyon Doty and A. J. H. Duganne, *A History of Livingston County, New York: from its Earliest Traditions, to Its Part in the War for Our Union: with an Account of the Seneca Nation of Indians, and Biographical Sketches of Earliest Settlers and Prominent Public Men* (Geneseo: Edward L. Doty, 1876), 676–77.

78. "Raffling for Turkeys," *Frank Leslie's Illustrated Newspaper,* Dec. 7, 1872, 205, 207.

79. *The Living Age,* Nov. 28, 1885, 576.

80. Lithograph by Sol Eytinge, *Harper's Weekly,* Jan. 3, 1874, f1; copy at the Library of Congress electronic database.

81. Mary L. Booth, *History of the City of New York, from Its Earliest Settlement to the Present Time* (New York: W. R. C. Clark, 1860), 192.

82. Frances Norton Mason, ed., *John Norton and Sons: Merchants of London and Virginia* (Richmond: Dietz Press, 1937), 142.

83. Christópher Marshall, *Extracts from the Diary of Christópher Marshall* (Albany: J. Munsell, 1877), 151.

84. Solomon Drowne, "Journal and Letters of Solomon Drowne on the Treaty of Fort Harmer," *Magazine of American History* 9 (1883): 287.

85. James Parker, "Excerpts from the Diary of James Parker of Shirley, Mass.," *New England Historical and Genealogical Register* 70 (July 1916): 212; James Parker, "Excerpts from the Diary of James Parker of Shirley, Mass.," *New England Historical and Genealogical Register* 70 (Oct. 1916): 295.

86. *The Violet: A Christmas and New Year's Gift, or Birthday Present* (Philadelphia: E. L. Carey and A. Hart, 1838), 36–52.

87. Eliza Leslie, *Miss Leslie's New Receipts for Cooking* (Philadelphia: T. B. Peterson and Brothers, 1854), 382–83, 388–89.

88. Mrs. J. C. Croly, *Jennie June's American Cookery Book* (New York: American News, 1866), 263; C. H. Cushing and B. Gray, comps., *The Kansas Home Cook-Book,* 5th ed. (Leavenworth, Kans.: Crew and Bro., 1886), 27–32, 303; Fannie Merritt Farmer, *Boston Cooking-School Cook Book* (Boston: Little, Brown, 1896), 520; Julia MacNair Wright et al., *Food for the Hungary: A Complete Manual of Household Duties Together with Bills of Fare for All Seasons by Marion Harland* ([New York]: L. M. Palmer, 1896), 443–48; *The Picayune Creole Cook Book,* 2d ed. (New Orleans: The Picayune, 1901), 43; Fannie Merritt Farmer, *What to Have for Dinner* (New York: Dodge Publishing, 1905), 109; *American Cookery* 19 (Nov. 1914): 299.

89. "Letter from Camp Anderson," *New York Times,* Jan. 3, 1862, 10.

90. John Faller as quoted in Kevin Rawlings, *We Were Marching on Christmas Day* (Baltimore: Toomey Press, 1997), 48.

91. Browning, *A Complete System of Raising Turkeys,* 27.

92. Frances Garvin Davenport, *Ante-Bellum Kentucky: A Social History, 1800–1860* (Oxford, Ohio: Mississippi Valley Press, 1943), 29.

93. *New York Times,* Dec. 19, 1915, as cited in Cathy Kaufman, "The Ideal Christmas Dinner," *Gastronomica* 4 (Fall 2004): 17.

Chapter 6: Hale's Turkey Tale

1. W. DeLoss Love Jr., *The Fast and Thanksgiving Days of New England* (Boston: Houghton, Mifflin, 1895), 464–510.

2. John Lothrop, *Scituate Church Records,* as in Love, *The Fast and Thanksgiving Days of New England,* 88–89.

3. Love, *The Fast and Thanksgiving Days of New England,* 76–77.

4. "From the South-Carolina Gazette, March 31: An Account of the Progress of the First Colony Sent to Georgia," *American Mercury,* May 17–24, 1733, 2 (first quotation); "Savannah," *New-England Journal,* Oct. 22, 1733, 2 (second quotation).

5. Joseph Plumb Martin, *Private Yankee Doodle; Being a Narrative of Some of the Adventures, Dangers, and Sufferings of a Revolutionary Soldier,* edited by George F. Scheer (Boston: Little, Brown, 1962), 100.

6. Shubael Breed, Norwich, Connecticut, to Mason Fitch Cogswell, New York, as quoted in Sandra L. Oliver, *Saltwater Foodways: New Englanders and Their Food at Sea and Ashore, in the Nineteenth Century* (Mystic: Mystic Seaport Museum, 1995), 242. An earlier description of a thanksgiving dinner is cited in Helen Evertson Smith, *Colonial Days and Ways as Gathered from Family Papers* (New York: Century, 1900). It was later frequently cited. The original diary that this selection was taken from has not been located, and several statements in the published description have led many observers to question the veracity of this account. It is more likely a late-nineteenth-century fictional creation.

7. "A Mouthful for the Poor!" *Continental Journal,* Dec. 7, 1786, 2.

8. *Norwich Weekly Register,* as quoted in the *Connecticut Courant,* Dec. 10, 1792, 2.

9. Samuel Griswold Goodrich, in *Yankee Life by Those Who Lived It,* edited by Barrows Mussey (New York: Stackpole Sons, [1937]), 133; "Thanksgiving-Day," *Norwich Packet,* Dec. 17, 1801, 3.

10. Jack Santino, *All Around the Year: Holidays and Celebration in American Life* (Urbana: University of Illinois Press, 1994), 168.

11. William Bentley, *The Diary of William Bentley, D.D.* (Salem: Essex Institute, 1905), 3:64, 3:202, 3:264 (quotation).

12. Edward E. Hale, *New England Boyhood* (New York: Cassell Publishing, 1893), 144–45.

13. Sarah Parker Goodwin, "Pleasant Memories," Memoirs of Sarah Parker Rice Goodwin, 1889, Goodwin Family Papers, Strawberry Banke Museum, Portsmouth, N.H., in Jane C. Nylander, *Our Own Snug Fireside: Images of the New England Home, 1760–1860* (New Haven: Yale University Press, 1994), 275.

14. U. P. Hedrick, *A History of Agriculture in the State of New York* (New York: New York State Agriculture Society, 1933), 217.

15. "Extracts from the Diary of Joseph Porter Dwinnell, 1837–1838," *Historical Collections of Danvers, Massachusetts* 26 (1938), entry for Nov. 31, 1837, in Nylander, *Our Own Snug Fireside,* 276.

16. Caroline Howard King, *When I Lived in Salem, 1822–1866* (Brattleboro: Stephen Day Press, 1937), 112.

17. Goodwin, "Pleasant Memories," 275.

18. Harriet Beecher Stowe, *Oldtown Folks* (Boston: Houghton, Osgood, 1878), 347.

19. *National Era,* Dec. 19, 1850, 203; *Christian Recorder,* Feb. 2, 1867.

20. Frederika Bremer, *The Homes of the New World: Impressions of America,* translated by Mary Howitt (New York: Harper and Brothers, 1853), 1:116.

21. Charles Mackay, *Life and Liberty in America; or, Sketches of a Tour in the United States and Canada, in 1857–8* (New York: Harper and Brothers, 1859), 66.

22. "A Merry Ode for Thanksgiving," *Norwich Packet,* Dec. 1, 1801, 4.

23. Lydia Maria Child, "The New-England Boys Song about Thanksgiving," *Flowers for Children* (New York: C. S. Francis; Boston: J. H. Francis, 1847), 2:25–28.

24. Plimoth Plantation at www.plimoth.org/Library/forefath.htm.

25. Daniel Webster, "Plymouth Oration," Dec. 22, 1820, as in *Daniel Webster, "the Completest Man,"* edited by Kenneth E. Shewmaker (Hanover: Dartmouth College and University Press of New England, 1990), 94–99.

26. William Apess, *Eulogy on King Philip, as Pronounced at the Odeon, in Federal Street, Boston* (Boston: The Author, 1836), in *On Our Own Ground: The Complete Writings of William Apess, a Pequot,* edited by Barry O'Connell (Amherst: University of Massachusetts Press, 1992), 286.

27. *A Relation or Iournall of the Beginning and Proceeding of the English Plantation Setled at Plimoth in New England* (London: John Bellamie, 1622), 60–65.

28. Alexander Young, *Chronicles of the Pilgrim Fathers of the Colony of Plymouth, from 1602–1625* (Boston: C. C. Little and J. Brown, 1841), 231.

29. William Bradford, *History of Plymouth Plantation* (Boston: Little, Brown, 1856). Bradford's journal was partially published along with Edward Winslow's letter in *The Journal of the Pilgrims at Plymouth, in New England, in 1620,* edited by G. B. Cheever (New York: J. Wiley, 1849).

30. William Bradford, *Of Plymouth Plantation 1620–1647,* edited by Samuel Eliot Morison (New York: Alfred A. Knopf, 1952), 90.

31. "Thanksgiving," *Gleason's Pictorial Drawing Room Companion,* Nov. 27, 1852, 345.

32. The "first Thanksgiving" was cited in historical works about the Pilgrims and New England. For instance, see Ashbel Steele, *Chief of the Pilgrims; or, The Life and Time of William Brewster* (Philadelphia: J. B. Lippincott, 1857), 270. It was also cited by immigrants who asked New Englanders how the Thanksgiving dinner arose. Bremer, *The Homes of the New World,* 1:116.

33. Mrs. S. J. Hale. *Northwood; or, A Tale of New England* (Boston: Bowles and Dearborn, 1827), 107–11.

34. Sarah Josepha Hale, *Northwood: or, Life North and South,* 2d ed. (New York: H. Long and Brother, 1852), iii; *Godey's Magazine* 41 (Dec. 1850): 326; Edward T. James, ed., *Notable American Women, 1607–1950* (Cambridge: Harvard University Press, 1971), 2:110–14.

35. Winslow Homer, *Thanksgiving Feast, Harper's Weekly,* Nov. 27, 1858, 760–61; Winslow Homer, *The Two Great Classes: Those Who have More Dinners Than Appetite,* and *Those Who Have More Appetite Than Dinners, Harper's Weekly,* Dec. 1, 1860, 760–61.

36. Hale, *Northwood; or, Life North and South,* iv; "Thanksgiving A New National Holiday," *Godey's Lady's Book* 61 (Sept. 1860): 271.

37. *Godey's Lady's Book* 59 (Nov. 1859): 466.

38. *Godey's Lady's Book* 63 (Nov. 1861): 441–42.

39. W. T. Crane, "Thanksgiving Festivities at Fort Pulaski, Georgia, Thursday, Nov. 27th, 1862," *Frank Leslie's Illustrated Weekly,* Jan. 3, 1863, 38.

40. Hale's 1863 letter to Seward has not been located. She reports in her letter to President Lincoln in 1863, however, that she had written to her "friend" Seward, requesting him to confer with the president. She again made reference to the 1863 letter to

Seward in a private letter to him in 1864 in which she again requested him to speak to the president. Hale then proceeded to recommend items for inclusion in the president's 1864 Thanksgiving proclamation. That implies that Seward was the one who prepared the previous Thanksgiving proclamation and Lincoln just signed it. Sarah J. Hale to Abraham Lincoln, Sept. 28, 1863, and Sarah J. Hale to William H. Seward, Oct. 9, 1864, "Making of America" data base, Library of Congress Web site.

41. *Godey's Lady's Book* 71 (Nov. 1865): 445.

42. L. H. Clark, *Military History of Wayne County, N.Y.: Military Register. Wayne County in the Civil War, 1861–1865* (Sodus, N.Y.: Lewis H. Clark, Hulett and Gaylord, 1883), 638.

43. Charles Cooper Nott, *Sketches in Prison Camps: A Continuation of Sketches of the War,* 2d ed. (New York: A. D. F. Randolph, 1865), 152.

44. *The New York Herald,* Jan. 3, 1864, as cited in Cathy Kaufman, "The Ideal Christmas Dinner," *Gastronomica* 4 (Fall 2004): 23–24.

45. George W. Blunt to Abraham Lincoln, Nov. 11, 1864, Abraham Lincoln Papers, Library of Congress.

46. *Report of the Committee on Providing a Thanksgiving Dinner for the Soldiers and Sailors, Presented December 14th, 1864* (New York: Union League Club, 1865), 3–4 (quotation), 25.

47. *Scene at Delmonico's Restaurant: Preparing Poultry to Be Cooked for Soldiers' Thanksgiving Dinner, Frank Leslie's Illustrated Weekly,* Dec. 3, 1864, 161.

48. *Report of the Committee on Providing a Thanksgiving Dinner for the Soldiers and Sailors,* 19.

49. Rutherford B. Hayes, *The Diary and Letters of Rutherford B. Hayes, Nineteenth President of the United States,* edited by Charles Richard Williams (Columbus: Ohio State Archeological and Historical Society, 1922), 2:540 (first quotation), 2:533 (second quotation).

50. Winslow Homer, *Thanksgiving Day in the Army, Harper's Weekly,* Dec. 3, 1864, 776–77, 780, 784.

51. *New York Times,* Nov. 24, 1864, 4.

52. *Southern Illustrated News,* Oct. 17, 1863, 120.

53. "Diary of Jason Niles," Southern Historical Collection, University of North Carolina, Chapel Hill, at http://docsouth.unc.edu/niles/nenu/html.

54. John Beauchamp Jones, *A Rebel War Clerk's Diary at the Confederate States Capital* (Philadelphia: J. B. Lippincott, 1866), 153.

55. *Charleston Mercury,* Nov. 28, 1864, as cited in Kaufman, "The Ideal Christmas Dinner," 23–24.

56. "About Thanksgiving," *Harper's Weekly,* Nov. 29, 1862, 755.

57. For instance, see "Turkey Jokes" at www.send4fun.com/turkeyjokesp.htm and "Thanksgiving Jokes: Thanksgiving Humor, Jokes about Thanksgiving" at www.quotesandjokes.com/thanksgiving-jokes.html.

58. F. S. Church, "The Turkeys' Revolt against Thanksgiving," *Harper's Weekly Supplement,* Nov. 30, 1872, 937.

59. "Thanksgiving," *Scribner's Magazine* 3 (Dec. 1871): 240–41.

60. *New York Times,* Nov. 20, 1887, 16.

61. *The Picayune Creole Cook Book,* 2d ed. (New Orleans: The Picayune, 1901), 433.

62. Fannie Merritt Farmer, *Boston Cooking-School Cook Book* (Boston: Little, Brown and Company, 1896), 520.

63. *The Picayune Creole Cook Book,* 433.

64. *Godey's Lady's Book* 71 (Nov. 1865): 445; Sarah Josepha Hale, "America's Thanksgiving Hymn," *Godey's Lady's Book* 85 (Nov. 1872), 462; Evert A. Duyckinck, *Cyclopadia of American Literature* (Philadelphia: T. E. Zell, 1875), 827.

65. *The Christian Recorder,* Feb. 2, 1867; *Thanksgiving: A Thanksgiving Dinner among Their Descendants* (lithograph), in *Harper's Weekly* 11 (Nov. 30, 1867): 753; Edward Everett Hale, "The Same Christmas in Old England and New," *The Galaxy* 5 (Jan. 1868): 51–52; "A New-England Farmers Thanksgiving in the Olden Times," *Hearth and Home,* Nov. 27, 1869, 769; "Thanksgiving-Day," *Harper's Weekly,* Dec. 6, 1873, 1084.

66. *Thanksgiving Day among the Puritan Fathers of New England, Harper's Weekly,* Dec. 3, 1870, 781.

67. David B. Scott, *A School History of the United States, from the Discovery of America to the Year 1870* (New York: Harper and Brothers, 1874), 85; "Thanksgiving-Day," *Harper's Weekly,* Dec. 6, 1873, 1084; William R. Bliss, "Thanksgiving: 'The Day We Celebrate,'" *New York Observer,* Nov. 28, 1872, 1; Leonard Bacon, *The Genesis of the New England Churches* (New York: Harper and Brothers, 1874), 349; *Journal of Health* 22 (Jan. 1876): 10; Charles Carleton Coffin, *Old Times in the Colonies* (New York: Harper and Brothers, 1881), 133.

68. I. N. Tarbox, "Our New England Thanksgiving, Historically Considered," *New Englander and Yale Review* 38 (Mar. 1879): 240–63; B. F. De Costa, "The Origin of Thanksgiving," *Magazine of American History with Notes and Queries* 8 (Nov. 1882): 757–63; C. L. Norton, "Thanksgiving Day, Past and Present," *Magazine of American History* 14 (1885): 556–61; M. Lowe, "Origin of Thanksgiving," *New England Magazine* 31 (Nov. 1904): 302–8; A. B. J. Jenner, "Origin of Thanksgiving Day," *Overland* n.s. 46 (Nov. 1905): 393–97.

69. Jane Austin, *Standish of Standish: A Story of the Pilgrims* (Boston: Houghton, Mifflin, 1889), 281, 283, 286.

70. For instance, see Hélène Adeline Guerber, *The Story of the Thirteen Colonies* (New York: American Book Company [1898]), 113–17; Kate D. Wiggin, ed., "First Thanksgiving Day," in *The Story Hour: A Book for the Home and the Kindergarten* (Boston: Houghton, Mifflin, 1891), 112–13; Elizabeth Pleck, "The Making of the Domestic Occasion: The History of Thanksgiving in the United States," *Journal of Social History* 32 (Summer 1999): 779–80.

71. Marjorie Benton Cooke, *The First Thanksgiving Dinner; a Play for Sixth to Twelfth Grade Schools* (Chicago: Dramatic Publishing Company, 1906), 10; Percival Chubb, *Festivals and Plays in Schools and Elsewhere* (New York: Harper and Brothers, 1912), 58; Ina Wolf, *The First Thanksgiving: A Miniature Musical Play in Four Sketches and Three Scenes for Fourth and Fifth Grade* (Cincinnati: Willis Music, 1931).

72. "Two Tired Little Turkeys," lyrics by William H. Gardner and music by Louis F. Gottschalk, in *Songs for Little Folks* (Philadelphia: Theodore Presser, 1904). An excellent summary of early literature appears in *Home Festivals: A Reference List on Hollowe'en, Thanksgiving and Christmas* (Riverside, Calif.: Riverside Public Library, 1913), 15–16.

73. "Pilgrim Pageant," *New York Times,* Dec. 27, 1920, 8.

74. Eric Hobsbawm and Terence Ranger, eds., *The Invention of Tradition* (New York: Cambridge University Press, 1983), 279–80; Diana Karter Appelbaum, *Thanksgiving; An American Holiday, an American History* (New York: Facts on File Publications, 1984), 218; Janet Siskind, "The Invention of Thanksgiving: A Ritual of American Nationality," *Critique of Anthropology* 12 (1992): 182–83, 186; Pleck, "The Making of the Domestic Occasion," 780–81.

75. "The First Thanksgiving Day, *New York Times,* Nov. 20, 1921, 87.

76. For instance, see the collection of First Thanksgiving stories in *Thanksgiving: Its Origin, Celebration and Significance as Related in Prose and Verse,* edited by Robert Haven Schauffler (New York: Moffat, Yard, 1907), 1–66.

77. Jennie Augusta Brownscombe's *The First Thanksgiving* is in the Museum of Pilgrim Treasures in Plymouth, Massachusetts; Jean Louis Gerome Ferris's *First Thanksgiving* is owned by a private collector. See, for example, the collection of First Thanksgiving stories in *Thanksgiving; its Origin, Celebration and Significance,* edited by Robert Haven Schauffler, 1–66.

78. Santino, *All Around the Year,* 173–74.

79. Love, *The Fast and Thanksgiving Days of New England.*

80. James Robertson, *American Myth, American Reality* (New York: Hill and Wang, 1980), 15.

81. Nora Zambreno, "We Can Do without the Turkey, but We Can't Do without the Ravioli! An Italian-American Family Celebrates Thanksgiving; I'm Not from Here: Reflections on a Western Sense of Place," M.A. thesis, Utah State University, 1999; Pleck, "The Making of the Domestic Occasion," 780–81 (quotation).

82. Robertson, *American Myth, American Reality,* 15.

Chapter 7: The Well-bred Turkey

1. Herbert Myrick, ed., *Turkeys and How to Grow Them* (New York: Orange Judd, 1897), 15.

2. James Earl Kennamer, Mary Kennamer, and Ron Brenneman, "History," in *The Wild Turkey: Biology and Management,* edited by James G. Dickson (Mechanicsburg, Pa.: Stackpole Books, 1992), 7.

3. J[ohn] Mortimer, *The Whole Art of Husbandry* (London: Printed by J. H. for H. Mortlock, 1708), 196.

4. Richard Bradley, *The Country Gentleman and Farmer's Monthly Director* (London: D. Browne, 1736), 62–63.

5. William Ellis, *The Country Housewife's Family Companion,* introduction by Malcolm Thick (1750, repr. Devon, U.K.: Prospect Books, 2000), 218.

6. *The Farmer's Magazine* (London) 4 (1779): 372.

7. René-Antoine Ferchault de Réaumur, *The Art of Hatching and Bringing up Domestick Fowls of All Kinds at Any Time of the Year* (London: C. Davis et al., 1750).

8. Edward Whitaker, *The Complete Grazier: or, Gentleman and Farmer's Directory* (London: J. Almon, 1767); *The Sportsman's Dictionary; or, The Gentleman's Companion* (Dublin: Peter Hoey, 1780); Samuel Cooke, John Houlston, Mary Bennell et al., *The Complete English Gardener . . . Together with the Whole Art of Breeding and Rearing Fowls, Ducks, Geese, Turkeys, Pigeons, and Rabbits* (London: Printed for J. Cooke, 1780).

9. John Laurence, *A New System of Agriculture, Being a Complete Body of Husbandry*

and Gardening (London: T. Woodward, 1726), 151; *Massachusetts Spy or Worcester Gazette,* May 15, 1799, 4; Hannah Glasse, *The Art of Cookery Made Plain and Easy* (Alexandria: Cotton and Stewart, 1805), 8; P. Thornton, *The Southern Gardener and Receipt Book* (Newark: A. L. Denis, 1845), 197–98.

10. Mortimer, *The Whole Art of Husbandry,* 197; Charles Millington, *The Housekeeper's Domestic Library; or, New Universal Family Instructor* (London: F. Flint, 1810), 361; Thornton, *The Southern Gardener and Receipt Book,* 198–99; Sarah Josepha Hale, *The New Household Receipt-Book* (New York: H. Long and Brother, 1853), 202; Mrs. J. C. Croly, *Jennie June's American Cookery Book* (New York: American News, 1878), 282; Lucy Nichols, *Our New Fireside Cook Book and Practical Receipts* (Boston: People's Publishing, 1882), 68; Alexis Soyer, *The Pantropheon; or, History of Food and Its Preparation, from the Earliest Ages of the World* (London: Simpkin, Marshall, 1853), 165.

11. [C. N. Bement], *The American Poulterer's Companion by Micajah R. Cock: Being a Practical Treatise on the Breeding, Rearing, Fattening, and Management of the Various Species of Poultry,* 2d ed. (New York: Harper and Brothers, 1845), 209–39.

12. *Boston Cultivator,* Sept. 15, 1849, 291; John C. Bennett, *The Poultry Book* (Boston: Phillips, Sampson, 1850), 77, 199.

13. Bennett, *The Poultry Book,* advertisement.

14. Ibid., 118.

15. For more information about John C. Bennett and hen fever, see chapter 11 in Andrew F. Smith, *The Saintly Scoundrel: The Life and Times of Dr. John C. Bennett* (Urbana: University of Illinois Press, 1997).

16. *Massachusetts Ploughman,* Mar. 23, 1850, n.p.; *Boston Traveller* as quoted in *The Northern Farmers' Almanac for 1851* (New York: A. B. Allen, 1850), n.p.; *Boston Cultivator,* Oct. 4, 1851, 316; *Northern Farmer,* 2d ser., 1 (Jan. 1854): 27.

17. [George Burnham], *The Poultry Breeder's Text Book* (Philadelphia: King and Baird, 1850); 53–57; George Burnham, *The History of the Hen Fever* (Boston: Hobart and Robbins, 1855); George Burnham, *Burnham's New Poultry Book* (New York: American News, 1871). The last two works went through several different printings; see also Edmund Saul Dixon, with large additions by J. J. Kerr, *A Treatise on the History of Ornamental and Domestic Poultry* (New York: C. M. Saxton, 1857).

18. Oscar August Hanke, "Press: Poultry Industry Growth Benefitted by Supportive and Involved Publications," in *American Poultry History, 1823–1973* (Madison, Wis.: American Poultry History Society, 1974), 106.

19. *The American Standard of Excellence: Giving a Complete Description of All Recognized Varieties of Fowls* ([Buffalo]: The Association, 1874).

20. *The American Standard of Perfection: A Complete Description of All Recognized Varieties of Fowls* (Buffalo: American Poultry Association, 1875), 199–210.

21. W. Clift, "Some Good Shore Narragansetts," *Poultry World* 2 (Dec. 1873): 163; *The American Standard of Perfection: A Complete Description of All Recognized Varieties of Fowls* ([Buffalo]: American Poultry Association, 1915), 359; H. S. Babcock, "The Bronze Turkey," in *Turkeys and How to Grow Them,* ed. Myrick, 16–18; Isabella Kruse Schaffner, *Turkeys in Texas: A History of the Turkey Industry in Texas* (San Antonio: Naylor, 1954), 4; Janet Vorwald Dohner, *The Encyclopedia of Endangered Livestock and Poultry Breeds* (New Haven: Yale University Press, 2001), 447, 452.

22. W. Clift, "The Narragansett Turkey," *Poultry World* 1 (Dec. 1872): 150–51; W. Clift, "Some Good Shore Narragansetts," *Poultry World* 2 (Dec. 1873): 163; Jacob Biggle, *Biggle Poultry Book: A Concise and Practical Treatise on the Management of Farm Poultry* (Philadelphia: W. Atkinson, 1895), 96; H. S. Babcock, "The Narragansett Turkey," in *Turkeys and How to Grow Them,* ed. Myrick, 31–34; *The American Standard of Perfection* (1915), 363; Carolyn J. Christman and Robert O. Hawes, *Birds of a Feather: Saving Turkeys from Extinction* (Pittsboro, N.C.: American Livestock Breeds Conservancy, 1999), 40–41; Dohner, *The Encyclopedia of Endangered Livestock and Poultry Breeds,* 451.

23. *The American Standard of Perfection* (1875), 202–3; Biggle, *Biggle Poultry Book,* 96; H. S. Babcock, "The Black Turkey," in *Turkeys and How to Grow Them,* ed. Myrick, 22–24; Christman and Hawes, *Birds of a Feather,* 34–35; Dohner, *The Encyclopedia of Endangered Livestock and Poultry Breeds,* 450–51.

24. *The American Standard of Perfection* (1875), 208; Biggle, *Biggle Poultry Book,* 95; H. S. Babcock, "The Buff Turkey," in *Turkeys and How to Grow Them,* ed. Myrick, 28–31; Christman and Hawes, *Birds of a Feather,* 39–40; Dohner, *The Encyclopedia of Endangered Livestock and Poultry Breeds,* 454.

25. *The American Standard of Perfection* (1875), 210; Biggle, *Biggle Poultry Book,* 96; Myrick, ed., *Turkeys and How to Grow Them,* 31; *The American Standard of Perfection* (1915), 365; Christman and Hawes, *Birds of a Feather,* 42–43; Dohner, *The Encyclopedia of Endangered Livestock and Poultry Breeds,* 455.

26. Christman and Hawes, *Birds of a Feather,* 41–42; Dohner, *The Encyclopedia of Endangered Livestock and Poultry Breeds,* 455.

27. *The American Standard of Perfection* (1875), 204; Biggle, *Biggle Poultry Book,* 96–97; *The American Standard of Perfection* (1915), 364; Christman and Hawes, *Birds of a Feather,* 43–44; Dohner, *The Encyclopedia of Endangered Livestock and Poultry Breeds,* 453.

28. *The American Standard of Perfection* (1915), 368; Christman and Hawes, *Birds of a Feather,* 35–36; Dohner, *The Encyclopedia of Endangered Livestock and Poultry Breeds,* 454.

29. M. C. Small, "Turkeys," in *American Poultry History,* 436.

30. Small, "Turkeys," 438; Dohner, *The Encyclopedia of Endangered Livestock and Poultry Breeds,* 455.

31. Small, "Turkeys," 439; Christman and Hawes, *Birds of a Feather,* 33.

32. Biggle, *Biggle Poultry Book,* 97 (quotation); Babcock, "The Narragansett Turkey," 31; Dohner, *The Encyclopedia of Endangered Livestock and Poultry Breeds,* 447.

33. A. Drew Davey, "Canada: A Comprehensive Overview of Canada's Progressive Industry," in *American Poultry History,* 591–92; Small, "Turkeys," 440; "Chronology: American Poultry History . . . ," in *American Poultry History,* 705–6.

34. Davey, "Canada," 591–92; Small, "Turkeys," 440; "Chronology," 705–6.

35. William Henry Burrows and Joseph P. Quinn, *Artificial Insemination of Chickens and Turkeys* (Washington: Government Printing Office, 1939).

36. "Big Butter-and-Egg Man," *Fortune Magazine* 28 (Oct. 1943): 237.

37. H. P. Griffin, "The Story of the Broad Breasted Bronze Turkey, When Breeders Forgot Color and Bred for Meat Qualities, Our Industry Took Its Biggest Stride," *Turkey World* (Oct. 1949); Small, "Turkeys," 440–42, 457.

38. Dohner, *The Encyclopedia of Endangered Livestock and Poultry Breeds,* 447, 452.

39. Christman and Hawes, *Birds of a Feather,* 43–44.
40. Beeton, *Book of Household Management,* 506.

Chapter 8: The Industrialized Turkey

1. J. H. Florea, "Education, Outstanding Teaching and Research Speeded Industry Commercialization," *American Poultry History, 1823–1973* (Madison, Wis.: American Poultry History Society, 1974), 52.
2. Samuel Cushman, *Turkeys* (Kingston: Agricultural Experiment Station of the Rhode Island College of Agriculture and Mechanic Arts, 1893).
3. W. A. Browning, *A Complete System of Raising Turkeys, Hens, Geese, &c* (Norwich, [Conn.]: Gordon Wilcox, 1873), 25.
4. Herbert Myrick, ed., *Turkeys and How to Grow Them* (New York: Orange Judd, 1897), 45.
5. Browning, *A Complete System of Raising Turkeys,* 26.
6. Fanny Field, *Practical Turkey Raising: Turkeys for Market and Turkeys for Profit* (Chicago: R. B. Mitchell, 1887), 1 (first quotation), 4 (second quotation).
7. Isabella Kruse Schaffner, *Turkeys in Texas: A History of the Turkey Industry in Texas* (San Antonio: Naylor, 1954), 8.
8. Stephen Beale, *Profitable Poultry Keeping,* edited by Mason C. Weld (New York: George Routledge and Sons, 1884), 226–28; Thomas R. Hazard, *The Jonny-cake Papers of "Shepherd Tom"* (Boston: Printed for the Subscribers, 1915), 72–73.
9. Jim Mason, "In the Turkey Breeding Factory," *Poultry Press* (Fall–Winter 1994): 1–2, 7; Tamara Jones, "The Stuffing of Scandal in which We Find the Juicy Tidbits about the National Turkey," *Washington Post,* Nov. 28, 1996, B17, as quoted in Karen Davis, *More than a Meal: The Turkey in History, Myth, Ritual and Reality* (New York: Lantern Books, 2001), 84–85, 97; Merk Veterinary Manual, 2003, at www.merckvetmanual.com/mvm/index.jsp?cfile=htm/bc/205700.htm.
10. Sivert Eriksen, "Disease," in *American Poultry History, 1823–1973,* 299–300.
11. E. M. Funk, "Hatcheries; Commercial Hatcheries Provided Ready-made Farmer Egg Machines," in *American Poultry History, 1823–1973,* 162–64.
12. Patrick Martins, "About a Bird," *New York Times,* Nov. 24, 2003, A23.
13. Beale, *Profitable Poultry Keeping,* 226–28; Thomas R. Hazard, *The Jonny-cake Papers of "Shepherd Tom"* (Boston: Printed for the Subscribers, 1915), 72–73.
14. "Big Butter-and-Egg Man," *Fortune Magazine* 28 (Oct. 1943): 123–25.
15. Beale, *Profitable Poultry Keeping,* 226–28; Hazard, *The Jonny-cake Papers of "Shepherd Tom,"* 72–73; Patrick Martins, "About a Bird," *New York Times,* Nov. 24, 2003, A23; Karen Davis, *More Than a Meal: The Turkey in History, Myth, Ritual and Reality* (New York: Lantern Books, 2001), 64–65.
16. "Big Butter-and-Egg Man," 228.
17. *Historical Statistics of the United States; Colonial Times to 1970* (Washington: U.S. Department of Commerce; Bureau of the Census, 1975), 1:425.
18. "Big Butter-and-Egg Man," 230.
19. Ibid., 237; M. C. Small, "Turkeys," in *American Poultry History, 1823–1973,* 460; *Historical Statistics of the United States; Colonial Times to 1970,* 1:424–45.
20. "Turkey on the Table Year Round," *Farmer's Bulletin No. 211* (Washington:

U.S.D.A., 1949); "Turkey on the Table the Year Round," *Home and Garden Bulletin No. 45* (Washington: U.S. Department of Agriculture, rev. 1958); Small, "Turkeys," 461; *Historical Statistics of the United States; Colonial Times to 1970*, 1:424–25.

21. Small, "Turkeys," 469.

22. Edwin Valentine Mitchell, *It's an Old New England Custom* (New York: Vanguard Press, [1946]), 29–30.

23. S. W. Hamilton, *Profitable Turkey Management*, 8th ed. (Cayuga: Beacon Milling, 1951), 91.

24. James Lesar and John A. McWethy, "Everyday Turkey," *Wall Street Journal*, July 24, 1951, 1.

25. *Christian Science Monitor*, Dec. 15, 1971, 8; Gladys Mason, "After Thanksgiving, Turkey Meatballs?" *Christian Science Monitor*, Nov. 22, 1972, B11.

26. "Big Butter-and-Egg Man," 123.

27. Ibid., 122.

28. Ibid.; *Famous Leaders of Industry* (Boston: L. G. Page, 1945), 311–23; *National Cyclopedia of American Biography* (New York: J. T. White, 1955), 40, 116–17.

29. Gerry Thomas, "TV Dinners: A Firsthand Account," personal communication sent to the author; author telephone interview with Gerry Thomas, Aug. 20, 2004.

30. Norge W. Jerome, "Frozen (TV) Dinners—The Staple Emergency Meals of a Changing Modern Society," in *Food in Perspective; Proceedings of the Third International Conference on Ethnological Food Research*, edited by Alexander Fenton and Trefor M. Owen (Edinburgh: John Donald Publishers, 1981), 145–46; Thomas, "TV Dinners"; telephone interview with Gerry Thomas, Aug. 20, 2004.

31. Thomas, "TV Dinners"; telephone interview with Gerry Thomas, Aug. 20, 2004.

32. *The American Agriculturalist*, as cited in *Turkeys and How to Grow Them*, ed. Myrick, vi.

33. Stanley J. Marsden, *Turkey Management* (Danville, Ill.: Interstate Publishers, 1939), 3.

34. Florea, "Education, Outstanding Teaching and Research Speeded Industry Commercialization," 65–67, 73–75; Small, "Turkeys," 457.

35. Norbest Web site at www.norbest.com/a_norbest_history.cfm.

36. Small, "Turkeys," 447–54.

37. Butterball Turkey Web site at www.butterball.com.

38. Eckrich Brand Web site at www.eckrichbrand.com/history.html.

39. Carolina Turkey Web site at www.carolinaturkey.com/history.asp.

40. *Agribusiness Examiner*, Nov. 26, 2002, 204; www.electricarrow.com/CARP/agbiz/204.htm.

41. Jennie-O Turkey Store Web site.

42. Ibid.

43. Ibid.

44. Norbest Web site.

45. Butterball Turkey Web site.

46. *Daily Gleaner*, Mar. 8, 1897, and the *Bedford* (Pa.) *Gazette*, May 2, 1955, as cited by Barry Popik in the American Dialect Society Archives, www.americandialect.org.

47. *Valley News,* Dec. 21, 1972, as cited by Barry Popik in the American Dialect Society Archives.

48. Leo Pearlstein, *Celebrity Stew* (Los Angeles: Hollywood Circle Press, 2002), 123–26; Leo Pearlstein and Lisa Messinger, *Mrs. Cubbison's Best Stuffing Cookbook; Sensational Stuffings for Poultry, Meats, Fish, Side Dishes, and More* (Garden City Park, N.Y.: Square One Publishers, 2005), 4–6.

49. "Creator of Stove Top Stuffing Dies," *New York Times,* Nov. 23, 2005.

50. Julie Vorman, "13 Percent of U.S. Turkeys Have Salmonella Group," Reuters, Nov. 19, 2001.

51. Centers for Disease Control Web site at www.cdc.gov/ncidod/dbmd/diseaseinfo/shigellosis_g.htm.

52. *Agribusiness Examiner,* issue 100, Dec. 21, 2000, at www.ea1.com/CARP/.

Chapter 9: The Social Turkey

1. Benjamin Franklin, *On the Art of Eating* (Princeton: Princeton University Press for the American Philosophical Society, 1958), 49, 63–64.

2. Benjamin Franklin to Peter Collinson, April 29, 1749, in Benjamin Franklin, *The Writings of Benjamin Franklin,* edited by Albert Henry Smyth (New York: Macmillan, 1905–7), 2:411; "A Child's Toy," *Chamber's Edinburgh Journal,* Jan. 3, 1852, 1.

3. Benjamin Franklin to Sarah Bache, dated Jan. 26, 1784, in Franklin, *The Writings of Benjamin Franklin,* 9:166–67.

4. Alexander Wilson, *American Ornithology; or, The Natural History of Birds of the United States* (Philadelphia: Bradford and Inskeep, 1808–24), 3:212–13; Godfrey Thomas Vigne, *Six Months in America* (London: Whittaker, Treacher, 1832), 1:2, 213; C. N. Bement, *The American Poulterer's Companion* (New York: Saxton and Miles, 1845), 209; James M. Phillippo, *The United States and Cuba* (London: Pewtress; New York: Sheldon, Blakeman, [1857]), 171.

5. Thomas Nast, *Uncle Sam's Thanksgiving Dinner, Harper's Weekly,* Nov. 20, 1869, 745.

6. Hotel San Remo menu, Thanksgiving Day 1898, New York Buttolph Menu Collection, General Research Division, New York Public Library.

7. Normal Rockwell, *Cousin Reginald Catches Thanksgiving Turkey, Country Gentleman,* Dec. 1, 1917, cover; Norman Rockwell, *Home for Thanksgiving, Saturday Evening Post,* Nov. 24, 1945, cover.

8. James Williams Abert, "Notes of Appendix No. 6 Ex. Doc. No. 41," in W. H. Emory, *Notes of a Military Reconnoissance* (Washington: Wendell and Van Benthuysen, 1848), 501–2.

9. *The New-York Mirror,* July 8, 1837, 16. Thanks to Barry Popik for locating this reference.

10. [Roderick Roundelay, ed.], *A Little Bit of a Tid-Re-I; or, A Chorus to the Times,* no. 2 (New York: n.p., 1824), 109.

11. *United States Democratic Review* 30 (Jan. 1852): 91.

12. *Daily Colonist* (Victoria, B.C.), Oct. 13, 1921, as cited in the online *Oxford English Dictionary.*

13. *New-Hampshire Gazette,* April 4, 1821, 4; Fanny Fern, *Little Ferns for Fanny's Little Friends* (Auburn, N.Y.: Miller, Orton and Mulligan, 1854), 124.

14. *The National Era,* Oct. 7, 1847, 1; Mary Irving, "A Story of Thanksgiving Day," *The National Era,* Jan. 3, 1850, 1; *Godey's Lady's Book* 44 (Jan. 1853): 41; *The Living Age,* Nov. 19, 1853, 487; Fern, *Little Ferns,* 128; Winslow Homer, *Wishbone, Harper's Weekly,* Dec. 3, 1864, 780; *Thanksgiving, Scribner's Magazine* 3 (Nov. 1871): 241.

15. Winslow Homer, *Thanksgiving Feast, Harper's Weekly,* Nov. 27, 1858, 760–61.

16. Homer, *The Wishbone,* 780.

17. Ebenezer Cooke, *The Sot-weed Factor; or, A Voyage to Maryland* (London: B. Bragg: London, 1708), 19–20.

18. Timothy Dwight, *The Triumph of Infidelity: A Poem* (Printed in the World, 1788).

19. Charles Mackay, *Life and Liberty in America; or, Sketches of a Tour in the United States and Canada, in 1857–8* (New York: Harper and Brothers, 1859), 66.

20. "A Merry Ode for Thanksgiving," *Norwich Packet,* Dec. 1, 1801, 4; *Harper's Weekly,* Dec. 3, 1864, 770.

21. Joseph Barber, *Crumbs from the Round Table* (New York: Leypoldt and Holt, 1866), 98–99; George Parsons Lathrop, *Dreams and Days: Poems* (New York: Charles Scribner's Sons, 1892), as at www.gutenberg.net/dirs/etext05/drmda10.txt; "The Turkey's Relief," *Table Talk* 20 (Nov. 1905): 422; Ruth Evelyn Henderson, "Celebrating Thanksgiving," *The English Journal* 14 (Nov. 1929): 715–16.

22. Henry Wadsworth Longfellow, *The Song of Hiawatha* (Boston: Ticknor and Fields, 1855), 148.

23. D. H. Lawrence, "Turkey Cock," *Poetry* 21 (Nov. 1922): 59–67; D. H. Lawrence, *The Plumed Serpent* (New York: A. A. Knopf, 1926), 93; James Thurber, "Two Turkeys," in *Fables for Our Time and Famous Poems: Illustrated* (New York: Harper, 1940).

24. Hundreds of children's and juvenile books have been published featuring turkeys. These include Edna Barth, *Turkeys, Pilgrims and Indian Corn: The Story of the Thanksgiving Symbols* (New York: Clarion Books, 1975); David Stemple and Ted Lewin, *High Ridge Gobbler: A Story of the American Wild Turkey* (New York: Collins, 1979); Steven Kroll, *One Tough Turkey: A Thanksgiving Story* (New York: Holiday House, 1982); Alison Prince, *The Turkey's Nest* (New York: Morrow, 1980); Brian Schatell, *Farmer Goff and His Turkey Sam* (New York: Lippincott, 1982); Sigmund A. Lavine, *Wonders of Turkeys* (New York: Dodd, Mead, 1984); Edna Miller, *Mousekin's Thanksgiving* (Englewood Cliffs: Prentice-Hall, 1985); Bob Reese, *Wild Turkey Run* (Provo: Aro Publishing, 1987); Dorothy Hinshaw Patent, *Wild Turkey, Tame Turkey* (New York: Clarion Books, 1989); Janice Lee Smith, *The Turkeys' Side of It: Adam Joshua's Thanksgiving* (New York: Harper and Row, 1990); Sylvie Wickstrom, *Turkey on the Loose* (New York: Dial Books for Young Readers, 1990); Penny Pollock, *The Turkey Girl: A Zuni Cinderella Story* (Boston: Little, Brown, 1995); Joy Cowley, *Gracias, the Thanksgiving Turkey* (New York: Scholastic Press, 1996); Ann M. Martin, *Karen's Runaway Turkey* (New York: Scholastic, 1999); Patrick Merrick, *Thanksgiving Turkeys* ([Chanhassen, Minn.]: Child's World, 1999); Dorothy Hinshaw Patent, *Wild Turkeys* (Minneapolis: Lerner Publications, 1999); Teresa Bateman, *A Plump and Perky Turkey* (Delray Beach: Winslow Press, 2001); Jim Arnosky, *All about Turkeys* (New York: Scholastic Press, 1998); Katy Hall, *Turkey Riddles* (New York:

Dial Books for Young Readers, 2002); and W. Nikola-Lisa, *Setting the Turkeys Free* (New York: Hyperion Books for Children, 2004).

25. *Cumberland Gazette,* Nov. 24, 1786, 2; "Boston," *Cumberland Gazette,* Nov. 22, 1787, 3; Samuel Griswold Goodrich, in *Yankee Life by Those Who Lived It,* edited by Barrows Mussey (New York: Stackpole Sons, [ca. 1937]), 133.

26. Goodrich, in *Yankee Life,* 133; *Frederick Douglass' Paper,* Nov. 25, 1853, and Dec. 14, 1855; *Scientific American,* Jan. 28, 1865, 71; "Thanksgiving in Prison," *Frederick Douglass' Paper,* Jan. 1, 1852.

27. Philip Hone, *The Diary of Philip Hone,* edited by Allen Nevins (New York: Dodd, Mead, 1927), 683–84.

28. "Thanksgiving in Prison."

29. *Frederick Douglass Paper,* Nov. 25, 1853, and Dec. 14, 1855; W. A. Browning, *A Complete System of Raising Turkeys, Hens, Geese, &c.* (Norwich, [Conn.]: Gordon Wilcox, 1873), 27.

30. *Scientific American,* Jan. 28, 1865, 71; *Evening Bulletin* (Decatur, Ill.), Dec. 26, 1896.

31. Chuck Pezzano, "Pins and Puns," *Bowling Digest* 20 (Feb. 2003): 58.

32. *Thanksgiving Dinner at the Five Points Ladies' Home Mission of the Episcopal Church, Harper's Weekly,* Dec. 23, 1865, 804; *New York Times,* Nov. 29, 1895, 2; W. S. L. Jewett, "Thanksgiving: A Thanksgiving Dinner among Their Descendants," *Harper's Weekly,* Nov. 30, 1867, 761.

33. *New York Times,* Nov. 30, 1894, 10, and Nov. 29, 1895, 2.

34. *Shooting the Christmas Turkey,* broadside (New York: Published by J[ames] Baillie, n.d.).

35. Ralph H. Avery to Thomas F. De Voe, in Thomas F. De Voe, dated June 24, 1858, in *The Market Assistant* (New York: Hurd and Houghton, 1867), 140.

36. Moses L. Lee to Abraham Lincoln, Wednesday, Feb. 27, 1861, ser. 1, General Correspondence, 1833–1916, in the Abraham Lincoln Papers, Library of Congress; *New York Times,* Nov. 19, 1898, 2.

37. Noah Brooks, "Lincoln's Reelection," *The Century* 49 (April 1895): 865; Louis A. Warren, *Lincoln's Youth: Indiana Years, Seven to Twenty One, 1816–1830* (New York: Appleton, Century, Crofts, [1959]), 225n; Noah Brooks, "Personal Reminiscences of Lincoln," *Scribner's Monthly* 15 (Mar. 1878): 677; Noah Brooks, *Washington in Lincoln's Time* (New York: Century, 1896), 217.

38. Thomas F. De Voe, *The Market Assistant* (New York: Hurd and Houghton, 1867), 140; Jacob Biggle, *Biggle Poultry Book: A Concise and Practical Treatise on the Management of Farm Poultry* (Philadelphia: W. Atkinson, 1895), 95; *New York Times,* Nov. 19, 1898, 2.

39. *New York Times,* Dec. 21, 1891, 1, Nov. 28, 1895, 1, Nov. 27, 1899, 2, Nov. 19, 1898, 2, and Nov. 28, 1901, 1; "President Back Again," *New York Times,* Jan. 1, 1901, 1.

40. Henry T. Finck, *Food and Flavor* (New York: Century, 1913), 477; Isabella Kruse Schaffner, *Turkeys in Texas: A History of the Turkey Industry in Texas* (San Antonio: Naylor, 1954), 49.

41. "Turkey Sent to President by Harding Girls Club of Chicago," *New York Times,* Nov. 27, 1928, 6, photograph in the Library of Congress's Making of America online archive; Norbest Web site at www.norbest.com/a_norbest_history.cfm.

42. Schaffner, *Turkeys in Texas,* 53; "This Roosevelt Turkey Never Got Its Feet to the

Ground; Pedigreed Bird One among Five which Were Sent to Chief Executive for Thanksgiving," *Los Angeles Times* Nov. 20, 1941, 21.

43. M. C. Small, "Turkeys," in *American Poultry History, 1823–1973* (Madison, Wis.: American Poultry History Society, 1974), 461.

44. "Turkey Gets Pardon," *Washington Post,* Nov. 21, 1963, C1; Leo Pearlstein, *Celebrity Stew* (Los Angeles: Hollywood Circle Press, 2002.), 103–5; Philip Potempa, "Advertising Campaigns Still Hold a Powerful Grip on Public Perception of Products," *Northwest Indiana Times,* Nov. 30, 2003, at www.thetimesonline.com/articles/2003/12/04/features/lifestyles_and_living/2057e2d63776551c86256dea0021ad62.txt.

45. Karen Davis, *More Than a Meal: The Turkey in History, Myth, Ritual and Reality* (New York: Lantern Books, 2001), 112–21.

46. "National Thanksgiving Turkey Spared Remarks by the President in Ceremonial Pardoning of the National Thanksgiving Turkey in the Rose Garden," Nov. 26, 2002, White House Press Release; www.photodc.com/screensaver/Turkey/default.asp

47. Elisabeth Bumiller, "Two Turkeys Pardoned, with First-Class Tickets," *New York Times,* Nov. 23, 2005.

48. Robert Hendrickson, *The Facts on File Encyclopedia of Word and Phrase Origins* (New York: Facts on File, 1997), 168.

49. *Turkeys in Season: An Original Ethiopian Whimsicality in Two Scenes* (New York: S. French, n.d.).

50. Mackinlay Kantor, *Turkey in the Straw: A Book of American Ballads and Primitive Verse* (New York: Coward-McCann, 1935).

51. Aaron Hougham, "Turkeys: Much Smarter Than You Think; OSU Poultry Scientist Gets the Word Out on Thanksgiving's Most Underappreciated Bird," *Daily Barometer,* Dec. 4, 2003, at www.upc-online.org/turkeys/120403notdumb.htm.

52. Walter Winchell, "A Primer of Broadway Slang: An Intimate Reveals Some of the Mysteries of the Much Quoted Theatrical Idioms," *Vanity Fair* 29 (Nov. 1927): 132.

53. Jerry Kluttz, "The Federal Diary; Gobbledygook Language Outlawed by Maverick," *Washington Post,* Mar. 30, 1944, 3; Maury Maverick, "The Case against 'Gobbledygook,'" *New York Times Magazine,* May 21, 1944, 11.

54. "Have You Tried the 'Long Boston' Dance?" *New York Times,* Jan. 29, 1911, SM9; "Chicago Society Women as the Portrait Painters See Them," *Chicago Daily Tribune,* Feb. 19, 1911, B7; "Turkey Trot at Newport," *New York Times,* Nov. 4, 1911, 13; "Approve the Turkey Trot; Philadelphia Society Leaders Are Taking Lessons in the Latest Dance," *New York Times,* Dec. 22, 1911, 13 (quotation); Warren G. Davenport, *Butte and Montana beneath the X-ray* (London: C. F. Cazenovei, 1909), 42.

55. Henry Lodge, "Oh You Turkey (a Rag Trot)," sheet music, Waterson Berlin and Snyder, 1914; Laura Guerite, *Modern Dances: The Tango and Turkey Trot Made Easy* (New York: n.p., 1913); Alfonso Josephs Sheafe, *The Fascinating "Boston"* (Boston: Boston Music, [1913]).

56. "The Turkey Trot," *Washington Post,* Dec. 1, 1910, 6. For European adoption of the turkey trot see Max Rivera, *Le tango et les danses nouvelles* (Paris: P. Lafitte et Cie, [1913]); and Francesco Giovannini, *Balli d'oggi* (Milan: n.p., 1914), 139–42.

57. *Mansfield News,* Sept. 27, 1910.

58. Edward F. Hannigan and Henry Moeller, as cited in Mordecai Fowler Ham, *The Modern Dance: A Historical and Analytical Treatment of the Subject; Religious, Social, Hygienic, Industrial Aspects as Viewed by the Pulpit, the Press, Medical Authorities, Municipal Authorities, Social Workers, Etc.,* 2d ed. ([San Antonio, San Antonio Printing, 1916]), 14; Norman Sargant and Tom Sargant, "Negro-American Music of the Origin of Jazz," *Musical Times,* Aug. 1, 1931, 752.

59. *Houston Chronicle,* as cited in Ham, *The Modern Dance,* 52.

60. "The Greatest of Them All," *Puck,* Jan. 31, 1912, 2.

61. Neil Simon, *Promises, Promises* (New York: Random House, 1969), which was based on a screen play entitled *The Apartment* written by Billy Wilder and I. A. L. Diamond. Music for *Promises, Promises* was composed by Burt Bacharach and the lyrics by Hal David; the show opened at the Schubert Theater on Broadway in December 1968.

62. Elyse Sommer, review of *Curtain Up* at www.curtainup.com/dinnerwithdemons.html.

63. Schaffner, *Turkeys in Texas,* 8–11.

64. Ibid., 45–49.

65. CBS News, Nov. 17, 2002, WGTN Web site at www.wgtn.net/Turkeyday.

66. *Life,* Nov. 23, 1953, 53, 55.

67. M. Chris Osment, *Arkansas Times,* Nov. 4, 2004.

68. WKRP Quotes Web site at www.tvsothertenpercent.tripod.com/wkrp/turkeys.html; Pat Kuchefski, "A Little Thanksgiving Day Fun," *Balloon Life* at www.balloonlife.com/publications/balloon_life/9801/9901/nessman.htm.

69. Urban Dictionary at www.urbandictionary.com/define.php?term=turkey+drop&r=f.

70. William Alcott, "Thanksgiving," *Moral Reformer and Teacher on the Human Constitution* 1 (Nov. 1835): 351–53.

71. Mrs. E. E. Kellogg, *Science in the Kitchen* (Battle Creek: Health Publishing, 1892), 544; Almeda Lambert, *Guide for Nut Cookery* (Battle Creek: Joseph Lambert, 1899), 112; Mrs. E. E. Kellogg, *Science in the Kitchen,* rev. ed. (Battle Creek: Modern Medicine Publishing, 1904), 409–10; Sarah Tyson Rorer, *Mrs. Rorer's Vegetable Cookery and Meat Substitutes* (Philadelphia: Arnold, 1909), 45; Helen Watkeys Moore, *Camouflage Cookery: A Book of Mock Dishes* (New York: Duffield, 1918), 60–61; Mrs. T. A. Gagnon, *Tried and Tested Recipes: Mrs. T. A. Gagnon's Cook Book for Practical Housekeeping* (Grafton, N.D.: Grafton News and Times Print, 1919), 52, 56.

72. The Farm Sanctuary at www.adoptaturkey.org.

73. Karen Davis, *Instead of Chicken, Instead of Turkey: A Poultryless "Poultry" Potpourri* (Summertown, Tenn.: Book Publishing, 1999); for more information about United Poultry Concerns see www.upc-online.org.

74. *America's Parade: A Celebration of Macy's Thanksgiving Day Parade* (New York: Life Books, 2001), 22, 29, 104.

75. For more information about the commercial aspects of Thanksgiving, see Melanie Wallendorf and Eric J. Arnould, "We Gather Together: Consumption Rituals of Thanksgiving Day," *Journal of Consumer Research* 18 (1991): 13–31.

76. U.S. Trademark Serial number 71495649; registration date, Aug. 16, 1949.

77. Wild Turkey Bourbon Web site at www.wildturkeybourbon.com.

Chapter 10: The American Turkey

1. For instance, see *Act 124: An Act for the Protection of Wild Deer, Turkey, and Bear* (Little Rock: Democrat P. and L. Company, [1915]).

2. J. D. Caton, "The Wild Turkey and Its Domestication," *American Naturalist* 11 (June 1877): 328.

3. Harold Titus, "The Gobbler Gets Attention," *Field and Stream* 45 (Dec. 1940): 26; Harold L. Blakley, "Status and Management of the Eastern Wild Turkey," *American Wildlife* 30 (1941): 141.

4. James Earl Kennamer, Mary Kennamer, and Ron Brenneman, "History," in *The Wild Turkey; Biology and Management,* edited by James G. Dickson (Mechanicsburg, Pa.: Stackpole Books, 1992), 14.

5. J. E. Kennamer and M. C. Kennamer, "Current Status and Distribution of the Wild Turkey," in William M. Healy and Georgette B. Healy, eds, *Proceedings of the Sixth National Wild Turkey Symposium, 26 February–1 March 1990, Charleston, South Carolina,* edited by William M. Healy and Georgette B. Healy (Edgefield, S.C.: The Federation, [1990]): 1–12; Kennamer, Kennamer, and Brenneman, "History," 16; telephone interview with Tom Hughs, biologist, National Wild Turkey Federation, Feb. 8, 2005.

6. James G. Dickson, "Introduction," in *The Wild Turkey; Biology and Management,* edited by James G. Dickson (Mechanicsburg, Pa.: Stackpole Books, 1992), 5; Rob Southwick et. al., *The 2003 Economic Contributions of Spring Turkey Hunting* (Fernandina Beach: Southwick Associates, 2003), v; telephone interview with Tom Hughs.

7. Larry Witucki, *Sourcebook: The U. S. Turkey Industry* (Washington: National Turkey Federation, 2004).

8. Stanley J. Marsden, *Turkey Management* (Danville, Ill.: Interstate Publishers, 1939), 58.

9. R. D. Crawford, "Turkey," in *Evolution of Domesticated Animals,* edited by Ian L. Mason (London: Longman Group, 1984), 325–34.

10. Carolyn J. Christman and Robert O. Hawes, *Birds of a Feather; Saving Turkeys from Extinction* (Pittsboro, N.C.: American Livestock Breeds Conservancy, 1999), 25–30.

11. For a summary of the survey, see www.feathersite.com/Poultry/SPPA/TurkCensusRept99.html.

12. American Livestock Breeds Conservancy at www.albc-usa.org/alerts/june11_03.htm.

13. A. L., "Bronze Bird," *Food and Wine* (Nov. 2004): 34; "Heritage Turkeys," *Bon Appétit* 49 (Nov. 2004): 72; Julia Boorstin, "Video Game," *Fortune Magazine,* Nov. 29, 2004, 68, 70.

14. For instance, see Slanker's Grass-Fed Meats Web site at www.slankersgrassfedmeats.com/id53.htm; Mary's Free-Range Turkey Web site at www.marysturkeys.com; and Eat Well Guide at www.EatWellGuide.org.

15. Marjorie Bender, email to author, Mar. 8, 2005.

16. A. D. Livingston. *Wild Turkey Cookbook* (Mechanicsburg, Pa.: Stackpole Books, 1995); Rick Black, *The Wild Turkey Cookbook* (Wever, Iowa: Black Iron Cookin', 2003).

17. *The Larro Turkey Book* (San Francisco: General Mills, 1947); Martha Logan, *All about Turkey: Butterball Swift's Premium* (N.l.: Swift, n.d.); *Turkey Made Easy* (Rich-

mond, Va.: Reynolds Metals, n.d.); Butterball Turkey Company, *The Butterball Turkey Cookbook* (New York: Hearst Books, 1992); Leo Pearlstein and Lisa Messinger, *Mrs. Cubbison's Best Stuffing Cookbook: Sensational Stuffings for Poultry, Meats, Fish, Side Dishes, and More* (Garden City Park, N.Y.: Square One Publishers, 2005).

18. S. I. Reese, *The Complete Turkey Cookbook: The Good Cook's Guide to Unusual Turkey Dishes and Exciting Accompaniments* ([Los Angeles]: Ward Ritchie Press [1971]); Johnnie F. Chandler, *Johnnie Bird's Turkey Rifics: Recipes for Preparing America's Favorite Bird so You'll Love Turkey, Too* (Waco, Tex.: Davis Brthers, 1973); *Turkey and Chicken Cookbook* (Garden City, N.Y.: Rockville House Publishers, 1978); Anita Borghese, *The Great Year-Round Turkey Cookbook* (New York: Stein and Day, 1979); Kathi Chapman, *Baron von Leftover: The International Turkey* (Honolulu: Pacific Printers, 1980); Barbara Gibbons, *The Year-round Turkey Cookbook: A Guide to Delicious, Nutritious Dining with Today's Versatile Turkey Products* (New York: McGraw-Hill, 1980); Susan O. Byrne and Barbara M. Mueller, *Turkey All Year* (Arlington: Barclay-Ramsey, 1984); Ken Wolfe and Olga Bier, *Chef Wolfe's New American Turkey Cookery* (Berkeley: Aris Books/Harris Publishing Company, 1984); Mary Ann Trombold, *Let's Talk Turkey: Gourmet Recipes* (Mercer Island, Wash.: Year-Round Press, 1985); Rick Rodgers, *The Turkey Cookbook* (New York: Harper Perennial, 1990); Franki Papai Seccunda, *The Everyday Turkey Cookbook* (New York: HPBooks, 1995).

19. Reece Williams, *The Ultimate Turkey Fryer Cookbook* (Des Moines: Meredith Press, 2003).

Turkey Breeding

Bender, Marjorie E. F. *Heritage Turkeys in America: The American Livestock Breeds Conservancy 2003 Heritage Turkey Census.* Pittsboro, N.C.: American Livestock Breeds Conservancy, 2003.

Brant, A. Wade. "A Brief History of the Turkey." *World's Poultry Science Journal* 54 (Dec. 1998): 365–73.

Breitburg, Emanuel. "The Evolution of Turkey Domestication in the Greater Southwest and Mesoamerica." In *Culture and Contact: Charles C. Di Peso's Gran Chichimeca,* edited by Anne I. Woosley and Jahn C. Ravesloot, 153–72. Albuquerque: University of New Mexico Press, 1993.

Crawford, R. D. "Introduction to Europe and Diffusion of Domesticated Turkeys from America." *Archivos de Zootecnia* 41 (1992): 307–14.

———. "Turkey." In *Evolution of Domesticated Animals,* edited by Ian L. Mason. London: Longman Group, 1984.

Davis, Karen. *More than a Meal: The Turkey in History, Myth, Ritual and Reality.* New York: Lantern Books, 2001.

Eiche, Sabine. *Presenting the Turkey: The Fabulous Story of a Flamboyant and Flavourful Bird.* Florence: Centro Di, 2004.

Fuller, Frank W. *Pheasants, Wild Geese, Turkeys, Ducks, Quails.* Salisbury, N.C.: Frank W. Fuller, 1939.

Hale, E. B., and M. W. Schein. "The Behaviour of Turkeys." In *The Behaviour of Domestic Animals,* edited by E. S. E. Hafez. London: Baillière, Tindall and Cox, 1962.

Hargrave, Lyndon L. "Turkey Bones from Wetherill Mesa." *American Antiquity* 31 (1965): 161–66.

Jull, Morley A. "Fowls of Forest and Stream Tamed by Man." *National Geographic* 57 (March 1930): 327–71.

Leopold, A. Starker. "The Wild Turkey of Mexico." In *Transactions of the Thirteenth North American Wildlife Conference,* edited by Ethel M. Quee, 393–400. Washington: Wildlife Management Institute, 1948.

Lovelace, Charles D. *Building the Largest Turkey Ranch in the World at Sunland, Texas.* Fort Worth: Utter and Evans, [ca. 1930].

Mahaney, Margaret. *Margaret Mahaney Talks about Turkeys.* Concord, Mass.: The author, 1915.

McKusick, Charmion R. *Southwest Indian Turkeys: Prehistory and Comparative Osteology.* Globe, Ariz.: Southwest Bird Laboratory, 1986.

Mickel, Earl, with Howard Pomtier. *Turkey Call Makers Past and Present: The Rest of the Best.* Beach Lake, Pa.: Earl Mickel, 1999.

Plouvier, Liliane. "Introduction de la dinde en Europe." *Scientiarium Historia* 21 (1995): 13–34.

Powell, Richard E. *Turkey Husbandry in Virginia and the Chesapeake Region, 1750–1830.* Colonial Williamsburg Research Report 327. Williamsburg, Va., 1992.

Reed, E. K. "Turkeys in Southwestern Archaeology." *El Palacio* 58 (1951): 195–205.
Reliable Poultry Journal Publishing Company. *Turkeys, All Varieties: Their Care and Management.* Quincy: Reliable Poultry Journal Publishing, 1904.
Schaffner, Isabella Kruse. *Turkeys in Texas: A History of the Turkey Industry in Texas.* San Antonio: Naylor, 1954.
Small, M. C. "Turkeys." In *American Poultry History 1823–1973: An Anthology Overview of 150 Years: People-Places-Progress,* edited by the American Poultry Historical Society, edited by Oscar August Hanke et al., [Lafayette, Ind.?]: American Poultry Historical Society, 1974.
Willis-Harris, William. *The Turkey: How to Breed and Rear Successfully.* Warnham, Sussex: Tunbridge Wells, 1890.
———. *The Turkey: How to Breed and Rear Successfully.* 2d ed. Pulboro, Sussex: The author, 1893.
Witucki, Larry. *Sourcebook: The U.S. Turkey Industry.* Washington: National Turkey Federation, 2004.

Turkey Husbandry

Bland, David C. *Turkeys: A Guide to Management.* Marlborough, Wiltshire: Crowood, 2000.
Browning, W. A. *A Complete System of Raising Turkeys, Hens, Geese, &c.* Norwich, Conn.: Gordon Wilcox, 1873.
Ensminger, Alpha A. *The Turkey Raiser's Guide.* Moran, Kans.: Banner Turkey Ranch, [1916].
[Field, Fanny]. *Practical Turkey Raising: Turkeys for Market and Turkeys for Profit.* Chicago: R. B. Mitchell, 1887.
Hamilton, S. W. *Profitable Turkey Management.* 8th ed. Cayuga, N.Y.: Beacon Milling, 1951.
Haynes, Cynthia. *Raising Turkeys, Ducks, Geese, Pigeons, and Guineas.* Blue Ridge Summit, Pa.: Tab Books, 1987.
Lamon, Harry Miles. *Turkey Raising.* New York: Orange Judd, 1922.
Marsden, Stanley J. *Turkey Management.* Danville, Ill.: Interstate Publishers, 1939.
Mercia, Leonard S. *Raising Your Own Turkeys.* Pownal, Vt.: Garden Way Publishing, 1981.
Myrick, Herbert, ed. *Turkeys and How to Grow Them: A Treatise on the Natural History and Origin of the Name of Turkeys, the Various Breeds, and Best Methods to Insure Success in the Business of Turkey Growing.* New York: Orange Judd, 1897.

On Wild Turkeys

Burger, George V. "The Introduction of Wild Turkeys in California." M.A. thesis, University of California, Berkeley, 1952.
Collinge, Chuck. *Nutmeg Turkeys: A Guide to the Wild Turkey in Connecticut, Their History, Habits and Hunting.* Ansonia, Conn.: Housatonic Books, 1992.
Dalke, P. D., A. Starker Leopold, and David L. Spencer. *The Ecology and Management of the Wild Turkey in Missouri.* [Jefferson City?]: Conservation Commission, Federal Aid Wildlife Program, State of Missouri, 1946.

Davis, Henry E. *The American Wild Turkey.* Georgetown, S.C.: Small-Arms Technical Publishing, 1949.

Eastern Wild Turkey Restoration in Eastern Texas. [Austin]: Texas Parks and Wildlife Department, 1989.

Grunkemeyer, Bill. *America's Bird the Wild Turkey.* Sheridan, Wyo.: Grunko Films, 1990 [videorecording: VHS tape].

Healy, William M., and Shawn Powell. *Wild Turkey Harvest Management: Biology, Strategies, and Techniques.* Sheperdstown, W.V.: U.S. Department of the Interior, U.S. Fish and Wildlife Service, [2000].

Hewett, Oliver H., ed. *The Wild Turkey and Its Management.* Washington: Wildlife Society, 1967.

Hoffman, Donald M. *The Wild Turkey in Eastern Colorado: A Research and Management Study.* [Denver]: State of Colorado, Department of Game and Fish, 1962.

Howard, Brad. *Wild Turkey Meleagris gallopavo.* Raleigh: Division of Conservation Education, North Carolina Wildlife Resources Commission, 1992.

Jonas, Robert James. *Merriam's Turkeys in Southeastern Montana.* [Helena?]: Montana Fish and Game Department, 1966.

Kooliath, Maria Rose Margaret. "The Seventeenth-Century Wild Turkey in Kanawha River Valley." M.S. thesis, St. Bonaventure University, 1975.

Kubisiak, John F., et al. *Wild Turkey Ecology and Management in Wisconsin.* Madison: Wisconsin Department of Natural Resources, Bureau of Integrated Science Services, 2001.

Land Management for Wild Turkeys in Alabama. Auburn: U.S. Department of Agriculture, Soil Conservation Service, 1983.

Latham, Roger M. *Complete Book of the Wild Turkey.* Harrisburg, Pa.: Stackpole Books, 1977.

Lewis, James C. *The World of the Wild Turkey.* Philadelphia: J. B. Lippincott, 1973.

Ligon, J. Stokley. *History and Management of Merriam's Wild Turkey.* Albuquerque: University of New Mexico Press, 1946.

Litton, George W. *Food Habits of the Rio Grande Turkey in the Permian Basin of Texas.* [Austin]: Texas Parks and Wildlife Department, 1977.

———, and Fielding Harwell. *Rio Grande Turkey Habitat Management.* [Austin]: Texas Parks and Wildlife Division, 1995.

Managing Your Land for Wild Turkeys. Madison: Wisconsin Department of Natural Resources, 1998.

Mosby, Henry S., and Charles O. Handley. *The Wild Turkey in Virginia: Its Status, Life History and Management.* Richmond: Pittman-Robertson Projects, Division of Game Commission of Game and Inland Fisheries, 1943.

National Wild Turkey Federation. *Guide to the American Wild Turkey.* Part 1: *Status—Numbers, Distribution, Season, Harvests and Regulations.* Edgefield, S.C.: National Wild Turkey Federation, 1992.

Porter, William F., and Kathleen K. Fleming, eds., *Making Tracks: Wild Turkey Management for the New Millennium: Proceedings of the Eighth National Wild Turkey Symposium, 5–9 June, 2000, Augusta, Georgia.* Edgefield, S.C.: National Wild Turkey Federation, 2001.

Rumble, Mark A., and Stanley H. Anderson. *Evaluating the Habitat Capability Model for Merriam's Turkeys.* Fort Collins, Colo.: U.S. Department of Agriculture, Forest Service, Rocky Mountain Forest and Range Experiment Station, [1995].

Sanderson, Glenn C., and Helen C. Schultz, eds. *Wild Turkey Management: Current Problems and Programs.* Columbia: University of Missouri Press, 1973.

Schorger, A. W. *The Wild Turkey: Its History and Domestication.* Norman: University of Oklahoma Press, 1966.

Seamster, Michael H. *The Wild Turkey in North Carolina.* Raleigh: Division of Wildlife Management, North Carolina Wildlife Resources Commission, 1993.

Shaw, Harley. *Stalking the Big Bird: A Tale of Turkeys, Biologists, and Bureaucrats.* Tucson: University of Arizona Press, 2004.

Southeastern Cooperative Wildlife Disease Study. *Southeastern Wild Turkey Populations.* [Athens, Ga.]: Southeastern Cooperative Wildlife Disease Study, [1980?].

Southwick, Rob, et al. *The 2003 Economic Contributions of Spring Turkey Hunting.* Fernandina Beach, Fla.: Southwick Associates, 2003.

Spicer, Robert L. *Wild Turkey in New Mexico: An Evaluation of Habitat Development.* Santa Fe: New Mexico Department of Game and Fish, 1959.

Spohr, Shelley M., Howard J. Kilpatrick, and Michael A. Gregonis. *Connecticut's Wild Turkey: History, Research, and Management.* Hartford: Bureau of Natural Resources, Wildlife Division, Department of Environmental Protection, [2002].

Thackston, Reggie, et al. *The Wild Turkey in Georgia: History, Biology and Management.* [Athens]: Georgia Department of Natural Resources; Georgia State Chapter National Wild Turkey Federation, [1991].

Triplett, Todd. *The Complete Guide to Turkey Taxidermy: How to Prepare Fans, Beards, and Body Mounts.* Guilford, Conn.: Lyons Press, 2003.

Turkey in South Carolina. Columbia: South Carolina Wildlife and Marine Resources Department, n.d.

Wheeler, Robert J. *The Wild Turkey in Alabama.* [Montgomery]: Alabama Department of Conservation, Game, Fish and Seafoods Division, 1948.

Williams, Lovett E., and David H. Austin. *Studies of the Wild Turkey in Florida.* Gainesville: University Press of Florida, 1988.

Zimmer, John T. *The Wild Turkey.* Chicago: Field Museum of Natural History, 1924.

Hunting Wild Turkeys

Blair, Gerry. *Turkey Hunting with Gerry Blair.* Iola, Wis.: Krause Publications, 1991.

Bland, Dwain. *Some Turkey Scratchings: A Guide Reminisces about Wild Turkeys.* Delmont, Pa.: Penn's Woods, 1983.

———. *Turkey Hunter's Digest.* Northbrook, Ill.: DBI Books, 1994.

Brady, James F. *Modern Turkey Hunting.* New York: Crown Publishers, 1973.

Bristol, Stewart J. *Hunting Wild Turkeys in New England.* Thorndike, Maine: North Country Press, 1986.

Burch, Monte. *Field Dressing and Butchering Upland Birds, Waterfowl, and Wild Turkeys: Step-by-step Instructions, from Field to Table.* Guilford, Conn.: Lyons Press, 2001.

Charles, Elliott. *Turkey Hunting with Charlie Elliott.* New York: David McKay, 1979.

Combs, Richard P. *Advanced Turkey Hunting.* Bellvale, N.Y.: Woods 'n' Water, 2001.

Eastman, Gordon. *Hunt the Wild Turkey.* Cody, Wyo.: Eastman's Outdoor World, 1989 [videorecording: VHS tape].

Elliott, Charles. *Turkey Hunting with Charlie Elliott.* New York: David McKay, 1979.

Everitt, Simon W. *Tales of Turkey Hunting,* edited by William H. Ball. Chicago: W. C. Hazelton, 1928.

Eye, Ray. *Practical Turkey Hunting Strategies: How to Effectively Hunt Birds under Any Conditions.* Guilford, Conn.: Lyons Press, 2003.

Fears, J. Wayne. *The Wild Turkey Book.* Clinton, N.J.: Amwell Press, 1981.

Hanankrat, William Frank. *The Education of a Turkey Hunter.* New York: Winchester Press, 1974.

Hanback, Michael. *Spring Gobbler Fever: Your Complete Guide to Spring Turkey Hunting.* Iola, Wis.: Krause Publications, 1996.

Harben, Frank P. *Hunting Wild Turkeys in the Everglades.* Safety Harbor, Fla.: Harben Publishing, 1982.

Harbour, Dave. *Advanced Wild Turkey Hunting and World Records.* New York: Winchester Press, 1983.

Higley, John. *Hunting Wild Turkeys in the West, Based on Thirty Years of Western Turkey Hunts.* Stevensville, Mont.: Stoneydale Press Publishing, 2001.

Humphrey, Bob. *New England Turkey Hunting: Strategies for Success: The Complete Guide to Turkey Hunting in New England.* Pownal, Maine: Sport-Ventures, 2003.

Huntington, Dwight W. *Game Farming for Profit and Pleasure: A Manual on the Wild Turkeys, Grouse, Quail or Partridges, Wild Ducks and the Introduced Pheasants and Gray Partridges.* Wilmington, Del.: Hercules Powder, 1915.

Keck, Rob. *Turkey Hunting.* St. Paul: 3M Leisure Time Products, 1989 [videorecording: VHS tape].

Kelly, Tom. *Tenth Legion: Tips, Tactics, and Insights on Turkey Hunting.* Fairhope, Ala.: Wing Feather Press, 1973.

Langston, Jay. *Turkey Hunter's Tool Kit: Calls and Calling.* Accokeek, Md.: Stoeger Publishing, 2003.

Lovett, Brian, ed. *The Turkey Hunters: The Lore, Legacy, and Allure of American Turkey Hunting.* Iola, Wis.: Krause Publications, 2003.

McDaniel, John M. *The American Wild Turkey: Reflections on the Bird, the Hunt, and the Hunter.* New York: Lyons Press, 2000.

———. *The Turkey Hunter's Book.* Clinton, N.J.: Amwell Press, 1980.

Mettler, John J. *Wild Turkeys Hunting and Watching.* Pownal, Vt.: Storey Books, 1998.

Pearce, Michael, and Ray Eye. *Hunting Wild Turkeys with Ray Eye.* Harrisburg: Stackpole Books, 1990.

Phillips, John E. *Outdoor Life Complete Turkey Hunting Outdoor Life.* New York: Stackpole, 1988.

———. *The Turkey Hunter's Bible.* New York: Doubleday, 1992.

———. *Turkey Hunting Tactics.* Minnetonka, Minn.: North American Outdoor Group, 1989.

Smith, Andrew F. "The Rise and Fall of the Wild Turkey." In *Nurture: Proceedings of the Oxford Symposium on Food and Cookery, 2004,* edited by Richard Hosking. Bristol, U.K.: Footwork, forthcoming.

Trout, John. *The Complete Book of Wild Turkey Hunting: A Handbook of Techniques and Strategies.* New York: Lyons Press, 2000.

Tucker, Ryan. *Turkey Hunters and the People We Meet: Stories of Turkeys, Those Who Hunt Them, and Friendships That Last Forever.* Milton Keynes, U.K.: Lightening Source, Print-on-Demand, 2003.

Turkey Hunting Tactics: Expert Advice for Locating, Calling, and Decoying Wild Turkeys. Minnetonka, Minn.: Creative Publishing International, 2001.

Turpin, Tom. *Hunting the Wild Turkey.* Delmont, Pa.: Penn's Woods, 1966.

Williams, Lovett E., Jr. *The Art and Science of Wild Turkey Hunting.* Cedar Key, Fla.: Real Turkeys Publishers, 1989.

———. *The Book of the Wild Turkey.* Tulsa, Okla.: Winchester Press, 1981.

———. *Wild Turkey Country.* Minnetonka, Minn.: Willow Creek Press, 1991.

Wolff, Ed, and Gary Holmes. *Hunting North American Wild Turkey.* Stevensville, Mont.: Stoney-Wolf Video Productions, 1988 [videorecording: VHS tape].

Cookbooks and Pamphlets

Borghese, Anita. *The Great Year-Round Turkey Cookbook.* New York: Stein and Day, 1979.

The Butterball Turkey Company. *The Butterball Turkey Cookbook.* New York: Hearst Books, 1992.

Byrne, Susan O., and Barbara M. Mueller. *Turkey All Year.* Arlington: Barclay-Ramsey, 1984.

Chandler, Johnnie F. *Johnnie Bird's Turkey Rifics: Recipes for Preparing America's Favorite Bird so You'll Love Turkey, Too.* Waco: Davis Brothers Publishing, 1973.

Chapman, Kathi. *Baron von Leftover: The International Turkey.* Honolulu: Pacific Printers, 1980.

Davis, Karen. *Instead of Chicken, Instead of Turkey: A Poultryless "Poultry" Potpourri.* Summertown, Tenn.: Book Publishing, 1999.

[General Mills]. *The Larro Turkey Book.* San Francisco: General Mills, 1947.

Gibbons, Barbara. *The Year-round Turkey Cookbook: A Guide to Delicious, Nutritious Dining with Today's Versatile Turkey Products.* New York: McGraw-Hill, 1980.

Good Cook's Library: Chicken and Poultry Cookbook. New York: Crescent Books, 1988.

Logan, Martha. *All about Turkey: Butterball Swift's Premium.* Nl: Swift, n.d.

Pearlstein, Leo, and Lisa Messinger. *Mrs. Cubbison's Best Stuffing Cookbook: Sensational Stuffings for Poultry, Meats, Fish, Side Dishes, and More.* Garden City Park: Square One Publishers, 2005.

Reese, S. I. *The Complete Turkey Cookbook: The Good Cook's Guide to Unusual Turkey Dishes and Exciting Accompaniments.* [Los Angeles]: Ward Ritchie Press [1971].

Roberson, John, and Marie Roberson. *Poultry Cook Book.* Greenwich, Conn.: Fawcett Publications, 1954.

Rodgers, Rick. *The Turkey Cookbook.* New York: HarperPerennial, 1990.

Seccunda, Franki Papai. *The Everyday Turkey Cookbook.* New York: HPBooks, 1995.

Trombold, Mary Ann. *Let's Talk Turkey: Gourmet Recipes.* Mercer Island, Wash.: Year-Round Press, 1985.

Turkey and Chicken Cookbook. Garden City: Rockville House Publishers, 1978.

Turkey Made Easy. Richmond, Va.: Reynolds Metals Company, n.d.

Williams, Reece. *The Ultimate Turkey Fryer Cookbook.* Des Moines: Meredith Press, 2003.

Wolfe, Ken, and Olga Bier. *Chef Wolfe's New American Turkey Cookery.* Berkeley: Aris Books/Harris Publishing, 1984.

On Thanksgiving

Adamczyk, Amy. "On Thanksgiving and Collective Memory: Constructing the American Tradition." *Journal of Historical Sociology* 15 (Sept. 2002): 343–65.

Agel, Jerome, and Jason Shulman. *The Thanksgiving Book: An Illustrated Treasury of Lore, Tales, Poems, Prayers, and the Best in Holiday Feasting,* edited by Melinda Corey. New York: Smithmark Books, 1987.

Appelbaum, Diana Karter. *Thanksgiving: An American Holiday, an American History.* New York: Facts on File Publications, 1984.

Baker, James W., and Elizabeth Brabb. *Thanksgiving Cookery.* New York: Brick Tower Press, 1994.

Barth, Edna. *Turkeys, Pilgrims and Indian Corn: The Story of the Thanksgiving Symbols.* New York: Clarion Books, 1975.

Blue, Kathryn K., and Anthony Dias Blue. *Thanksgiving Dinner.* New York: HarperPerennial, 1990.

Curtin, Kathleen, Sandra L. Oliver, and Plimoth Plantation. *Giving Thanks: Thanksgiving Recipes and History from Pilgrims to Pumpkin Pie.* New York: Clarkson Potter, 2005.

De Costa, B. F. "The Origin of Thanksgiving." *Magazine of American History with Notes and Queries* 8 (Nov. 1882): 757–63.

Dew, Robb Forman. *A Southern Thanksgiving: Recipes and Musings for a Manageable Feast.* Reading: Addison-Wesley Publishing, 1992.

Dickson, Paul. *The Book of Thanksgiving.* New York: Perigee Book, 1995.

Greninger, Edwin T. "Thanksgiving: An American Holiday." *Social Science* 54 (Winter 1979): 3–15.

Home Festivals: A Reference List on Hollowe'en, Thanksgiving and Christmas. Riverside, Calif.: Riverside Public Library, 1913.

Jenner, A. B. J. "Origin of Thanksgiving Day." *Overland* 46 (Nov. 1905): 393–97.

Linton, Ralph, and Adelin Linton. *We Gather Together: The Story of Thanksgiving.* New York: Schuman [1949].

Love, W. DeLoss, Jr. *The Fast and Thanksgiving Days of New England.* Boston: Houghton, Mifflin, 1895.

Norton, C. L. "Thanksgiving Day, Past and Present." *Magazine of American History* 14 (1885): 556–61.

Pleck, Elizabeth. "The Making of the Domestic Occasion: The History of Thanksgiving in the United States." *Journal of Social History* 32 (Summer 1999): 773–89.

Rodgers, Rick. *Thanksgiving 101: Celebrate America's Favorite Holiday with America's Thanksgiving Expert.* New York: Broadway Books, 1998.

Schauffler, Robert Haven, ed. *Thanksgiving: Its Origin, Celebration and Significance as Related in Prose and Verse.* New York: Moffat, Yard, 1907.

Smith, Andrew F. "The First Thanksgiving." *Gastronomica* (Fall 2003): 79–85.

Tarbox, I. N. "Our New England Thanksgiving, Historically Considered." *New Englander and Yale Review* 38 (March 1879): 240–63.

Wallendorf, Melanie, and Eric J. Arnould, "'We Gather Together': Consumption Rituals of Thanksgiving Day." *Journal of Consumer Research* 18 (1991): 13–31.

National Organizations and Associations

American Poultry Association (APA)
P.O. Box 2209
Mango, FL 33550-2209
1-508-473-8769
Web site: www.ampltya.com
Email: apanetcontact@home.com

American Poultry Historical Society (APHS)
Division of Animal and Veterinary Science
Agricultural Science Building
University of West Virginia
Morgantown, WV 26506-6108
1-304-293-5229

American Poultry U.S.A. (APUSA)
P.O. Box 16805
Jackson, MS 39236
1-601-956-1715

National Broiler Council (NBC)
Madison Building, No. 614
1155 15th St., NW
Washington, D.C. 20005
1-202-296-2622

National Contract Poultry Growers Association
1592 Haw Branch Rd.
Sanford, NC 27330
1-888-787-9813
Email: ncpga@afo.net

National Poultry Improvement Plan (NPIP)
USDA, Aphis-VS
Presidential Building 205
Hyattsville, MD 20782
1-301-436-7768

National Turkey Federation
1225 New York Avenue NW, Suite 400
Washington, D.C. 20005
1-202-898-0100
Web site: www.turkeyfed.org/

National Wild Turkey Federation
P.O. Box 530
Edgefield, SC 29824-0530
1-800-THE-NWTF
Web site: www.nwtf.org

Poultry Breeders of America (PBA)
1530 Cooledge
Tucker, GA 30084
1-404-493-9401

Poultry Science Association, Inc.
1111 N. Dunlap Ave.
Savoy, IL 61874
1-217-356-3182
Web site: www.poultryscience.org

Turkey Market Development Council
1026 Poultry Science Building
Purdue University
West Lafayette, IN 47906
1-317-494-8567

U.S. Poultry and Egg Association
1530 Cooledge Rd.
Tucker, GA 30084
1-770-493-9401

USA Poultry and Egg Export Council
2300 West Park Place Blvd
Suite 100
Stone Mountain, GA 30087
1-770-413-0006

World's Poultry Science Association, U.S.A. Branch (WPSA)
U. S. Department of Agriculture
Presidential Building 205
Hyattsville, MD 20782
1-301-436-7768

Major Turkey Businesses

Butterball Turkey Company / ConAgra Foods
2001 Butterfield Rd.
Downers Grove, IL 60515-1049
1-800-BUTTERBALL

Cargill, Inc./HoneySuckle White
1505 Old Missouri Rd.
Springdale, AR 72765-0225
1-800-338-9937

Carolina Turkeys
1628 Garner Chapel Rd.
Mt. Olive, NC 28365
1-800-523-4559

Cooper Farms
P.O. Box 547
22348 Country Rd. 140
Oakwood, Ohio 45873
1-419-594-3325

El Jay Poultry Corporation/Oak Valley Farms
1010 Haddonfield Berlin Rd.
P.O. Box 778
Voorhees, NJ 08043
1-856-435-0900

Empire Kosher
RR 5, Box 228
Mifflintown, PA 17059
1-717-436-5921

Farbest Foods, Inc.
P.O. Box 480
Huntingburg, IN 47542-0480
1-812-683-4200

Foster Farms
1000 Davis St.
Livingston, CA 95334
1-800-255-7227

House of Raeford Farms, Inc.
P.O. Box 100
520 E. Central Avenue
Raeford, NC 28376
1-800-8-TURKEY

Iowa Turkey Products, Inc.
P.O. Box 339
715 W. Tilden St.
Postville, IA 52162-0339
1-319-864-7676

Jaindl's Turkey Farm
3150 Coffetown Rd.
Orefield, PA 18069
1-610-395-3333

Jennie-O Turkey Store
P.O. Box 778
2505 Willmar Avenue SW
Willmar, MN 56201
1-800-328-1756
Web site: www.jennieoturkeystore.com

Kopp's Turkey Sales
10964 Campbell Rd.
Harrison, OH 45030
1-513-367-4133

Kraft/Oscar Mayer
P.O. Box 7188
Madison, WI 53707
1-608-241-3311

Michigan Turkey Producers, LLC
2140 Chicago Drive, SW
Wyoming, MI 49509
1-616-245-2221

Norbest, Inc.
P.O. Box 1000
Midvale, UT 84047
1-801-566-5656
Web site: www.norbest.com

Northern Pride, Inc.
P.O. Box 598
Thief River Falls, MN 56701
1-218-681-1201

Perdue Farms
P.O. Box 1537
Salisbury, MD 21802-1537
1-800-4PERDUE

Pilgrim's Pride Corporation—Turkey Division
110 S. Texas St.
P.O. Box 93
Pittsburg, TX 75686
1-800-824-1159

Plainville Farms
7830 Plainville Rd.
Plainville, NY 13137
1-800-724-0206

Sara Lee Brand
900 N. North Branch St.
Chicago, IL 60622
1-888-SLMEATS (888-756-3287)
Web site: www.saralee.com/saraleebrand/product_list.aspx?category=19

West Liberty Foods
207 West 2d St.
P.O. Box 318
West Liberty, IA 52776-0318
1-888-511-4500

Willow Brook Foods
P.O. Box 50190
405 North Jefferson
Springfield, MO 65805
1-800-423-2362

Organizations Engaged in Protection or Heritage Turkey Preservation

All American Turkey Growers Association
1-785-965-2628
Email: brahmabrahma@hotmail.com

American Livestock Breeds Conservancy (ALBC)
P.O. Box 477

Pittsboro, NC 27312
1-919-542-5704
Web site: www.albc-usa.org

Farm Sanctuary
Adopt-a-Turkey Project
P.O. Box 150
Watkins Glen, NY 14891
1-607-583-2225
Web site: www.adoptaturkey.org

Society for the Preservation of Poultry Antiquities (SPPA)
1878 230th St.
Calamus, IA 52729
Web site: www.feathersite.com/Poultry/SPPA/SPPA.html

Society for the Preservation of Poultry Antiquities (SPPA)
P.O. Box 102
Murphysboro, IL 62966
1-618-684-3811

Slow Food U.S.A.
Heritage Turkeys 1-718-260-8000
Web site: www.slowfoodusa.org/ark/turkeys.html

United Poultry Concerns
P.O. Box 150
Machipongo, VA 23405-0150
1-757-678-7875
Web site: www.upc-online.org
Email: info@upc_online.org

Index

ANDREW SMITH is a freelance writer and speaker on culinary matters. He teaches culinary history and professional food writing at the New School in Manhattan. He has written eight books on culinary history, including *Peanuts: The Illustrious History of the Goober Pea,* and is editor-in-chief of the *Oxford Encyclopedia on Food and Drink in America.* He serves on the editorial board for the Association for the Study of Food Society (ASFS) journal *Food, Culture and Society* and is chair of the Culinary Trust, the philanthropic arm of the International Association of Culinary Professionals (IACP).

The Food Series

A History of Cooking *Michael Symons*
Peanuts: The Illustrious History of the Goober Pea *Andrew F. Smith*
Marketing Nutrition: Soy, Functional Foods, Biotechnology, and Obesity *Brian Wansink*
The Turkey: An American Story *Andrew F. Smith*